European Integration in a Global Economy

CESEE and the Impact of China and Russia

Edited by

Ewald Nowotny

Governor, Oesterreichische Nationalbank, Austria

Peter Mooslechner

Director, Economic Analysis and Research Department, Oesterreichische Nationalbank, Austria

Doris Ritzberger-Grünwald

Head of the Foreign Research Division, Oesterreichische Nationalbank, Austria

PUBLISHED IN ASSOCIATION WITH THE OESTERREICHISCHE NATIONALBANK

Edward Elgar
Cheltenham, UK • Northampton, MA, USA

Published by
Edward Elgar Publishing Limited
The Lypiatts
15 Lansdown Road
Cheltenham
Glos GL50 2JA
UK

Edward Elgar Publishing, Inc.
William Pratt House
9 Dewey Court
Northampton
Massachusetts 01060
USA

A catalogue record for this book
is available from the British Library

Library of Congress Control Number: 2012938082

ISBN 978 1 78100 949 9

Typeset by Servis Filmsetting Ltd, Stockport, Cheshire
Printed and bound by MPG Books Group, UK

Contents

Contributors

Sergey Aleksashenko, Ex-scholar-in-residence, Carnegie Moscow Center, and Director of Macroeconomic Studies at Moscow's Higher School of Economics, Russia

Anders Åslund, Senior Fellow, Peterson Institute for International Economics, Washington, DC

Menzie D. Chinn, Professor, University of Wisconsin, and NBER, USA

Ágnes Csermely, Director of Monetary Strategy and Economic Analysis, Magyar Nemzeti Bank (National Bank of Hungary), Hungary

Luc Everaert, Assistant Director, International Monetary Fund, Washington, DC.

Péter Harasztosi, Economist, Magyar Nemzeti Bank (National Bank of Hungary), Hungary

Willem J. Kooi, Economist, Globalisation–Trade–Development, European Commission, Brussels, Belgium

Iikka Korhonen, Head of Bank of Finland Institute for Economies in Transition (BOFIT), Helsinki, Finland

Erkki Liikanen, Governor, Suomen Pankki (Central Bank of Finland), Helsinki, Finland

Gian Maria Milesi-Ferretti, Assistant Director, International Monetary Fund, Washington, DC

Peter Mooslechner, Director of the Economic Analysis and Research Department, Oesterreichische Nationalbank (Central Bank of Austria), Austria

Christoph Moser, Post-doctoral Researcher at ETH Zurich, KOF Swiss Economic Institute, Zurich, Switzerland

Frank Moss, Director General International and European Relations, European Central Bank, Germany

Ewald Nowotny, Governor, Oesterreichische Nationalbank (Central Bank of Austria), Austria

Gianni Franco Papa, Head of CEE Division, UniCredit S.p.A., Vienna, Austria

Gábor Pellényi, Senior Economist, Magyar Nemzeti Bank (National Bank of Hungary), Hungary

Doris Ritzberger-Grünwald, Head of the Foreign Research Division, Oesterreichische Nationalbank (Central Bank of Austria), Austria

Andrew K. Rose, B.T. Rocca Professor, Associate Dean and Chair of the Faculty, Haas School of Business, University of California, Berkeley, USA

Christian Schitter, Analyst, EMC, Commerzbank AG Corporate & Markets London Branch, UK

Gunther Schnabl, Full Professor for Economic Policy and International Economics, Faculty of Economics and Management, University of Leipzig, Germany

Jean-Luc Schneider, Deputy Director, Economics Department, Organisation for Economic Co-operation and Development, Paris, France

Alasdair Scott, Senior Economist, International Monetary Fund, Washington, DC

Maria Silgoner, Economist, Foreign Research Division, Oesterreichische Nationalbank (Central Bank of Austria), Austria

Dejan Šoškić, Governor, National Bank of Serbia, Serbia

Katharina Steiner, Economist, Foreign Research Division, Oesterreichische Nationalbank (Central Bank of Austria), Austria

Loukas Stemitsiotis, Head of Unit, Globalisation – Trade – Development, European Commission, Brussels, Belgium

Altin Tanku, Director, Research Department, Bank of Albania, Albania

Markus Taube, Professor, University of Duisburg-Essen, Germany

Julia Wörz, Economist, Foreign Research Division, Oesterreichische Nationalbank (Central Bank of Austria), Austria

Holger Zemanek, Economist, University of Leipzig, Germany

Min Zhu, Deputy Managing Director, International Monetary Fund, Washington, DC

Preface

This book discusses selected aspects of European economic integration from a global perspective, investigating the impact of China and Russia as emerging global economic players on the catching-up process in Central, Eastern and South-Eastern Europe (CESEE). Contributions focus on global imbalances and accompanying policy challenges, competitiveness and trade, the sustainability of current growth strategies, and banking and financial stability in the light of the economic and financial crisis that started to evolve in 2008.

To adopt this broader view of European economic integration is not only necessary because of the crisis in which spillovers and contagion are one of the major issues. Even under normal circumstances a country-by-country approach involves a certain risk: the risk of overlooking fundamental economic developments that take place elsewhere and might affect the CESEE region as a whole. Developments in Russia, and even more so in China, seem to fall into this category. Given their huge size and market potential alone, it is quite obvious that economic developments in these two countries will have an impact on the CESEE region. In turn, the CESEE region as a whole – and the euro area as well – may have an impact on Russia and China, too. Therefore we found it was high time to analyse this triangle of regions – CESEE, China and Russia.

China started to successfully enter the stage of the global economy in the 1990s and has since succeeded in delivering rather sophisticated goods to a number of markets. Sooner rather than later the emerging and developing economies will overtake the advanced economies in terms of output, thereby significantly shifting the balance of economic activity in the world. While this growing share necessarily comes at the expense of Europe and the USA, the global economy must not be understood as a zero-sum game. With China becoming more affluent, the export markets for European goods and services are growing, too.

China in particular has been recording impressively high growth rates, although admittedly from a low starting point. Still, as a result of its strong growth performance China will turn into an increasingly attractive destination for exports from the CESEE region. At the same time, however, the rising importance of the Chinese and Russian economies represents a challenge in its own right. The main export destinations of China and the CESEE countries overlap, so that the two economic areas compete for the same markets.

Russia, another global player in Europe, has a key role in securing the supply of energy and thus in securing CESEE growth. But this richness in energy masks several economic challenges, and sometimes even prevents their solution: as there is a lack of productive investment, actual growth is rather unstable. Demographic developments are also worrying: Russia will see a serious decline not only in its population, but also in its labour force. Immigration will not suffice to compensate for this decline. Russia's current account increasingly depends on oil exports. As a consequence, oil prices have an impact on the balance of payments and, in turn, high oil price volatility leads to a high volatility of the exchange rate of the Russian ruble. Moreover, the federal budget heavily depends on oil revenues, contributing to the Dutch disease phenomenon.

In terms of trade, one of the key issues covered by this book, the intensification of already existing trade relationships has contributed most significantly to export growth from CESEE, China and Russia to the EU-15 market, with EU accession in particular temporarily leading to a notable contribution of new trade relationships to the export growth of the new EU countries. Regarding the commodity breakdown of exports to the EU-15, Russia has increasingly specialized in natural resources, while CESEE and China have diversified their export base, intensifying direct competition in capital goods, machinery and vehicles. In particular, CESEE shows a weaker competitiveness effect than China in one of its main export categories, which is transport equipment.

While the trade performance of the CESEE countries used to benefit from their proximity to the EU-15 and the low output volatility, trade with the EU-15 declined strongly in the course of the recent crisis. Compared with developments in other emerging market regions, CESEE exports have so far recovered less dynamically. At the same time, the trade integration of the CESEE countries with China has clearly increased during the crisis. One of the main challenges for future trade developments in CESEE is the ongoing improvement of the value-added content of their exports, which implies that the CESEE countries will be confronted with higher competition from other emerging markets, including China.

In general, global growth gravity is moving away from the advanced economies to the emerging economies, narrowing the gap between these two groups, while both are currently facing a growth slowdown. This development causes global demand structures to change as lifestyles in the emerging markets adjust to people's increasing incomes. Both trade patterns and global financial flows are becoming more emerging markets oriented. China thus needs to adopt a new growth model based rather on domestic consumption than on external demand and investment. To this end, China needs to move up the value chain, open up its services sector and use fiscal policy to provide its people with solid education, health care and pension systems.

This demonstrates that China's growth model has had its merits as well as its limits, as the current approach has reached the point of diminishing returns. In the current global macro environment, the scope for export-led growth is constrained. Another reason for reducing the export contribution to growth is that the export sector is a very capital-intensive sector. The foreseeable reorientation of US demand away from consumption adds to this effect. China is facing a stark choice between bearing increasingly large capital losses in its foreign exchange reserves and tolerating immediate losses in terms of a significant drop in its current account surplus and large revaluation losses. Hence China would benefit from a reorientation toward domestic demand and from liberalizing the services sector. A faster appreciation of the Chinese yuan renminbi would not only reduce global imbalances, but would facilitate East Asian adjustment via the exchange rate channel.

The final section of the book is devoted to financial market issues. Next to trade, capital inflows and institution building, sound financial markets are a precondition for emerging market economies walking the catching-up path successfully. A comparison between the financial markets of all three regions shows significant differences. In CESEE, financial markets deepened continuously before the crisis, mostly with the support of foreign investments in the banking sector. During the crisis the banking sector was not heavily affected due to its business model – concentration on lending activities. In Russia, quite to the contrary, the presence of foreign banks is relatively low and banking sector developments depend on international financial markets rather than on European banking groups. With a GDP contribution of less than 10 per cent, Russia's financial sector is still weak, and for banking supervision there is still room to improve. China's financial markets are slowly but continuously opening up. They also proved to be an important element in weathering the storm during the crisis, as they kept on lending. Due to their peculiarities they can hardly be compared with banking sectors in other countries. In any case, all policy measures that helped to calm the situation in the global financial markets were also helpful in stabilizing the banking sectors of CESEE, Russia and China.

Overall, convergence not only in Europe, but also globally, takes time and requires constant efforts in order to be sustainable. Therefore maintaining competitiveness is key. Internal devaluation aimed at regaining competitiveness can work if the right conditions and policies are in place, but it is generally not a recipe for the long run. Instead, strengthening the economy in each and every respect should be the motto. As shown by many examples in this book, economic integration with neighbouring countries, but also with those far away, pays off. The masterpiece is complete when this goes along with avoiding unbalanced growth and income.

Ewald Nowotny
Peter Mooslechner
Doris Ritzberger-Grünwald

PART I

CESEE, China and Russia – shifts in global
activity

1. The economic impact of China and Russia on the catching-up process in CESEE

Ewald Nowotny[1]

The purpose of this chapter is to investigate the economic impact of China and Russia as emerging global economic players on the catching-up process in Central, Eastern and South-Eastern Europe (CESEE). The focus is on CESEE as a whole, because a country-by-country approach would involve the risk of overlooking fundamental economic developments that take place elsewhere but might affect the region as a whole. Developments in Russia, and even more so in China, seem to fall into this category. Given their huge size and market potential alone, it is quite obvious that economic developments in these two countries will have an impact on the CESEE region. In turn, the CESEE region as a whole – and the euro area as well – may well have an impact on Russia and China, too.

From the perspective of the CESEE area, the question arises as to whether competition from the two large and growing emerging market economies of China and Russia constitutes a drawback for CESEE, or whether opportunities prevail.

I briefly address this question by first comparing some key indicators for the three economic areas in question and then looking more closely at the economic impact of China and Russia on CESEE. Although we all have an idea about the size of these areas, it is useful to look at the actual statistics.

In Figure 1.1 we can see at first glance that the CESEE-10 – that is the group of CESEE EU member states – are very small in terms of population and landmass compared to China and Russia. China stands out with its large population (almost 20 per cent of world population), which means, of course, that the country's workforce is enormous.

Turning to GDP per capita (see Figure 1.2), we see a different picture. While the CESEE-10 cover a comparatively small area, in 2010 their GDP per capita in purchasing power terms was on average almost three times higher than that of China. It is clear that the income level in Russia was

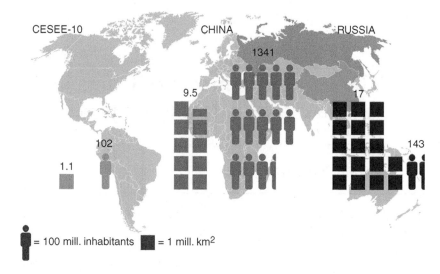

Source: OeNB calculations based on IMF data.

Figure 1.1   Country size and population in 2010

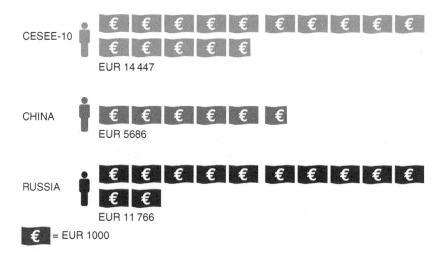

Note: Figures in purchasing power terms. CESEE-10 figures are GDP-weighted averages.

Source: As for Figure 1.1.

Figure 1.2   GDP per capita in 2010

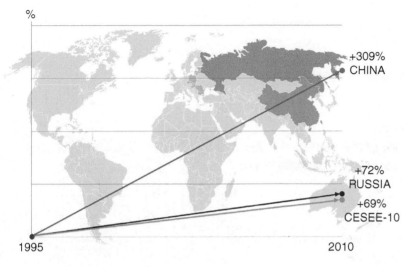

%

+309%
CHINA

+72%
RUSSIA

+69%
CESEE-10

1995   2010

Note: 1995 = 100.

Source: As for Figure 1.1.

Figure 1.3   Real GDP growth

close to the GDP-weighted average in the CESEE-10. But does this mean
that CESEE (and Russia) can be complacent?

No: on the contrary, China's impressive growth path since the mid-
1990s constitutes a challenge to all other economies, including CESEE and
Russia. Data on GDP growth (see Figure 1.3) show that China stands out
with a remarkable real GDP growth of 309 per cent over the period from
1995 to 2010. China had chosen a highly controlled opening-up strategy.
The Chinese growth model relies upon a large pool of domestic savings
and investment (which, to a large extent, comes from abroad), lower
labour costs and thus labour-intensive exports.

By contrast, in CESEE and Russia, central planning was overthrown in
the late 1980s and early 1990s, when a major shift in economic, political,
cultural and sociological paradigms occurred in these countries. Russia's
growth model has, to a large extent, rested on industrial production and,
increasingly, on energy exports. In the CESEE-10, by contrast, capital
inflows – mainly from Western Europe – together with institutional reforms
and EU accession have spurred export-led growth. Even if CESEE and
Russia started out from higher GDP per capita levels than China, their
growth performance has still been remarkable. The financial crisis, however,
has challenged the current growth models not only in these regions.

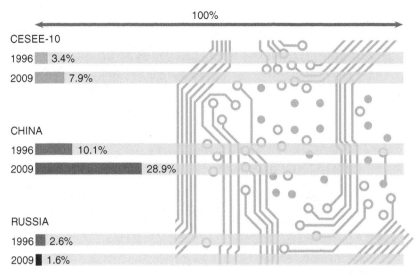

100%

CESEE-10

1996 3.4%

2009 7.9%

CHINA

1996 10.1%

2009 28.9%

RUSSIA

1996 2.6%

2009 1.6%

Note: CESEE-10 exports include intra-CESEE-10 trade.

Source: OeNB calculations based on IMF and World Bank data.

Figure 1.4   Share of high-tech exports in total exports

While China has weathered the financial crisis quite well,[2] CESEE and Russia were directly hit.[3] Despite these differences, all three markets face common challenges both in the real economy and on the financial market, such as rising external imbalances and decelerating external demand for goods, particularly in the face of downward-revised GDP growth forecasts in many export destinations.

Of course, the speed of growth and the quality of institutional and economic adjustment will determine which will be the leading economy in 20 to 30 years.

Against this backdrop, I now briefly discuss the economic impact China and Russia might have on CESEE. In doing so, I will mainly focus on trade, FDI and financial interlinkages.

A closer look at the trade performance of the CESEE-10, China and Russia since the mid-1990s shows that the CESEE-10 have doubled their share in world exports,[4] while Russia's market share has increased only slightly – and has, to a large extent, been driven by the increase in world energy prices. China is expanding its role as an exporter not only of traditional labour-intensive products, but also of high-tech goods (see Figure 1.4).

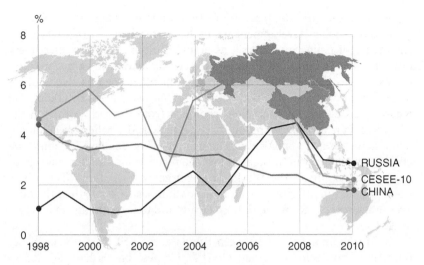

Note: CESEE-10 figures are GDP-weighted averages.

Source: OeNB calculations based on UNCTAD, IMF and national statistical offices data.

Figure 1.5 Annual FDI inflows in per cent of GDP

On the one hand, internationally operating firms have relocated the final production stage not only of labour-intensive goods, but also of high-tech products from industrial countries, other Asian tiger economies and possibly CESEE to China. On the other hand, not only this relocation but also the production or final assembly of new technology-intensive products in China accounts for this strong rise in China's export market share.

Whether this development will cause CESEE export market shares to decrease largely depends on whether the CESEE countries compete in similar product categories that have the same export destinations.

We now turn to a key term in this discussion: foreign direct investment (FDI). Particularly in CESEE and in China, increasing openness to FDI has contributed largely to growth performance (see Figure 1.5). Many empirical analyses have provided evidence on the relationship between FDI and growth. However, not only the fact that capital inflows take place, but in particular the way this capital is put to use plays a major role in achieving sustainable convergence.[5] Direct FDI linkages between CESEE, China and Russia are very small in terms of volume.[6]

An initial conclusion is that the relocation of production sites, catching up in technology-intensive production and dynamic export growth in general are challenges to any economy. At the same time, they can be seen as opportunities to adapt institutional settings to promote sustainable, growth-enhancing development in the home markets. In this sense, the emergence of China and Russia as global economic players offers clear opportunities. China and Russia can become attractive target markets for exports – from CESEE as well as from other regions. Not only is China expanding its role as a supplier of goods, but both China and Russia increasingly demand final products from abroad. Although the EU-15 remain the major trading partner for CESEE, the region should make active use of China's and Russia's growing demand for imported goods – particularly in the light of the recent economic and financial crisis. Russia's accession to the World Trade Organization (the WTO) which was approved in 2011, will open new possibilities to strengthen the linkages in the real economy via FDI and trade and to foster financial linkages as well.

So far, the financial ties between Russia and CESEE have been closer than those between China and CESEE. Chinese banks have started to invest in CESEE only recently. Moreover, China's increasing investment in several sectors in Europe proves that the financial linkages between these two economic areas will gain importance in the future.

I have tried to present a snapshot of recent economic developments of – and interlinkages between – CESEE, China and Russia. Of course, the relations among these three markets have to be seen in a much broader context of international policy cooperation and coordination, such as the efforts by the G-20 to rebalance their economies.

NOTES

1. Katharina Steiner, of the Oesterreichische Nationalbank's staff, contributed to these remarks.
2. Despite a decline in real GDP growth against pre-crisis levels, China nevertheless recorded positive annual growth rates of between 9 per cent and 10.5 per cent over the period from 2009 to 2010 (IMF). Most recently, however, real GDP growth slowed down again from 9.5 per cent in the second quarter to 9.1 per cent in the third quarter of 2011.
3. In 2009, GDP growth turned negative at –3.8 per cent on average in CESEE and –7.8 per cent in Russia.
4. CESEE doubled its market share from 1.9 per cent in 1995 to 3.9 per cent in 2010.
5. See e.g. J. Firdmuc and M. Reiner (2011), 'FDI, trade and growth in CESEE countries', *Focus on European Economic Integration* Q1/11, OeNB, 70–89.
6. China's stock of FDI in CESEE is very small and has been decreasing since 2000.

2. Global shifts in the balance of economic activity through the emergence of China and Russia

Erkki Liikanen

Even though the euro area and the OECD countries more generally have been caught up in a period of low growth and even crisis for some time now, it is also important to keep an eye on other, more dynamic parts of the world in the process of analysing European integration. One of the key defining trends of the past two decades in the global economy has been the emergence of China. Chinese manufacturing goods are competing at higher and higher levels of sophistication, and the effects are being felt all over Europe and the rest of the world.

At the same time, Russia's economic growth has also been impressive, and the country has become even more important for those in Europe. Russia is particularly important as a source of energy and its growing standards of living have enabled many countries – including Finland – to export more there.

Furthermore, we should not forget that other emerging markets and developing countries succeeded in growing at a rapid pace during recent years and even decades. During the 'Great Recession' the largest emerging market economies continued to grow, while advanced OECD countries contracted. According to IMF forecasts, the economic size – adjusted for purchasing power parities – of emerging and developing economies will exceed that of the advanced countries as early as 2012 (see Figure 2.1). This rapid change continues to affect the Central and Eastern European economies as well, whether they are inside the EU or not.

While this is a significant shift in the balance of economic activity in the world, we need to also remember that we are witnessing a return to the situation that persisted for most of the past two millennia. China accounted for more than one quarter of global output until the beginning of the nineteenth century, and the country is now on its way to a similar share of total output (see Figure 2.2).

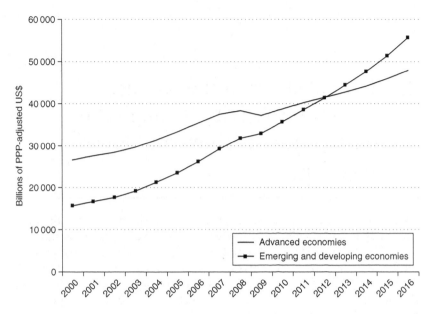

Source: IMF International Financial Statistics, September 2011 version.

Figure 2.1   World GDP

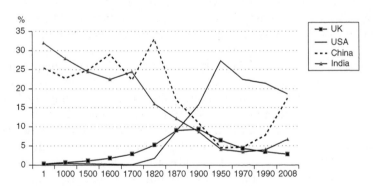

Source: Angus Maddison statistics on historical economic data.

Figure 2.2   Share of global output

While this growing share necessarily comes at the expense of Europe and the USA, we need to remind ourselves that the global economy is not a zero-sum game. A more affluent China also means larger export markets for European goods and services. Moreover, China is not alone. Other

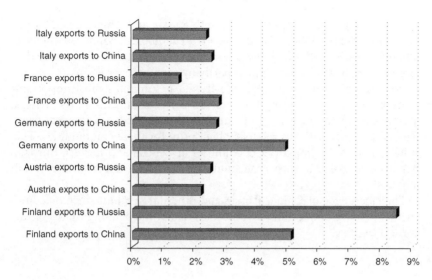

Source: Eurostat.

Figure 2.3 Share of Russia and China in total exports in 2010

large emerging economies like Russia and Brazil have generally enjoyed rapid growth during recent years, partly because of their prudent economic policies, which have allowed them to fulfil their catch-up potential.

The catch-up has not been limited to the so-called BRIC countries (Brazil, Russia, India and China), of course. Many smaller countries in Eastern Europe, Asia and Sub-Saharan Africa have become more integrated into the world economy, and – as a result – have been able to increase the welfare of their citizens. In many ways this volume is dedicated to discussing the results of this global shift of the balance of economic activity.

Given the importance of these rapidly growing economies, it is no surprise that their share in the foreign trade of the EU countries has also grown. In 2010, China accounted for 8.4 per cent of all exports for the EU as a whole, while Russia's share was 6.4 per cent. On the import side both countries were even more important, and China accounted for almost 19 per cent of all imports to the EU. Russia's share was 10.5 per cent. On the export side only the USA was a more important trading partner than China, and on the import side China was clearly the most important trading partner, while the US and Russian shares were practically equal. It is obvious that we have become more dependent on the large emerging economies, especially China and Russia (see Figure 2.3).

Given the growing importance of both Russia and China, it is interesting that within both the EU and the euro area, different countries still have different economic ties with these two emerging giants. Partially these differences are driven by geography, partly by economic structure.

For example, on the import side Russia is Finland's most important trading partner, accounting for some 18 per cent of all imports. This is mainly due to the high level of natural gas and crude oil imports from Russia, together with the relatively high price for these commodities. The situation is similar in many EU countries in Central and Eastern Europe, but even in Austria Russia accounts for less than 2 per cent of total imports.

The emergence of China, Russia and other large middle-income countries as major global economic powers is one of the defining trends of the current century.

PART II

Global imbalances and policy challenges

3. The global outlook, a growth strategy for Europe, and the role of China[1]

Min Zhu, Alasdair Scott and Luc Everaert

This chapter covers three deeply interrelated topics: the global outlook; the views of the IMF on the growth strategy in Europe; and the nature and the role of Europe's increasing economic links with China. The current crisis in Europe has raised questions about growth prospects for economies in the 'south' of the euro area. It comes on the heels of the challenges posed by the emergence of China, to which European economies have reacted differently. But now the deterioration of euro area prospects is challenging China in turn. China is not likely to be able to escape spillovers from the crisis in the euro area – Europe and China are strongly linked by trade and, increasingly, by capital.

The problems are interrelated – that much is clear. But it is perhaps less obvious that solutions are also interrelated. We believe that the policies that Europe and China could adopt to remedy their imbalances will also help each other. Hence, authorities in the two economies have a great opportunity. But to see this opportunity, we must first look at the current situation, and the deep forces that have driven us to it.

1. THE GLOBAL OUTLOOK

If our remarks about great opportunities sound too optimistic, let us be clear: the world economy is in a very dangerous phase. Major advanced economies are locked in a vicious cycle of weak economic activity and financial stress, with the potential to get much worse. And the room for policy error has simply ceased to exist.

The first aspect of the crisis is sovereign debt. In the euro area, sovereign funding costs have soared, despite interventions by the ECB (European Central Bank): yields on Spanish 10-year sovereign bonds are over 6 per cent, and Italian yields have seen peaks over 7 per cent. Spreads over

German bonds have increased to the point where clearing houses are demanding higher collateral in order to facilitate trades. Prices for sovereign insurance have increased substantially, and show that the crisis has spread from the periphery to the core.

In turn, sovereign concerns have reignited fears over the health of the area's banks. The European Banking Authority estimated that banks need more than €100 billion to reach a core tier 1 capital ratio of 9 per cent. Term funding needs for 2012 are estimated to be in the order of half a trillion euros. Euro funding rates are at record levels, dollar funding rates are rising, and banks in some economies have already lost access.

The situation in financial markets has interacted with a deteriorating real economy. Growth in major advanced economies has slowed dramatically. Global growth in 2010 was a solid 5 per cent, which included a contribution from advanced economies of just over 3 per cent. Encouragingly, advanced growth in the USA was 3.0 per cent, with 1.8 per cent in the euro area and 4.0 per cent in Japan. It looked as if the extraordinary policy interventions in 2008 and 2009 had succeeded, and private demand would be able to take over from public support.

Then there were two major shocks: Japan was struck by the Tohoku earthquake and tsunami, and we were reminded how interconnected modern supply lines are. Japanese 'parts paralysis' caused production of Fords to cease in Australia, falls in mining stocks, and speculation that the launch of the new iPad would have to be delayed. We were also reminded of the sensitivity of energy costs to political events: during the second quarter of 2011, oil prices briefly rose more than 25 per cent above the levels that prevailed in January, in part because of unrest in some oil-producing countries. But with the restoration of supply from Japan and lower oil prices, there were signals that the recovery would continue.

Instead, output growth slowed as consumers remained reluctant to open their wallets and concerns over sovereigns and banks grew. Activity has declined severely in recent months. PMI (Purchasing Managers' Index) indices that were typically reading in the high 50s in the first quarter of 2011 now indicate that firms expect no improvement in demand. In the euro area, that number has retreated below 50 to 47 – firms expect contraction. Indeed, industrial production in the euro area declined 2 per cent in September alone, the largest decline since the start of 2009.

Underlying these developments is the broad structural change we are observing in the global economy. We have been observing much stronger growth in emerging markets compared to developed economies. As a result, the share of emerging and developing economies in global GDP has increased rapidly from 38 per cent in 2001 to 49 per cent in 2011.

Commensurately, consumption in the emerging markets has been growing at a much faster pace too, with China alone contributing a remarkable 1.1 percentage points to the 3.2 per cent growth in global consumption in 2011.

Indeed, emerging economies show stronger fundamentals, but vulnerabilities are also increasingly evident. Some economies show signs of overheating pressures, including strong credit growth and rising current account deficits. This has been fuelled in part by a renewed 'search for yield' that has encouraged capital flows to emerging economies. Currently, there is a cyclical slowdown in emerging economies. In particular, China is trying to cool its economy without a hard landing. Inflation receded to 5.5 per cent in October 2011, while industrial production remained robust at nearly 20 per cent from the year earlier – an astonishing figure in comparison to advanced economies – but there are concerns about the state of the property market and bank exposures.

The combination of increased investor fear, growing signs of weakness in major advanced economies, and cyclical cooling in emerging economies can be measured in losses to household wealth. The Euro Stoxx 50 index has fallen by over 20 per cent this year (2011). Even the investor who diversified by 'buying the world', as measured by the MSCI world index, is down 9 per cent for the year. The appetite for taking on risk is shrinking: the VIX index – the 'fear index' – had been back in the mid-teens at the start of the year, an average level by historical standards, but leapt back up above 40 during the summer of 2011, an increase not seen since the collapse of Lehman Brothers in September 2008.

Against this backdrop, IMF staff project continued imbalanced growth. The *World Economic Outlook* projections published in October 2011 show an anaemic recovery in major advanced economies, together with a cyclical slowdown in emerging economies. Global growth falls to 4 per cent in 2011. More worryingly, growth in advanced economies is projected to be only 1.5 per cent in 2011, and less than 2 per cent in 2012. These forecasts were based on the euro area growing by about 1 per cent in 2012, a forecast that now looks optimistic. Indeed, the euro area is more likely to stagnate in 2012.

And risks are firmly to the downside. Spillovers from further euro area deterioration would be severe and widespread. We do not think that emerging economies have 'decoupled'; if anything, weaker global demand and more difficult international financial conditions could expose underlying vulnerabilities from excessive credit growth in some emerging economies.

Restoring growth is therefore essential. Low growth has obvious implications for financial balances and debt sustainability. But let us not forget that it has social implications as well – European unemployment is over

10 per cent, and the youth unemployment rate is twice that, representing 5.5 million people. So we need not just growth but inclusive growth to avoid losing a generation.

2.   A GROWTH STRATEGY FOR EUROPE

It is obvious that Europe faces a number of pressing immediate challenges. In the euro area, authorities have announced plans to recapitalize banks and strengthen funding, while fiscal consolidation efforts have been stepped up. Overcoming the current crisis in a way that restores lustre to European integration and viability to its economic and monetary union is indispensable. It is clear, however, that a long-lasting solution will require measures to restore and rebalance growth.

The challenge is substantial. Let us present two facts to frame the discussion. First, before the crisis, aggregate growth in mature European economies had been steady, but modest, at around 2 per cent. Second, there is considerable heterogeneity in growth rates across Europe. It has been solid in 'northern' economies. Eastern European economies experienced booms, then sharp slumps during the crisis, from which they are recovering. Growth in key 'southern' European economies has been slow. To illustrate, if we were to rank growth rates from 2000 to 2010, we would see that Italian growth was below 1 per cent, whereas growth in Latvia was nearly 10 per cent.

Two implications follow from these two facts. First, higher growth on average will be needed to ensure debt sustainability, preserve living standards and social models, and shoulder the costs of aging populations. Second, more uniform growth within the euro area is needed to make the monetary union robust, given low labour mobility and fiscal integration.

So what can be done to maintain and increase average European growth rates? Simple 'growth accounting' tells us that both inputs and productivity are issues. Labour utilization rates in the euro area are relatively low, in terms of both hours worked and participation in the labour force. Participation rates by women and older workers are noticeably low. But labour inputs are only part of the story. Total factor productivity growth fell below that of the USA since the mid-1990s, whereas it had been higher before. Staff research indicates that human and capital invested in information and communications technology plays a key role in explaining this change.

The story gets more interesting when we start to think about the differences in growth rates across countries. Labour inputs do not explain them – hours worked are higher in the south than in the north, and, in many cases, so too is labour participation. To explain these differences – and to understand what markets are so worried about – we need to understand differences in productivity growth and capital accumulation.

A natural framework for thinking about productivity and capital accumulation is in terms of convergence. It turns out that convergence works very well in explaining the differences between eastern and mature European economies. Relatively poor eastern economies, with lower capital stock and higher returns, have had larger investment ratios and net capital inflows, financed, in part, by northern economies such as Germany and the Netherlands. Fixed investment has also brought increases in human investment – changes in total factor productivity have been higher in eastern economies. But the convergence story does not work so well for explaining growth within the euro area. For example, Italy and Portugal have grown more slowly than expected, whereas the Slovak Republic has grown faster than income disparities would predict.

Initially, convergence appeared to be working for southern economies, too. These countries ran increasing current account deficits since the advent of the European Monetary Union, going from balance in 1994 to an average deficit of 10 per cent in 2008. But it did not bear fruit: growth in deficit economies – mainly the south – lagged that of northern neighbours running surpluses. Expanded credit was used to finance housing investment and consumption in southern economies, not capital and human investment.

Why such differences? Lower nominal interest rates, following the accession to the euro, and perhaps over-optimism about future incomes, may have encouraged consumption and booms in real estate. In the absence of independent monetary policy, rapid credit expansion in some euro area economies was associated with relatively low real interest rates – much lower than would have been suggested appropriate by guides such as the Taylor rule.

Crucially, rising costs saw falling competitiveness *vis-à-vis* northern euro area economies. Unit labour costs in Greece rose by 38 per cent from 2000 to 2009, by about one third for Ireland, Italy and Spain, and 27 per cent for Portugal. Because of such increases, these economies saw their real effective exchange rates rise by 15 per cent from 2000 to 2008 – by nearly 25 per cent in the cases of Italy and Spain. By contrast, the real effective exchange rates of surplus economies decreased by 10 per cent.

Consequently, tradables sectors in deficit economies – especially in manufactures – suffered. From the advent of the euro up until the crisis hit, average labour productivity growth in manufacturing in Greece, Italy, Spain and Portugal, relative to the euro area average, was minus 3 per cent – each year. Exports of goods as shares of GDP actually fell in deficit economies over the decade, while increasing in surplus economies from twice to three times those of deficit economies. In short, there is clear evidence that the degree of trade integration has been associated with very different growth fortunes.

The preceding story is useful for description, but it is not an explanation, and we need to press further. Why were capital inflows not used for investment, and why did some countries miss out on trade? Work by staff economists and others points to problems with product and capital markets. There is evidence of considerable barriers to competition, in part from heavy and inconsistent regulation. In turn, heavily regulated economies have been less flexible and less integrated into the global economy; strong performers have been well integrated. It therefore seems plausible that rigidities in product markets and obstacles to market entry lowered incentives for the absorption of capital to productive investment.

Indeed, assessment of structural factors shows that there is a significant 'reform gap' for Europe and the southern economies in particular. The ideal of the European single market has not been realized, especially in services. The list of gaps includes: labour markets that do not deliver; business, network, retail sector and professional services regulation; infrastructure bottlenecks; and human capital development and returns to innovation.

An illustration of the combined effects of these barriers is seen in margins. Margins in services are higher in the euro area than they are in the USA. In particular, financial intermediation and insurance, retail sector, transportation, and R&D margins are higher. For example, gross retail margins in the USA have been estimated at 1.19, but 1.95 in Italy. Interestingly, manufacturing margins in Europe are similar to those in the USA, even in the south – but, as we have already noted, southern-economy manufacturing has lost competitiveness as productivity has declined and costs have risen.

Moreover, financial integration in the EU is incomplete and uneven. Some elements of the financial system are highly integrated: as we have seen, capital flows across borders easily, and banks can transact freely in the money market. But securitization is very much a national affair, and cross-border retail banking is virtually non-existent – cross-border provision of retail financial services amounts to less than 1 per cent of total loans. Cross-border mergers and acquisitions are still limited, with foreign acquisitions accounting for only 20 per cent of banking activity.

What does this analysis say about policies? The IMF has been emphasizing action on several fronts:

- raising labour market participation rates;
- addressing labour market segmentation, informal economy and inadequate wage flexibility;
- renewed efforts on human capital and returns to R&D;
- lowering remaining barriers to competition, particularly in network industries, retail trade and regulated professions;
- growth-friendly tax reform;
- steps to deepen financial integration, such as by reducing public ownership and involvement in the banking sector.

Such a list clearly overlaps and is ambitious. European authorities will need to show determined political action to overcome previous poor coordination and conflicting priorities. But for a more dynamic and stronger economy it will be crucial to ensure Europe's cohesion and allow the countries to grow out of the sovereign debt crisis.

3. THE ROLE OF CHINA

We now want to turn to the role of China. China is increasingly visible in Europe. There have been high-profile purchases of European firms, such as Volvo. Chinese banks are now mixed in with more familiar names in the City of London. China has a crucial role in 'processing trade' – i.e. as the final stage in a production process that starts in neighbouring Asian economies. China is now the EU's second largest trading partner behind the USA and the EU's biggest source for exports, mainly of machinery and transport equipment. To put this in perspective: EU exports to China were worth over €130 billion in 2010, which, as you will recall, is in the middle of the range of the amount needed to recapitalize European banks, or, alternatively, nearly as large as the Portuguese economy. And of course, in an environment in which advanced-economy growth is so weak, Chinese growth rates are striking. China's growth was 10.3 per cent in 2010, twice the global rate of growth.

Hence, if we are to ask: 'Can China help Europe?', one might answer: it already does, by supporting growth in the world economy. Moreover, for those northern economies that have been able to take advantage of Chinese demand for high-value-added manufactures, China is a lifeline. Take luxury automobiles, for example: China is now Audi's largest market. Imports of some of its models have doubled in only a year. BMW produces limited edition models – at much higher premiums than the standard models – solely for the Chinese market.

However, the emergence of China also presents challenges. IMF staff research suggests that the rapid rise in imports from China explains a large share of the rising trade deficits of periphery euro area economies. Exports of Greece, Italy and Portugal may have been challenged by Chinese exports.

Going forward, there will be two major issues for Europe and China: the need for China's external rebalancing, and the need for European – particularly intra-euro area – rebalancing. The good news is that there is a policy path that would result in benefits for both Europe and China.

On Chinese rebalancing: it is in China's interest to move away from export-oriented growth towards greater reliance on domestic demand. China's export markets in advanced economies are growing at a much slower pace than before, and the pace is expected to remain slow for some time. On the other hand, China has relatively low private consumption – only about one third of GDP. Of the 10 per cent plus growth in 2010, private consumption growth only contributed 2 percentage points. Instead, the economy's resources are excessively directed toward investment, which stands at 47 per cent of GDP.

China faces additional important medium-term challenges. Demographic pressures are set to increase substantially as the society begins to age. There are serious resource constraints that will affect the ability to increase production while keeping costs down. Wages are increasing at a rate that is exceeding productivity increase. A part of the investment in the economy is financed by local governments in a way that increases their indebtedness in a non-transparent manner, bringing into question the sustainability of such financing.

To address these challenges, China has to move away from an export-led growth model to a domestic-consumption-driven growth model. There are a number of critical policies China should implement, many of which are embraced in the recent 12th Five-Year Plan, but let us highlight three that require special urgency.

- First, reforms should continue to be implemented to create more complete social safety nets. The pension and health care systems in particular need to be enhanced. Such changes would lower households' incentive to save and encourage consumption.
- Second, the service sector needs to be opened up to full competition. The manufacturing sector is linked to the global production chain and feels the full force of competition. Services, on the other hand, are directed mostly to domestic markets and have been protected from competition, with reduced incentives to grow. Therefore, currently the service sector has the best potential to grow at a fast pace, create the most number of jobs, and help achieve inclusive growth.

● Third, industries should strive to increase their value added. By producing goods with more value per worker and thus climbing up the value-added curve, firms can continue to support strong wage growth without losing competitiveness, and such sustainable wage growth will encourage more consumption.

Overall, Europe stands to benefit considerably from this rebalancing, especially as Chinese consumers find themselves able to afford products from advanced economies. Staff analysis suggests that reforms that achieve external rebalancing could therefore be 'win–win' for both China and the rest of the world.

It also represents a major opportunity for intra-euro area rebalancing, and this brings us back to growth. The challenge to periphery euro area economies is to take advantage of the rise of the Chinese consumer class. Hence the potential for rebalancing in Europe is closely tied to the opportunity for rebalancing in China, and it is therefore doubly imperative that the growth-enhancing reforms in Europe are pursued to take advantage of this historic opportunity.

To summarize, measures are urgently needed to raise potential growth in Europe. But we say this not simply because growth is good. We say it because there are deep imbalances that culminated in the financial crisis that must be rectified. The world needs to rebalance in order for there to be stability and inclusivity. First, the major advanced economies are still struggling under the weight of debt from the crisis. With public support at its limits, private demand must take over. Second, growth must be more uniform within the euro area for the monetary union to be sustainable. Third, external imbalances must diminish; for example, China must move away from externally driven growth to domestic growth. But as imposing as these challenges are, they also bring opportunities. There is a small business owner in Spain that could benefit from the Chinese householder. Given the right policies, cooperative and coordinated, we can realize those benefits.

NOTE

1. As delivered by Min Zhu on 21 November 2011 at the Conference on European Economic Integration (CEEI), Vienna, Austria.

4. China, East Asia and global rebalancing

Menzie D. Chinn[1]

In 2010, policy makers around the world were confronted with a series of challenges that, while substantial, seemed relatively well defined. International organizations such as the IMF and the OECD highlighted the challenges of managing a two-speed recovery: emerging markets raced ahead, while the advanced economies plodded along. Global financial imbalances, particularly current account imbalances, were a worry, but there were some signs that both growth and rebalancing in the USA and China would prove durable.

The prospects for sustained and global recovery seem much less definite at the time of writing. In the first half of 2011, most forecasters revised downward their estimates for growth in the USA and particularly in Europe, where recession is now more likely than not. Anxiety surrounding the durability of Chinese growth was rising toward the end of 2011. Against this backdrop, the resurgence in the US trade deficit combined with the reluctance of the Chinese to accelerate currency appreciation suggests that the challenges to sustaining both growth and rebalancing are much more profound than policy makers earlier thought.

The failure in the USA to maintain (let alone increase) short-term fiscal and monetary stimulus – despite ample evidence of economic slack and little evidence of inflation or crowding out – and the difficulties euro area policy makers have encountered in forging a resolution to the debt crisis means that, if a global recovery with rebalancing is to be effected, it is incumbent upon policy makers in other countries to step into the breach.

In my view, those measures include greater fiscal stimulus in the current account surplus countries and greater currency appreciation on the part of the East Asian economies. If one takes the European situation as one where policy makers have difficulty in doing anything more than muddling through the next few years, East Asia will be pivotal. In this respect, the fate of the world economy rests upon policy makers in China and East Asia to a greater extent than at any time in the past.

1.   INTERNAL AND EXTERNAL BALANCE

One of the ways the challenges policy makers currently face can be organized is into two dimensions – internal and external balance. Internal balance refers to getting output up to normal levels of output, namely potential GDP; in the absence of other shocks, that level of output should be consistent with non-accelerating inflation. External balance refers to getting the current account to levels consistent with what is consistent with a given country's level of development and fiscal policies. A rough impression of the amount of slack in the world economy can be gleaned from Figure 4.1, which shows the growth rates for the advanced and emerging market economies.

Figure 4.1 highlights the dichotomous nature of the world economy: the advanced economies are projected to grow slowly, with correspondingly high levels of economic slack, while numerous emerging market economies are growing sufficiently fast so that they are operating above potential GDP. The key asymmetry is that output gaps in the advanced economies are negative, while those in the emerging economies are largely positive.

The current account imbalances are shown (as a share of world GDP) in Figure 4.2. The global recession, which hit the USA particularly hard,

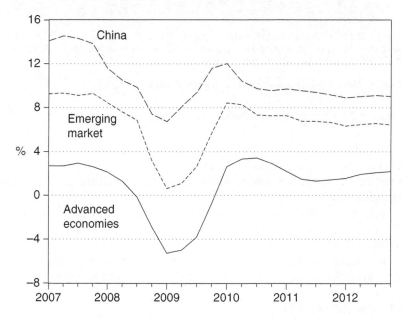

Source: IMF, *World Economic Outlook*, September 2011.

Figure 4.1   Annual growth rates

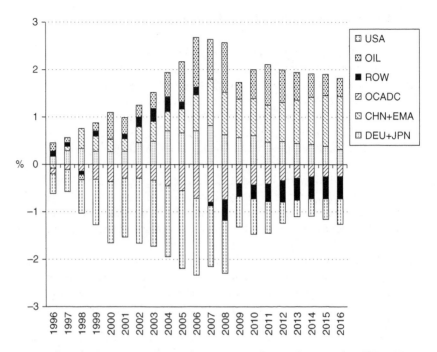

Notes: Data for 2011–16 are IMF projections. OIL: oil-exporting countries; DEU+JPN: Germany plus Japan; OCADC: other advanced developed countries; CHN+EMA: China plus other emerging Asia; ROW: rest of the world.

Source: IMF, *World Economic Outlook*, September 2011.

Figure 4.2   Current account balances as a share of world GDP

has reduced the US current account deficit. However, the IMF forecasts a resurgence in the US deficit, and a concomitant increase in China plus emerging Asia.

Thus the challenge is to push output upward toward potential in the advanced economies, while simultaneously reducing current account deficits in the USA. Within the euro area, current account imbalances also have to be reduced. In contrast, the challenge for policy makers in select emerging market economies is to engineer a glide path toward potential GDP.

1.1   The Advanced Economies

The USA is the key to rebalancing the world economy. However, effective policy making has been hampered by misconceptions regarding the current state of the economy. First, concerns about overheating in the USA are much, much too overblown. The IMF indicates a 2011 output gap of only about –4 percentage points of GDP, while the OECD and the Congressional Budget Office (CBO) indicate a greater extent of slack, at –5 and –6 percentage points.

The fear that the economy is coming close to its speed limit is linked to the fear that the natural rate of unemployment has spiked, driven by the suspicion that with the change in the composition of output, the labour market mismatch has increased. The argument has some content, given the large proportion of long-term unemployed – the highest on record. However, most estimates do not ascribe more than a small proportion of the increase in unemployment to a rise in the natural rate.[2]

The evidence of substantial slack in the US economy is buttressed by the reality of flat inflation, and the absence of any evidence of rising inflationary expectations. Survey-based measures of inflationary expectations have not budged, even at the ten-year horizon. Market-based measures, such as the spread between inflation-indexed bonds and Treasury yields, buttress this conclusion. If anything, fears of *deflation* have risen.

The fear that the USA is very close to a tipping point with respect to government debt, which has constrained fiscal policy, is misguided. The USA has long faced a long-term fiscal problem largely due to rising entitlement spending and refusal to raise sufficient tax revenues; the recession, and particularly the 2001 and 2003 tax cuts, merely magnified the problem. The USA still possesses some latitude for fiscal stimulus in the short term, as documented by Ostry et al. (2010). If there is a medium-term problem, the solution is not to retrench now, but to conduct countercyclical fiscal policy, while setting forth a plan for medium-term fiscal consolidation.

In terms of the current account, prospects for rebalancing are more difficult to assess, in part because the process depends upon what happens in the rest of the world. The IMF projects a gradual increase of the US current account deficit. Given the current constellation of exchange rates, particularly with respect to China, and the failure of Europe to expand rapidly, it is hard to see why these projections should prove substantially incorrect.[3]

One thing that would change the outlook is a sustained and prolonged depreciation in the US dollar. While real oil imports have stabilized and even dropped, oil still accounts for a large share of the trade deficit. Hence the US trade deficit remains very susceptible to a rebound in oil prices.[4] Perhaps more importantly, the troubles in the euro area have induced a flight to dollar-denominated assets that have stymied further dollar depreciation.

The key development over the past year has been the gradual unfolding of the drama in the euro area. It is clear that even if the leaders of the euro area come to an agreement on how to resolve the sovereign debt crisis, Europe is in for a long period of fiscal consolidation – partly self-defeating in terms of really addressing the debt problem – which will result in recession in the short term. Depending on the parameters of the final agreement, and actions of the European Central Bank, Europe is likely to face a long period of less-than-robust growth (see Eichengreen, 2011).

In fact, this scenario is probably the most optimistic one. In the view of many observers, euro area policy makers have not faced up to the immediate challenges of the debt crisis, and in the minds of some, there is not even a long-run solution. The stronger set of fiscal rules announced in late 2011 sounds to outsiders like a warmed-up version of the Stability and Growth Pact. They certainly do not constitute a 'fiscal union' in the common sense of the term, where fiscal transfers offset asymmetric shocks. At the same time, there is no acknowledgement – at least not publicly – that attaining internal equilibrium by adjustment of nominal wages and prices is likely to be incredibly prolonged and painful, and hence politically untenable. Even with a successful recapitalization of the euro area banks, this contractionary approach to fiscal policy will assure stagnant growth in the euro area. This will reduce the scope for rebalancing on the part of the US and East Asian economies, and at the same time places greater pressure for action on policy makers in these countries.

1.2   China and the East Asian Economies

The problems facing the emerging market economies are substantially different from those facing the advanced economies. Of the BRICs, Brazil, Russia and India are already slowing, while the first and last remain above potential. In contrast, China is probably above potential, but growth is slowing rapidly.

China merits extensive discussion for several obvious reasons. First, its rapid growth and heft in the global macroeconomy makes the world economy's fate dependent in part on China's fate. Second, China has a role in global current account imbalances, both directly and, by affecting the conduct of the other East Asian economies, indirectly. The key point is that if China can effect rebalancing toward domestic sources of demand *and* sustain growth, the chances of avoiding a global recession are greatly enhanced. In particular, as China supplies fewer tradable goods to the rest of the world, the scope for expenditure-switching in Europe and the USA will be increased.

There are a couple of ways to examine this issue of rebalancing of the Chinese current account. The first is the conventional elasticities

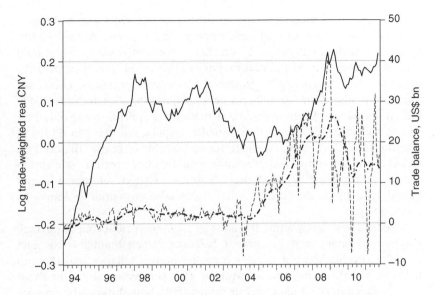

Note: Up is appreciation, left scale. Monthly trade balance, and 12-month moving average (in US$ bn, right scale).

Source: IMF, *International Financial Statistics* and author's calculations.

Figure 4.3   Log CNY real effective exchange rate and Chinese trade balance

approach, where the impact of Chinese currency misalignment is assessed in a partial equilibrium approach. The second is a more macroeconomic one, in which one views the current account as the outcome of saving and investment and government budget decisions. The latter approach does not necessarily exclude the former; rather it changes the focus.

What is the evidence in favour of the view that Chinese misalignment of the renminbi (RMB) has driven the surge in the Chinese trade surplus? The trade-weighted real value of the renminbi, and the Chinese trade balance, are illustrated in Figure 4.3.

The fact that the renminbi appreciates even as the trade balance surges does not invalidate the proposition that exchange rates can have an impact. Exchange rates typically appreciate as countries experience rapid economic growth.[5] Nonetheless, the empirical evidence regarding the strength of exchange rate effects on Chinese trade is not definitive. Studies using Chinese data pre-dating the Great Recession find some effects of the exchange rate on Chinese exports, but do not typically find correspondingly large and statistically significant effects of the exchange rate on Chinese imports.

More recently, using data spanning the recent recession and sharp drop-off and rebound in Chinese imports and exports, Ahmed (2009) finds that in the long run, a 1 percentage point increase in the annual rate of appreciation of the real exchange rate would have a cumulative negative effect on real export growth of 1.8 percentage points. This result means that, after four years, 20 per cent yuan appreciation induces a $400 billion decrease in Chinese exports. Cheung et al. (2010), using data pre-dating the Great Recession, find a smaller impact, but updated results in Cheung et al. (forthcoming) suggest a measurable response. In addition, it is likely that a renminbi appreciation would induce a region-wide appreciation of currencies against the US dollar. That development would definitely facilitate the further dollar depreciation essential to American rebalancing.[6]

A second way to examine the issue of Chinese rebalancing is through the lens of saving and investment balances, which highlights the fact that the current account is related to the budget balance and the gap between private saving and investment. This perspective shifts the focus to the behaviour of Chinese private saving (both household and corporate sector), as well as government saving. In contrast to the mid-2000s, when the surge in corporate saving was identified as a key factor, more recent analyses have focused on the elevated levels of all three components (Ma and Yi, 2010; Prasad, 2009).

Some of these trends are due to the trend decrease in the share of labour income in Chinese GDP. This phenomenon, combined with the relatively high household saving rate, means that merely trying to raise the household saving rate (by improving the social safety net, and by increasing access to consumer credit) cannot in and of itself solve the problem. Hence rebalancing involves a rebalancing of the domestic shares of income, away from capital.

This point has become increasingly central as the debate has moved to whether wage rates are rising. Those familiar with the Lewis (1954) and the Fei and Ranis (1964) model of development will recall that, as wages rise, the share of income going to capital decreases. If the propensity to save of labour is less than that of capitalists, then the saving rate should decline (Kroeber, 2010). It might be that this process is happening as a natural outcome arising from the exhaustion of labour close to the coastal provinces. Even if that is true, the process of raising household savings (in aggregate terms, not just as a share of household income) can be accelerated by aggressive government action, to reduce uncertainty by developing the health and social insurance networks, as suggested by Prasad (2009).

In sum, there is scope for Chinese government policy to accelerate

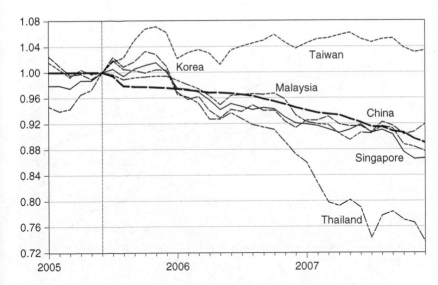

Figure 4.4 Exchange rates (against the US$, rescaled to 2005M06 = 1.00)

rebalancing. In the short term, this involves faster currency appreciation:[7] over the longer term, allowing state-owned enterprises to pay dividends, reducing the monopoly power of the state-owned corporations, and accelerating the development of a social safety net and provision of social services (which will reduce incentives for household saving while reducing government saving).[8]

How does the rest of East Asia fit in? The most important thing to realize is that in terms of currency values, where China goes, so too does East Asia. This assertion is illustrated by two graphs – the first following the 2005 de-pegging of the RMB (see Figure 4.4), and the second following the 2010 de-pegging (see Figure 4.5).

For the USA, East Asia constitutes about the same amount of imports. Thus substantive adjustment requires exchange rates to move for the entire East Asian production complex.

Hence, while some aspects of East Asia's external imbalances will respond only to structural changes, more readily effected measures can have an immediate effect. Exchange rate movements can induce the textbook expenditure-switching, as long as other countervailing policies are not implemented. This is an important factor, given the dire need for aggregate demand in the developed economies, in particular Europe.

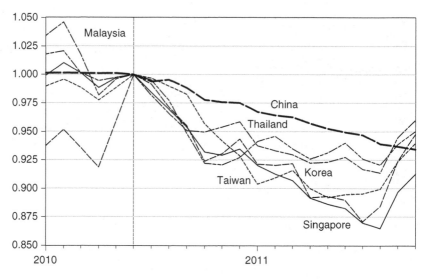

Figure 4.5   Exchange rates (against the US$, rescaled to 2010M06 = 1.00)

2.   POLICY CHALLENGES

Many of the recommendations that have been laid out have been raised numerous times before. Is there any reason why these policies might be implemented more readily than before, especially against a backdrop of decelerating world growth? In fact, most commentary right now suggests that Chinese authorities will stop RMB appreciation in the face of slowing domestic growth and the decline in the trade surplus. Clearly, slower appreciation will not enhance rebalancing. On the other hand, there are several reasons for hope.

The first reason is that there is an increasing recognition within China that the current development model is reaching an end-point. First, the slowing world economy makes continued reliance on exports as the engine of growth increasingly risky. Second, the high level of invest-ment, allocated in the current fashion, is resulting in declining rates of return on capital. Finally, the costs of building up massive stocks of low-yield foreign exchange reserves are becoming readily apparent to Chinese policy makers (e.g. Yu, 2011). In the past, those policy makers have implemented changes slowly and deliberately. That caution has served the Chinese well; however, in the current macroeconomic and political environment, I believe speed is of the essence – so that a cautious approach to policy modification may ironically prove to be *in*cautious.

Moving forward, I think the following key points need to be recalled.

First, we should not take the recent decline in the Chinese current account surplus as a sustainable trend. It is possible that it is due to stock-piling of commodities, or other temporary factors. Hence we need to continue to press for greater appreciation of the RMB.

Second, the foregoing should not be taken to mean that Chinese revaluation would alone eliminate the imbalances; rather it would facilitate East Asian adjustment more generally by allowing other currencies to appreciate against the dollar. With relative prices altered, labour and capital would more probably move. Third, adjustment will be even more important if Europe (and the USA?) go into outright recession, despite the fact that political concerns will make policy implementation more difficult.

NOTES

1. The chapter is based on a paper presented at the Suomen Pankki/OeNB conference 'European Integration in a Global Economic Setting – CESEE, China and Russia', Vienna, 21–22 November 2011. I thank Gunther Schnabl and conference participants for helpful comments.
2. Weidner and Williams (2011) work off Okun's Law to calculate an increase of 2.5 percentage points from 2007Q4 to 2011Q1. A more micro-based approach is adopted by Dowling et al. (2010), who directly address the skills mismatch issue. They estimate the natural rate has risen 1.5 percentage points.
3. Bertaut et al. (2009) use the Fed's partial equilibrium model to forecast a similar trajectory for the US current account deficit.
4. Some demand-side management proposals are in Chinn (2005).
5. The most common explanation for this phenomenon is the Balassa–Samuelson effect, which posits that rapid growth of productivity in the tradables sector, relative to the non-tradables, appreciates a currency. See Cheung et al. (2010) for a discussion.
6. See Thorbecke (2010). China's weight in US trade is about 17.9 per cent, while the weight of China plus the newly industrialized countries (NICs; excluding Hong Kong) and South-East Asian countries is about 39.9 per cent. See Federal Reserve Board at: http://www.federalreserve.gov/releases/H10/Weights/.
7. There has been some debate whether such appreciation endangers China's growth too much. On one side is Dani Rodrik (2008). On the other side is IMF (2010) and Eichengreen and Rose (2010).
8. Chinn and Ito (2007, 2008) document the fact that for developing countries, increases in government spending can induce a reduction in the current account balance. They also verify that for countries like China, financial development cannot be depended upon to reliably reduce Chinese current account balances, in contradiction to the Bernanke (2005) saving glut thesis.

REFERENCES

Ahmed, Shaghil (2009), 'Are Chinese exports sensitive to changes in the exchange rate?', International Finance Discussion Paper No. 987, December.

Bernanke, Benjamin (2005), 'The global saving glut and the U.S. current account', Remarks at the Sandridge Lecture, Virginia Association of Economics, Richmond, VA, 10 March.

Bertaut, Carol, Steve Kamin and Charles Thomas (2009), 'How long can the unsustainable U.S. current account deficit be sustained?', *IMF Staff Papers*, **56**(August), 596–632.

Cheung, Yin-Wong, Menzie Chinn and Eiji Fujii (2010), 'China's current account and exchange rate', in Robert Feenstra and Shang-Jin Wei (eds), *China's Growing Role in World Trade*, Chicago, IL: University of Chicago Press for NBER, pp. 231–71.

Cheung, Yin-Wong, Menzie Chinn and Xingwang Qian (forthcoming), 'Are Chinese trade flows different?' *Journal of International Money and Finance*.

Chinn, Menzie (2005), 'Getting serious about the twin deficits', Council Special Report No. 10, New York: Council on Foreign Relations, September.

Chinn, Menzie and Hiro Ito (2007), 'Current account balances, financial development and institutions: assaying the world "Savings Glut"', *Journal of International Money and Finance*, **26**(4), 546–69.

Chinn, Menzie and Hiro Ito (2008), 'Global current account imbalances: American fiscal policy versus East Asian savings', *Review of International Economics*, **16**(3), 479–98.

Dowling, Thomas, Marcello Estevão and Evridiki Tsounta (2010), 'The Great Recession and structural unemployment', United States: Selected Issues Paper, IMF Country Report No. 10/248, July.

Eichengreen, Barry (2011), 'Disaster can wait, project syndicate, December 9, 2011', http://www.project-syndicate.org/commentary/eichengreen37/English.

Eichengreen, Barry and Andrew Rose (2010), '27 up: the implications for China of abandoning its dollar peg', mimeo, UC Berkeley.

Fei, John C.H. and Gustav Ranis (1964), *Development of the Labor Surplus Economy: Theory and Policy*, Homewood, IL: Richard D. Irwin.

International Monetary Fund (2010), 'Getting the balance right: transitioning out of sustained current account surpluses', *World Economic Outlook*, April, Washington, DC: IMF, ch. 4.

Kroeber, Arthur (2010), 'Economic rebalancing: the end of surplus labor', *China Economic Quarterly*, **14**(1), 35–46.

Lewis, W. Arthur (1954), 'Economic development with unlimited supplies of labor', *Manchester School of Economic and Social Studies*, **22**, 139–91.

Ma, Guonan and Wang Yi (2010), 'China's high saving rate: myth and reality', BIS Working Paper No. 312, June.

Ostry, Jonathan D., Atish R. Ghosh, Jun I. Kim and Mahvash S. Qureshi (2010), 'Fiscal space', Staff Position Note 10/11, Washington, DC: International Monetary Fund, September.

Prasad, Eswar (2009), 'Rebalancing growth in Asia', NBER Working Paper No. 15169.

Rodrik, Dani (2008), 'The real exchange rate and economic growth', *Brookings Papers on Economic Activity*, Fall, 365–412.

Thorbecke, Willem (2010), 'Investigating the effect of exchange rate changes on trans-Pacific rebalancing', unpublished manuscript, Asian Development Bank Institute, Tokyo.
Weidner, Justin and John C. Williams (2011), 'Update of "How big is the output gap?"', mimeo, San Francisco: Federal Reserve Bank of San Francisco, 7 July. http://www.frbsf.org/publications/economics/letter/2009/el2009-19_update.pdf.
Yu, Yongding (2011), 'Global challenges facing China', mimeo, October. http://www.die-gdi.de/CMS-Homepage/openwebcms3_e.nsf/(ynDK_contentByKey)/MSIN-8KZD5L/$FILE/Workshop_Financial-Stability-in-Emerging-Markets_21.10.2011_Yongding%20Yu_Global%20Challenges%20Facing%20China.pdf.

5. Global imbalances, capital flows and the crisis

Gian Maria Milesi-Ferretti

This chapter discusses developments in global imbalances as well as imbalances in the euro area. It builds on Lane and Milesi-Ferretti (2011) and Chen et al. (2012). It starts by presenting some stylized facts on global imbalances and imbalances within the euro area, and then turns to a discussion of factors that help explain their behaviour.

Figure 5.1 shows the evolution of 'global imbalances', showing current account surpluses and deficits in the main countries and regions. In particular, the chart divides European countries in two groups: one comprising current account surplus countries in the European Union (in particular Germany, the Netherlands, Denmark and Sweden) as well as Switzerland, and the other comprising deficit countries (Greece, Ireland, Italy, Portugal, Spain, the UK and countries in Central and Eastern Europe). Current account balances are scaled by world GDP.

According to this metric, imbalances reached a peak in 2007–08, and have since shrunk. One important factor explaining the contraction of imbalances in 2009 was the collapse in commodity prices – particularly oil – in the period following the collapse of Lehman Brothers. This decline implied an improvement in current account balances in deficit countries – almost all of which are oil importers – and a corresponding decline in surpluses in oil-exporting countries. Commodity prices including oil rebounded in 2010, and so did the surpluses in oil exporters, but the contraction in imbalances has persisted. Despite the contraction in current account deficits and surpluses, the overall creditor and debtor positions have continued to increase even after the crisis (see Figure 5.2).

Both figures show clearly the increase in imbalances in European countries, with those in the euro area playing a prominent role. In discussing these imbalances, much emphasis has been put – correctly – on intra-euro area factors. For example, a number of papers have stressed the loss in competitiveness of countries such as Greece, Ireland, Italy, Portugal and Spain *vis-à-vis* Germany due to their higher wage and price increases during this period. Current account deficits widened significantly

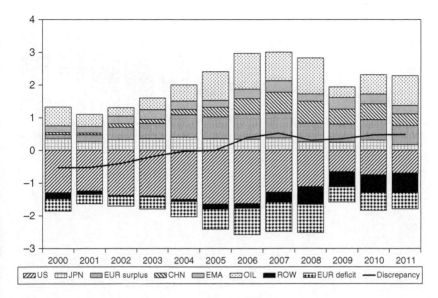

Notes: The composition of country groups is as follows:
EUR surplus: Austria, Belgium, Denmark, Finland, Germany, Luxembourg, Netherlands, Sweden, Switzerland.
EUR deficit: Greece, Ireland, Italy, Portugal, Spain, UK, Bulgaria, Czech Republic, Estonia, Hungary, Latvia, Lithuania, Poland, Romania, Slovak Republic, Turkey, Ukraine.
EMA (emerging Asia): Hong Kong SAR of China, Indonesia, Korea, Malaysia, Philippines, Singapore, Taiwan province of China, Thailand.
OIL (oil exporters): Algeria, Angola, Azerbaijan, Bahrain, Republic of Congo, Ecuador, Equatorial Guinea, Gabon, Iran, Kazakhstan, Kuwait, Libya, Nigeria, Norway, Oman, Qatar, Russia, Saudi Arabia, Sudan, Syria, Trinidad and Tobago, United Arab Emirates, Venezuela, Yemen.
ROW: remaining countries.

Source: IMF, *World Economic Outlook*, October 2011.

Figure 5.1   Global current account imbalances (in per cent of world GDP, 2000–11)

in southern euro area countries, where sizeable declines in interest rates were accompanied by decreasing saving rates and in some cases higher investment rates.

In a recent paper (Chen et al., 2012) we also stress the significance of global factors. It is important to recognize that the euro area as a whole is actually a very open economy, with significant trade and capital flows with countries outside the euro area. Indeed, euro area deficit countries ran significant trade imbalances *vis-à-vis* countries outside the region.

The first global factor is the exchange rate of the euro. We document

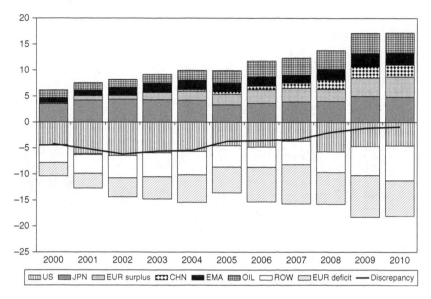

Source: Lane and Milesi-Ferretti (2007), External Wealth of Nations Database (updated to 2010). See note to Figure 5.1 for composition of country groups.

Figure 5.2   Net foreign asset positions (in per cent of world GDP, 2000–10)

that for countries such as Greece, Ireland, Italy, Portugal and Spain, the appreciation in the real effective exchange rate (measured against all trading partners) between 2000 and 2010 was driven to a significant extent by the nominal appreciation of the euro *vis-à-vis* other currencies. Inflation differentials mattered as well – and, of course, went the 'wrong' way – but they were not the only factor contributing to real appreciation in euro area deficit countries.

The second global factor is the growing importance of China in the world economy, which affected euro area countries in an asymmetric fashion. Specifically, China increased significantly its imports of capital goods from Germany and other countries in the euro area 'core', but its exports competed with those from Southern European countries, which specialized in relatively lower-tech products.

The third global factor, which like the second also affected different parts of the euro area asymmetrically, was the increase in commodity prices, especially oil. Countries in the euro area core, especially Germany, rely less on imported energy than Southern European countries, and hence the effect of the oil price increase on import values was smaller. But in addition Germany is a producer of the type of investment goods that were in high demand from commodity exporters, so much so that its trade balance *vis-à-vis* these countries improved in the past decade despite the massive increase in oil and commodity prices.

In summary: while intra-euro area factors played an important role in explaining the current account imbalances of individual euro area countries, so did a host of other 'global' factors. So, while in the aggregate the euro area current account remained broadly balanced throughout the period, the current account deficits and surpluses in the region reflected the global shocks, which help explain the global widening of current account balances.

It is interesting to contrast the behaviour of trade flows for euro area countries with the behaviour of capital flows. While 'southern' euro area countries incurred trade deficits also *vis-à-vis* countries outside the region, the lion's share of the external financing came from countries in the 'core' euro area. A simple example: a Greek resident would sell a Greek government bond to, say, a French bank, and use the euros to buy oil from Saudi Arabia, and the euros that Saudi Arabia receives for oil are redeposited in a French or a German bank. With this circuit, the Greek deficit is financed within the euro area, even though the current account imbalance is incurred *vis-à-vis* other countries, while external investors acquired claims on core euro area countries. A telling statistic in this regard concerns the investment in euro area bonds (Figure 5.3): investors from outside the euro area bought primarily from 'core' euro area countries, whose investors in turn bought bonds issued by southern euro area countries.

What factors were behind these developments? Clearly the elimination of currency risk played a big role in increasing the substitutability between bonds issued by different euro area countries in the eyes of investors. Still, the evidence suggests that such substitutability increased by more for 'internal' euro area investors than for external investors, with very large purchases in core euro area countries of bonds issued by southern euro area countries. One possible reason is the collateral role that these bonds played for euro area banks in accessing liquidity from the European Central Bank – on the same terms as, say, German bonds – a role that would be of lesser importance to outside investors. Another possible reason is the expectation that these bonds would be repaid via bailouts in difficult times.

Having focused on some of the factors that contributed to the increase in euro area imbalances prior to the crisis, we now turn to the factors explaining the reduction in imbalances after the crisis. In Lane and Milesi-Ferretti (2011) we examined in particular whether 'excessive' current account balances pre-crisis were unwound after the crisis, and how that

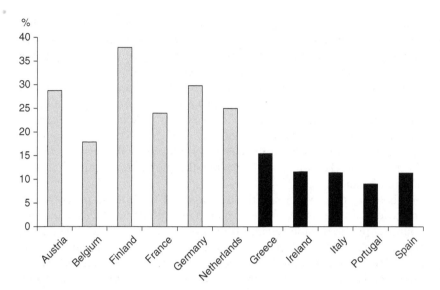

%

Note: Total holdings of domestic debt securities by non-euro area residents as a ratio of total holdings of domestic debt securities by non-residents.

Source: Chen et al. (2012) based on IMF, *Coordinated Portfolio Investment Survey* and *Balance of Payments Statistics.*

Figure 5.3   Holdings of domestic portfolio debt instruments by non-euro area countries (in per cent of total foreign holdings, end-2008)

unwinding occurred. Pre-crisis excesses were fuelled by easy credit (leading to very low spreads even for large debtors), asset price bubbles in a number of countries, reflecting in some cases housing booms, as well as very rosy growth expectations. To obtain a metric for how these excesses were reflected in the current account balance, we took a set of standard current account determinants and through econometric analysis we estimated the pre-crisis current account balance explained by fundamental variables such as demographics, level of development, fiscal balances and oil prices. We then took the residual part of the current account in the pre-crisis period and examined the extent to which such residual is correlated with changes that have occurred since the onset of the crisis.

Figure 5.4, taken from that work, is a scatter plot showing on the horizontal axis the current account residual for the pre-crisis period (2005–08). On the vertical axis is shown how much the current account balance has changed between 2010 and the period 2005–08. For example, countries such as Bulgaria, Iceland and Latvia in the upper left corner had,

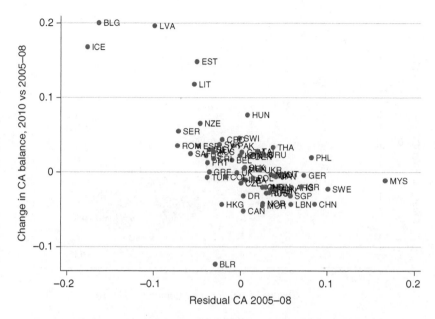

Note: Scatter of changes in the current account balance between 2005–08 and 2010 against the 2005–08 residual from a current account balance regression.

Source: Lane and Milesi-Ferretti (2011).

Figure 5.4   Change in current account balance and current account gap

according to this metric, much larger current account deficits than those one would have expected on the basis of their fundamentals, and at the same time experienced an enormous current account correction between 2010 and the period 2005–08 (of the order of 20 per cent of GDP). More generally, the picture conveys a strong correlation between pre-crisis 'residuals' and the subsequent correction in the current account balance, providing a more decentralized picture of the overall contractions and imbalances seen in Figure 5.1.

How did this change in the current account since the crisis come about? In Figure 5.5, the vertical axis plots the change in the current account balance between 2007 and 2010, and the horizontal axis shows how much domestic demand has changed in these countries during the same period. The figure shows that countries such as Bulgaria, Latvia, Estonia, Lithuania and Iceland (top left corner), which had big changes in the current account, also experienced very sharp declines in real domestic demand between 2007 and 2010. In the opposite corner

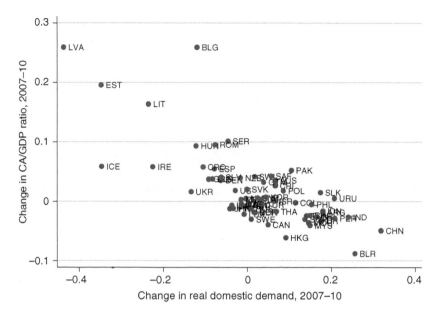

Note: 'Change in real domestic demand 2007–10' is the log change in real domestic demand between 2007 and 2010. 'Change in CA/GDP ratio 2007–10' is the difference between the CA/GDP ratio in 2010 and 2007.

Source: Lane and Milesi-Ferretti (2011) based on IMF, *Balance of Payments Statistics* and *World Economic Outlook*.

Figure 5.5   Change in current account/GDP and change in real domestic demand relative to trading partners (2007–10)

are countries such as China and Singapore, which experienced a big reduction in their current account surplus and very strong increases in domestic demand.

With, say, current account deficits falling sharply, one would indeed expect domestic demand to contract. But how about GDP? Figure 5.6 provides the answer. The figure is equivalent to Figure 5.5, except that it has GDP rather than domestic demand on the horizontal axis. The overall message is that the big compression in imbalances on the deficit side was associated in many countries with a big compression in domestic demand and an outright decline in GDP.

Did real exchange rates help cushion the adjustment by shifting demand between tradables and non-tradables across countries? To address this question we compare two scatter plots for non-pegs (Figure 5.7) and one for pegs (Figure 5.8). On the vertical axis we again have the change in the

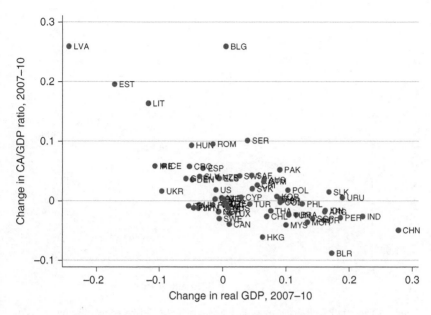

Note: 'Change in real GDP 2007–10' is the log change in real GDP between 2007 and 2010. 'Change in CA/GDP ratio 2007–10' is the difference between the CA/GDP ratio in 2010 and 2007.

Source: Lane and Milesi-Ferretti (2011) based on IMF, *Balance of Payments Statistics* and *World Economic Outlook*.

Figure 5.6   Change in current account/GDP and change in real GDP relative to trading partners (2007–10)

current account balance (between 2007 and 2010), and on the horizontal axis we have the change in the real effective exchange rate over the same period. Now, if you just run a regression you get a strong negative relation between the real exchange rate and the current account change – relative prices moved in the 'right' direction. However, if we simply omit Iceland we are left with a pretty weak relation between real exchange rate adjustment and the current account change. It seems therefore that expenditure compression in deficit countries was much more important than expenditure-switching. If we focus on countries with an exchange rate peg, the evidence against expenditure-switching is much stronger – the real exchange rate change is actually positively correlated with the change in the current account balance. Now, of course, some of these countries peg to the euro, and hence experience an appreciation if the euro appreciates. What the figure shows is that exchange rate movements (or

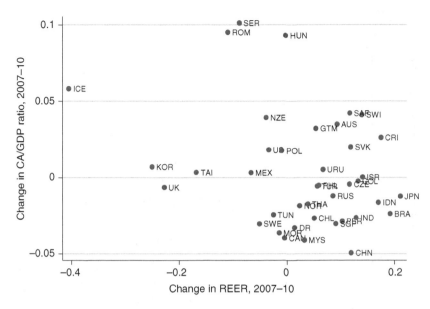

Note: 'Change in REER 2007–10' is the log change in the CPI-based real effective exchange rate index between 2007 and 2010. 'Change in CA/GDP ratio 2007–10' is the difference between the CA/GDP ratio in 2010 and 2007.

Source: Lane and Milesi-Ferretti (2011) based on IMF, *International Financial Statistics, Balance of Payments Statistics* and *World Economic Outlook*.

Figure 5.7 *Change in current account/GDP and change in real exchange rates (2007–10): floating and intermediate exchange rate regimes*

lack thereof) did not contribute to helping rebalance, at least during this sample period.

In summary, our research documents a very strong current account adjustment after the crisis. We have shown data for 2010, but estimates for 2011 (where final outcomes are still not available at the time of writing) suggest the same conclusion. The current account adjustment is correlated with pre-crisis 'excesses'. However, the adjustment has taken place in deficit countries primarily through compression of demand and output. One can certainly make the case that in some of these countries this was unavoidable, given that output and demand were growing above trend and the output gap was positive. This notwithstanding, the high level of unemployment and under-utilization of resources in these countries highlights the cost of the adjustment and the difficulty in reallocating resources across sectors, all the more

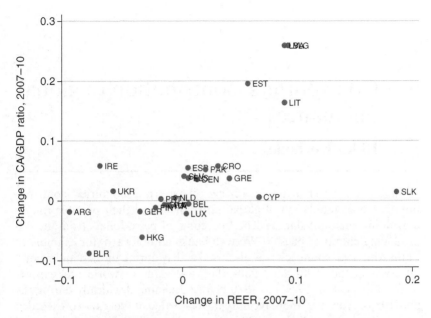

Note: 'Change in REER 2007–10' is the log change in the CPI-based real effective exchange rate index between 2007 and 2010. 'Change in CA/GDP ratio 2007–10' is the difference between the CA/GDP ratio in 2010 and 2007.

Source: Lane and Milesi-Ferretti (2011) based on IMF, *International Financial Statistics, Balance of Payments Statistics* and *World Economic Outlook.*

Figure 5.8   Change in current account/GDP and change in real exchange rates (2007–10): pegged exchange rate regimes

so in the absence of significant moves in relative prices to ease such reallocation.

REFERENCES

Chen, Ruo, Gian Maria Milesi-Ferretti and Thierry Tressel (2012), 'External imbalances in the euro area', forthcoming in *Economic Policy.*

Lane, Philip R. and Gian Maria Milesi-Ferretti (2007), 'The external wealth of nations mark II', *Journal of International Economics*, **73**(2), 223–50.

Lane, Philip R. and Gian Maria Milesi-Ferretti (2011), 'External adjustment and the global crisis,' IMF Working Paper 11/197, forthcoming in *Journal of International Economics.*

6. Oil exporters' contribution to global imbalances

Iikka Korhonen

In this chapter I shall briefly review oil-exporting countries' contribution to the accumulation of global imbalances and their possible role in unwinding such imbalances. The 'recycling' of petrodollars from the oil-producing countries back to Western banks and onward, for example to Latin American countries, was discussed widely during the first and second oil crises in the 1970s and 1980s. The real value of world fuel exports reached its peak in 1979 and 1980 before declining drastically during the mid-1980s. However, more recently the real value of fuel exports exceeded its previous peak as early as 2005 as the volume of fuel exports grew and the price of crude oil continuously increased between 2000 and 2008 (see also IMF, 2006). Moreover, prices of many raw materials follow the price of oil relatively closely, which can reinforce the effects of oil price on global imbalances.

OIL EXPORTERS' CURRENT ACCOUNT BALANCES EBB AND FLOW WITH THE PRICE OF OIL

Figure 6.1 shows the evolution of current account balances in the world's major economic areas in nominal US dollars. We can see that in nominal terms global imbalances remained relatively stable up until the beginning of the 2000s, when they started to increase. On the surplus countries' side, China has received a great deal of attention in the media and policy debates, but in fact OPEC together with other major oil exporters (Russia, Norway and Kazakhstan) have had larger combined current account surpluses than China. As is well known, Japan, Germany and the newly industrialized countries of Asia have also had relatively large current account surpluses. In the case of Japan the surpluses (even in nominal terms) have been quite high since the mid-1980s, whereas for Germany the large current account surpluses did not emerge until the mid-2000s. For Germany the economic reforms of the early 2000s, especially in the labour

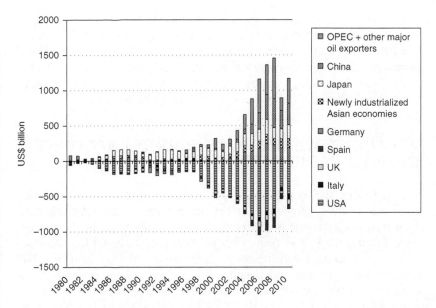

Source: IMF, *International Financial Statistics.*

Figure 6.1 Global current account balances, 1980–2010, US$ billion

market and wage setting, have often been credited with sparking off the country's tremendous export growth.

Oil exporters' current account surpluses started to grow in earnest in 2004 and reached their peak in 2008, together with the price of oil. However, the price of oil declined from over US$140 per barrel in July 2008 to approximately US$30 in January 2009. This drastic deterioration in the terms of trade of oil producers led to a marked decrease in the level of current account surpluses, both as a percentage of GDP and in dollar terms. Nevertheless, it must be noted that oil producers also recorded current account surpluses in 2009. Declining oil prices had an immediate effect on the exchange rates of the oil-exporting countries. This relatively tight link between oil producers' real exchange rate and the price of oil has been documented, for example, in Korhonen and Juurikkala (2009), as well as in Koranchelian (2005). For the link between other raw materials and exchange rates, see, for example, Chen and Rogoff (2003).

Among current account deficit countries, the role of the USA is dominant. It has had a current account deficit for more than three decades, and the deficit started to widen as early as the 1990s. However, in nominal

terms the deficit reached its peak in 2006 (US$800 billion), before con-
tracting during the Great Recession of 2008 and 2009. Some European
countries also had current account deficits contributing to the global
imbalances, but their absolute size was still much smaller than the deficits
in the USA. Interestingly enough, the euro area as an aggregate has had a
practically balanced current account for most of its existence.

WHY DON'T WE SEE MORE CURRENT ACCOUNT DEFICITS IN OIL-EXPORTING COUNTRIES?

Just surveying the aggregate current account balance of oil-producing
countries would suggest that current account deficits are relatively rare.
However, the aggregate numbers mask certain differences between countries. During the period from 1980 to 2010 only three OPEC countries
had current account deficits, on average (Angola 0.8 per cent of GDP,
Indonesia 0.5 per cent and Ecuador 2.8 per cent). Some countries – for
example Kuwait and Libya – had average current account surpluses of
more than 10 per cent of GDP. In the late 1980s and early 1990s many
oil exporters saw either low current account surpluses or outright deficits,
as oil prices declined. Figure 6.2 charts the evolution of current accounts
in the largest oil-exporting countries as a percentage of GDP. We can see
that after 1999 none of the countries have had current account deficits, but
during the mid-1990s only Kuwait was able to garner substantial current

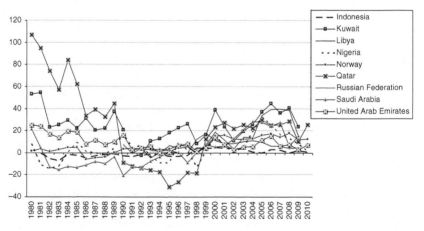

Source: IMF, *International Financial Statistics.*

Figure 6.2   Current account, 1980–2010, percentage of GDP

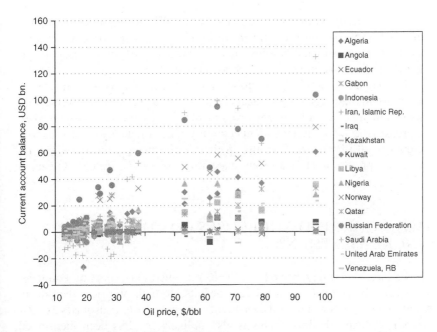

Source: IMF, *International Financial Statistics.*

*Figure 6.3   Current account, 1980–2010, US$ billion, and price of oil,
US$/barrel*

account surpluses. Nevertheless, one should note that even the largest
oil exporter, Saudi Arabia, ran substantial current account deficits in the
1980s after the second oil crisis. One can hypothesize that more credit-
worthy countries are 'allowed' to have larger current account deficits, at
least for some time. Countries finance these deficits by running down their
foreign assets or then by borrowing from abroad. However, since the late
1990s oil exporters have had no need to do this.

There are several potential reasons for this. First, perhaps oil prices
have been so high that oil exporters have been able to run current account
surpluses, no matter what. However, this cannot be the whole truth, as
countries did not have current account deficits in 2009, when the price of
oil decreased drastically. In many oil-exporting countries the real depreciation of the domestic currency helped in maintaining current account
surpluses. Nevertheless, the link between the price of oil and the current
account balance exists. Looking at the absolute level of current account
balances (Figure 6.3), we can see that there is clearly a positive correlation
between the size of the surplus (in billions of US dollars) and the level of

oil prices, across countries and across time. Whenever the oil price was above US$50 per barrel, current account deficits were practically non-existent. At oil price levels below this threshold, country-year observations with negative current account increase clearly.

The second possible explanation is that after the various economic crises in emerging markets, oil producers have been much more risk-averse, and have sought to avoid current account deficits, as they are perceived to increase risks in an oil-dependent economy. The popularity of various sovereign wealth funds (SWFs) also in the oil-producing countries supports this interpretation. (For a recent exposition on SWFs, see e.g. Kunzel et al., 2011.)

WILL CURRENT SURPLUSES CONTINUE TO INCREASE, THEN?

If we have seemingly moved into a regime where oil-exporting countries are unlikely to run current account deficits, do high oil prices then mean that oil exporters will record ever-higher current account surpluses as their export revenues balloon? This is also unlikely. As has been mentioned above, in oil-exporting countries the real exchange rate tends to react to changes in oil price. The real exchange rate is then intimately linked to the purchasing power of the country's residents *vis-à-vis* foreign goods, that is, imports. While, for example, a policy of fixed nominal exchange rates can delay the adjustment of the real exchange rate, at some point higher inflation will lead to an appreciation of the real exchange rate in this case as well. Adjustment may take time, but it will happen. Therefore one could expect to find a positive correlation between the price of oil and the value of imports, even if the correlation between oil price and export value is contemporaneous.

Figure 6.4 shows the lagged change in the price of oil (on the horizontal axis) in dollars (per barrel), while the vertical axis depicts the contemporaneous change in a country's current account balance. A negative change means a smaller surplus or perhaps even a larger deficit. The correlation between these two variables is negative for almost all countries over time, and from the figure we can see that if the absolute size of the oil price change is larger than $15, the current account is very likely to move in the *opposite* direction in the following year. Obviously, many other factors influence a country's current account balance, but the self-correcting mechanism of oil price changes also seems obvious. Oil-producing countries cannot, or will not, run large current account deficits. Moreover, large export revenues will inevitably spark a boom in imports, helped by

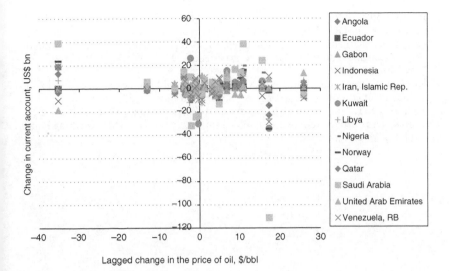

Source: IMF, *International Financial Statistics* and own calculations.

Figure 6.4   Changes in current account balance and lagged change in the price of oil

stronger real exchange rates. This self-correcting mechanism will then keep the current account surpluses in check.

CONCLUDING REMARKS

Oil-exporting countries have contributed to global imbalances. However, for most of the 2000s this was because the price of oil increased continuously. Higher oil prices inevitably invite more imports, and as the price of oil stops increasing, this effect may come to dominate, leading to smaller current account surpluses. This means that if the oil price does not rise in the coming years (as suggested by current futures prices), oil exporters' current account surpluses will shrink. This will be the oil producers' contribution to the adjustment of global imbalances.

REFERENCES

Chen, Yu-chin and Kenneth Rogoff (2003), 'Commodity currencies', *Journal of International Economics*, **60**, 133–60.

International Monetary Fund (2006), *World Economic Outlook*, April, Washington, DC: IMF.

Koranchelian, Taline (2005), 'The equilibrium real exchange rate in a commodity exporting country: Algeria's experience', IMF Working Paper 05/135, Washington, DC.

Korhonen, Iikka and Tuuli Juurikkala (2009), 'Equilibrium exchange rates in oil-dependent countries', *Journal of Economics and Finance*, **33**, 71–9.

Kunzel, Peter, Yinqiu Lu, Iva Petrova and Jukka Pihlman (2011), 'Investment objectives of sovereign wealth funds – a shifting paradigm', IMF Working Paper 11/19, Washington, DC.

7. German unification and intra-European imbalances

Gunther Schnabl and Holger Zemanek

The Greek euro tragedy and the European debt crisis have revived the discussion on the optimal adjustment to asymmetric shocks in a heterogeneous currency area. In the current discussion, the benefits of macroeconomic stability (McKinnon, 1963) and lower transaction costs for factor movements within the European Economic and Monetary Union (EMU) (European Commission, 1990) have been eclipsed by the costs of lost monetary policy independence as an adjustment tool after asymmetric shocks (Mundell, 1961). While some proponents have argued that Greece should exit the EMU to prevent a supranational transfer union, the European Commission (2010) urges the crisis countries to impose austerity in private and public spending to cure the real overvaluation of their abrogated currencies. To prevent further imbalances, France and other international partners have called upon Germany to reduce its surplus in the current account by raising wages and consumption (G20, 2011). In contrast, the German chancellor Merkel highlights the importance of exports for the German growth model.

To analyse the consequences of the current policy propositions on the intra-European current account imbalances, we look back to the 1990s when German unification constituted an asymmetric shock to Europe. It will be argued that the legacy of German unification remains an important reason for the current divergence of European current accounts and thereby the current European debt crisis. It will be shown that the adjustment channels of asymmetric shocks in the European (Monetary) Union go far beyond Mundell's (1961) seminal theory of optimum currency areas, extending to capital markets, fiscal policies and monetary policy.

Based on this finding, it will be argued that the French and G20 policy proposition to restrict German current account surpluses is in the interests of German savers and taxpayers, as international risk exposure would be reduced. However, the policy tools available to the German authorities to scale down the German current account surplus may be very limited because of the European institutional framework. Furthermore, if a reduction of the German current account surplus could be achieved through expansionary wage and/or fiscal policies, this may not be in the interests of its neighbours. A move of Germany towards expansionary macroeconomic policies would impose austerity on the rest of Europe, unless, as the likelihood of a new wave of crisis increases, the European Central Bank felt urged to engineer a new round of monetary expansion.

1.   INTERTEMPORAL SAVINGS AND THE GERMAN UNIFICATION SHOCK

German unification is a textbook case for the advantage of intertemporal savings in a heterogeneous currency area. Before unification, West Germany traditionally generated large saving and current account surpluses through its highly productive export industry (Figure 7.1). The resulting net capital exports led to a gradual build-up of international assets, *inter alia* versus its European partners. From 1980 to 1990 the net international assets of West Germany increased from €24 billion to

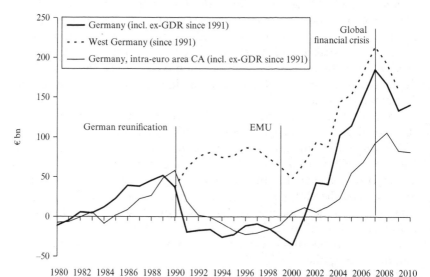

Source: Eurostat, Bundesbank and Destatis, own calculation based on regional national account figures.

Figure 7.1   German current account balance in € billion (1980–2010)

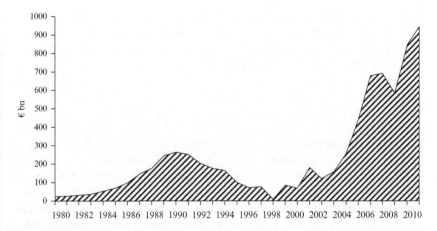

Source: IMF.

Figure 7.2 *German net international investment position in € billion (1980–2010)*

roughly €250 billion, as shown in Figure 7.2. When in 1990 the asymmetric unification shock hit, West Germany's international assets could be repatriated to meet the immense financing needs to rebuild the new eastern part of unified Germany.

As a result, the current account balance of unified Germany switched from a €40 billion surplus in 1990 to a €20 billion deficit in 1991, while the West German current account balance further increased to a surplus of around €60 billion in 1991 (Figure 7.1). This implies three main macroeconomic financing sources of unification: first, the current account surplus of West Germany increased; second, the West German current account surplus was redirected from West Germany's (European) trading partners towards East Germany; third, West German international assets were repatriated. German net international assets declined from €250 billion in 1990 to close to zero in 1998 (Figure 7.2).

For Europe, the German unification shock constitutes a textbook asymmetric shock in the sense of Mundell (1961) as Germany boomed whereas its neighbours were in recession. In contrast to Mundell (1961), the shock spread over Europe primarily via capital markets (rather than goods markets). As German net capital exports turned into net capital imports overnight, the supply of German capital to European capital markets dried up and the German Mark came under appreciation pressure. In the European Monetary System (EMS) of the early 1990s, which aimed to keep nominal exchange rates between the European currencies fixed, interest rates increased. The currencies other than the Mark came under depreciation pressure (Figure 7.3) and the central banks (other than the Deutsche Bundesbank) lost foreign reserves.

This process was further compounded when the Deutsche Bundesbank tightened money supply to contain inflationary pressure. Many European countries were dragged even deeper into recession, while Germany enjoyed its unification boom. EMS members who were regarded as unwilling to follow the German monetary policy stance – such as the UK and Italy – became victims of speculative attacks and currency crises.

The crisis of the EMS was resolved by realignments of the EMS central parities and by widening the EMS bandwidths. In Figure 7.3 the real exchange rate against the Mark is defined as national euros per German euros. The exchange rate alignment is clearly visible for Finland, Greece, Ireland, Italy, Portugal and Spain. That solution fits the textbook model by Mundell (1961), who argued that, given price and wage stickiness, exchange rate adjustments are necessary to cope with asymmetric shocks. Mundell (1961) also argued that the depreciation of the currency of the recession country is welcomed by the booming country, as the appreciation helps to reduce inflationary pressure. Indeed, in the short term the appreciation of the German Mark partially contained the inflation arising from the unification boom.

Yet Germany followed the UK and other European partner countries into the recession as the demand for German products declined. The real appreciation of the German Mark – which was caused by the realignments against the EMS crisis currencies, rising inflation in Germany and an appreciation of the German Mark against the dollar (and all currencies pegged to the dollar) – became a drag on German exports. The real appreciation of the German Mark and wage increases beyond productivity increases eroded Germany's traditionally strong international competitiveness, turning the German current account balance negative for a long period. This trend is particularly visible if the real effective exchange rate of the German Mark is calculated based on unit labour costs (ULC) as in Figure 7.4. When in the mid-1990s the turmoil of the German unification shock and the EMS crisis had settled down and growth in the EU resumed, government debt in Germany (as well as in most European countries) had substantially increased (Figure 7.5). Germany had become plagued by the legacy of the unification boom in the form of high unit labour costs, high unemployment and high public debt.

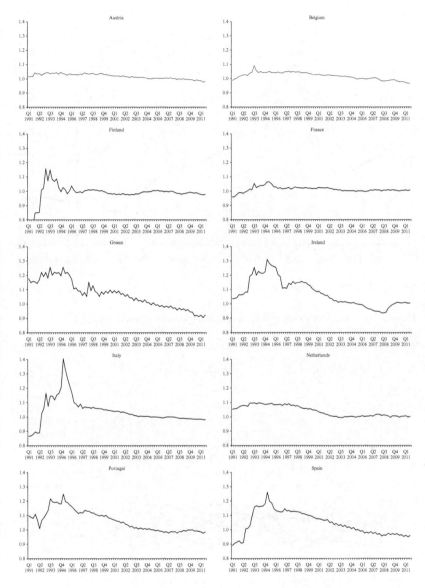

Note: Bilateral real exchange rates in national currency per German Mark are converted by national EMU entry exchange rates.

Source: IMF.

Figure 7.3 Bilateral real exchange rates against Germany based on CPI (national euro per German euro)

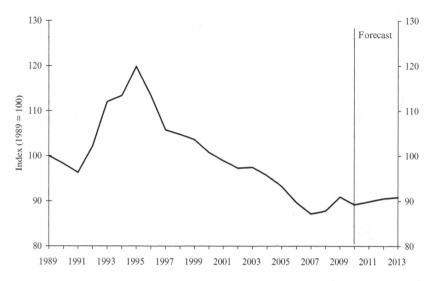

Source: European Commission.

Figure 7.4   German real effective exchange rate (based on ULC)

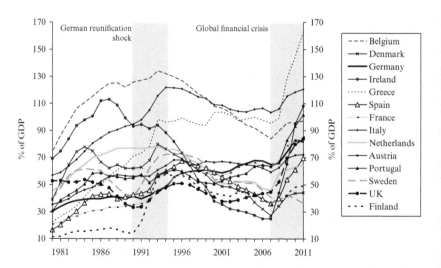

Source: European Commission.

Figure 7.5   Gross public debt in per cent of GDP

2. INTRA-GERMAN ADJUSTMENT TO THE UNIFICATION SHOCK

The economic consequences of the German unification process were not only perpetuated by a Mundell (1961) type asymmetric shock across Europe, but also within Germany, as East German demand suddenly shifted from East German products to West German products. The political dynamics of German unification did not allow for an adjustment via exchange rates as proposed by Mundell (1961). In the German monetary union, the nominal exchange rate for East German cash, bank deposits, wages and pensions was fixed far above the market rate at 1:1 and 1:2, respectively. By then, the market exchange rate between the West and East German Mark was assessed at around 1:10 (Koedijk and Kool, 1992).[1] The political decision in favour of the 1:1 exchange rate had been made in the belief that this would increase the East German standard of living in a timely manner (again to prevent large-scale migration from East to West). West German politicians had made respective promises in the pre-election campaign in early 1990 (Tietmeyer, 2000).

Furthermore, wages were not fully adjusted to divergent productivities. The strongly overvalued entry of the East German Mark into the German monetary union in combination with lower productivity of East German industry would have required a substantially lower wage level in the eastern part of Germany. Because of the strong bargaining power of the unified German trade unions, wages in East Germany increased far beyond the levels justified by industrial productivity (to prevent large-scale migration from East to West).[2] Furthermore, rigid West German labour market regulations were carried over to East Germany, as trade unions pushed for a quick equalization of working conditions.

The German monetary union in combination with wage equalization required alternative adjustment mechanisms. As in Mundell's (1961) seminal theory, labour migration from East to West as well as public transfers (explicit and implicit via social security systems) in the opposite direction (to prevent even more migration) became the most important adjustment channels. Until 2008 East Germany lost (in net terms) around 6 per cent of its population, particularly due to migration to the western part of Germany. Within a completely integrated labour market and given a highly developed transport infrastructure, thousands of workers started to commute from East to West.

The public transfers for East Germany consist of payments for the extraordinary burden related to German unification (Solidarpakt I+II)

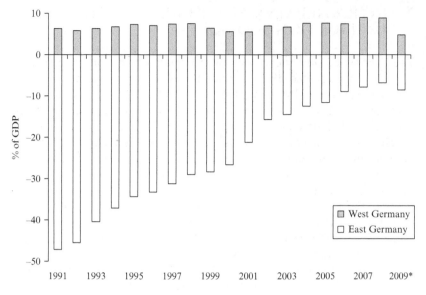

Note: * provisional figures.

Source: Destatis, own calculations based on regional national account figures.

*Figure 7.6   Current account balance of West and East Germany as
              per cent of GDP*

and payments via the German regional tax equalization system
(Länderfinanzausgleich) (Bundesfinanzministerium, 2010). In total, since
1990, transfers from West to East are estimated at about €15 to €17
billion annually. Transfers corresponded to more than 20 per cent of
the current aggregated public budgets of East German federal states
in 2008.[3] Additionally to the outright transfers, implicit transfers arose
from the adoption of the West German social security system in East
Germany.

In Figure 7.6 overall net transfers (private and public) are approximated
by the East German current account balance. Based on this proxy, by
1990 net transfers constituted almost 50 per cent of East German output.
Although net transfers gradually declined to less than 10 per cent of East
German output, the persistence of public transfer flows remains a source
of discomfort in the western part of Germany, which generates the largest
share of German tax revenues. All in all, the overall volume of net transfers from West to East Germany is estimated to amount to €1300 billion
between 1991 and 2009.

The intra-German adjustment to the unification shock based on high wage levels and public debt can be seen as the starting point for the divergence of intra-European current account balances. The 1:1 German monetary union combined with the real effective appreciation of the German Mark (Figure 7.4) and low productivity of the industries in the eastern part of the country had eroded the international competitiveness of unified Germany. During the post-unification recession, unemployment rocketed, in particular in the eastern part where most state-owned enterprises went bankrupt following the sudden real wage hikes, which were not backed by respective productivity increases. The East German unemployment rate jumped from virtually zero in 1990 to 10 per cent in 1991 and reached almost 20 per cent in 1997. The unemployment rate of unified Germany was dragged to previously unheard-of peaks, from about 7 per cent in 1990 to more than 12 per cent in 1998.

German public debt had increased sharply during the unification process (Figure 7.5), from 41 per cent of GDP in 1990 to 60 per cent in 1998. During the second half of the 1990s, the advent of EMU and the Stability and Growth Pact enhanced the need for fiscal consolidation. The hike in both unemployment and public debt drastically reduced the bargaining power of trade unions. The consolidation of public budgets seemed even more necessary in the face of the Stability and Growth Pact, which Germany itself had initiated and now seemed to be unable to comply with. To reduce public spending, public wage growth was kept very moderate. Private sector wages were not only constrained by public wage austerity but also by high unemployment figures and the integration of the Central and Eastern European countries into the EU. As a result, overall German real wage growth remained very moderate. The resulting gloomy business sentiment put a drag on domestic investment, which made – in the context of global financial exuberance – investment in foreign government bonds look very attractive (Sinn, 2010).

Due to rising productivity, unit labour costs have not significantly increased since 1995, and have strongly declined versus other EU members, as suggested by Figure 7.4. A lasting trend of real depreciation of the German Mark set in, which was mainly perpetuated by a gradual relative decline in unit labour costs. This trend continued after the German Mark had been converted into the euro and the German current account returned to unprecedented surpluses (Figure 7.7), while Germany's neighbours generated rising deficits. Thus the distortions caused by the adjustment to German unification based on public debt and high wages constituted the origin of the divergence of intra-European current accounts since the late 1990s, as Germany sought to regain its international competitiveness.

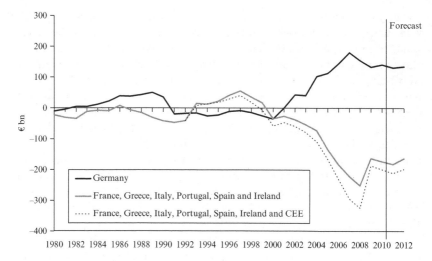

Note: CEE countries are Czech Republic, Slovak Republic, Slovenia, Bulgaria, Estonia, Hungary, Latvia, Lithuania, Poland and Romania.

Source: IMF.

Figure 7.7 European current account balances

3. LONG-TERM CONSEQUENCES FOR THE EURO AREA

The introduction of the euro further promoted the divergence of current account balances in the EMU, as suggested in Figure 7.1 and Figure 7.7. Although a common monetary policy was implemented and euro area money and capital markets became (more) integrated, differences in wage growth remained in place. In Germany, overall wage growth remained moderate as a legacy of the post-unification distortions, which were perceived as in urgent need of attention. In contrast, wage growth in many other countries of the euro area remained high, as the result of the inflation indexation of wages and high public sector wage growth (Zemanek, 2010a).

High wage growth at the E(M)U periphery became possible because of private and public austerity in Germany, which slowed German domestic investment and led to immense German current account surpluses and net capital exports (Figures 7.1 and 7.2). After the net international investment position of Germany had declined close to zero in 1998, with the start of EMU, Germany's net international assets dramatically increased to more than €900 billion by 2009 (Figure 7.2). Gros (2010), who refers to the current crisis as 'the long shadow of the fall of the wall', argues that the worldwide credit boom since 2003 has made the euro crisis possible: the rise of intra-European current account imbalances was enhanced by the low interest rate policy in the USA after the burst of the new economy bubble, which was translated into a (rather) low interest rate policy in the euro area (Freitag and Schnabl, 2011).

German net savings were funnelled via integrated capital markets *inter alia* to Southern, Central and Eastern Europe. The elimination of exchange rate risk and the common monetary policy as conducted by the European Central Bank improved macroeconomic conditions and therefore credit conditions in former high-inflation countries such as Greece, Portugal, Spain, Ireland, Bulgaria and Hungary. Lower borrowing constraints as a result of financial deepening accelerated southward, eastward and westward capital flows. EMU and EU membership seemed to have nourished the notion of enhanced international capital allocation efficiency and international risk sharing.

The common monetary policy of the European Central Bank was not able to steer against rising wages and inflation at the E(M)U periphery as German low wage and price growth kept average euro area inflation close to its target. Given that capital flows were unidirectional instead of mutual (and therefore wage policies in EMU could diverge), the one-size monetary policy of EMU led to a divergence of real interest rates, which further aggravated asymmetric economic development. The nominal differences in wage and price inflation translated into real divergences. The German Mark gradually depreciated against all other euro area and EU currencies, as shown in Figures 7.3 and 7.4. Current accounts continued to diverge (Zemanek et al., 2010), as shown in Figure 7.7.

In later papers, Mundell (1973a, 1973b) argued that a higher degree of capital market integration in a monetary union helps to absorb asymmetric shocks via cross-country financial asset holdings[4] (McKinnon, 2004). In respect of EMU, Mundell (1973a, 1973b) implies that Germany would have increased its assets in Greece and Greece would have increased its assets in Germany after both countries had entered the monetary union. With each country holding claims on output of the other, asymmetric shocks or adverse business cycles are shared by varying capital income and capital valuation. This international risk-sharing mechanism should have helped to absorb asymmetric shocks and to smooth consumption over time.

However, in contrast to Mundell (1973a, 1973b), the capital market integration process in EMU was *de facto* not a mutual one. Capital flows were unidirectional, in particular German capital flowing to Southern and Western Europe as well as – often via Austria – to Central and Eastern European countries. In contrast, very little capital seems to have moved in the opposite direction. In effect, integrated capital markets allowed – fuelled by the global credit boom – the current account balances to diverge as shown in Figure 7.7. Because of the resulting asymmetric distribution of risk, instead of risk sharing, capital markets further aggravated the crisis once the mood had changed and the crisis struck (Zemanek, 2010b).

Apparently, during the crisis, market participants and lenders seem to have interpreted all EMU countries as being jointly liable for a single member country's debt. Markets seem to have ignored the European Treaty, which explicitly excludes bailouts for the euro area (Article 125, Treaty on the Functioning of the European Union). The Greek government, Greek banks and German banks seem to have anticipated supranational support (or bailout), because on a global level past balance-of-payment crises had been mostly monetized by rising public debt in combination with interest rate cuts (Hoffmann and Schnabl, 2011).[5] Thus moral hazard is likely to have inflated the dimension of the current crisis, as expansionary monetary policy compressed risk premiums. That might be particularly true as the shock did not appear suddenly and exogenously as modelled by Mundell (1961), but potential for crisis was gradually built up by diverging current accounts and rising intra-euro area liabilities (Zemanek, 2010a; Zemanek et al., 2010).

Although it remains unclear who will pay for the costs of the European debt crisis, West German savers and taxpayers bear an overproportional risk if the fast-rising European public debt burden is to be worked off by raising taxes, perpetuated wage restraint or inflation. West German taxpayers wonder if Greece will follow the East German example, with adjustment costs being borne on a supranational level by taxpayers and with net transfers becoming even more persistent than in the case of East Germany. The stake at risk can be quantified as a substantial part of Germany's net international assets, as shown in Figure 7.2, that is, a sum of up to €900 billion, which comes close to the total cost of German unification. The process of devaluing German international savings would be accelerated if Greece, Ireland, Portugal, Spain or others were to default. If the ECB responds to the threat of default of EMU and/or EU members with monetary expansion, the devaluation of savings will take place via higher inflation or new boom-and-bust cycles. In all cases, intertemporal allocation would be transformed into intra-European redistribution.

4.   ECONOMIC POLICY IMPLICATIONS: TOWARDS EVEN MORE MONETARY EXPANSION?

The adjustment mechanisms of asymmetric shocks in the EMU are complex and go beyond Mundell (1961) and Mundell (1973a, 1973b). Because financial markets seem to regard country-specific liabilities as union-wide liabilities, asymmetric shocks in the E(M)U are more likely to be absorbed by rising public debt or inflation. German unification as well as the European debt crisis, which was sparked by the Greek tragedy, have increased and will increase public debt throughout Europe. When public debt in Europe threatens to reach unsustainable limits, at the latest during a new round of crisis, debt reduction by increasing inflation becomes more likely.

Intertemporal saving will not pay off if public debt and/or inflation are used to prevent credit defaults during crisis. From this point of view, the French and G20 proposal to increase wages and private consumption in Germany can be seen to be in the interests of German savers and taxpayers. The declining German current account surplus would reduce potential future credit risk for Germany in general and German savers and taxpayers in particular. However, a declining German current account surplus cannot be achieved by economic policy action for three reasons. First, German wages are negotiated by enterprises and trade unions without political interference. Even if France demands higher German wages, the German government has only limited scope to encourage private sector wage increases. Generous public wage increases are likely to encourage higher private sector wages, but they are constrained by the Stability and Growth Pact, which seems to have become even more binding after the most recent crisis.

Second, the German current account surplus may shrink if German savers anticipate further defaults of German international savings. If this were the case, savings would be invested at home, for instance in the real-estate sector, where prices are cheap from a European perspective and therefore have already picked up. Yet the German real-estate sector may not be large enough to absorb all German savings. Third, even if wages in Germany rise, it is not certain whether Germans will translate higher wages into more domestic demand. If Germans stick to their saving habit while wages rise, the current account surplus will persist, as suggested by Figure 7.7. A huge public investment programme, as after unification, would be necessary to redirect German capital towards domestic investment. As the marginal efficiency of public investments is in general below private investments and decreasing over time, a large-scale Keynesian investment programme may not be seen as a desirable option.

But unintended repercussions on the whole of Europe are likely when the German current account turns negative. As during the unification boom, rising real interest rates, slowing growth and increasing unemployment throughout Europe may be the consequence. This is not the scenario that French politicians have in mind. Therefore they may want to consider the backlash of their idea, unless they have already anticipated that the reversal of German capital flows will trigger a new crisis in fragile countries such as Ireland, Greece, Spain and in Central and Eastern Europe. Then the threat of a new crisis will be the catalyst for even further monetary expansion by the ECB. That could be equivalent to a move from a German-type 'hard-nosed' central bank to a more inflation-benign central bank, as prevailed in France and many current EMU members before 1999.

NOTES

1. The estimation is based on a black market rate as the East German Mark was not freely convertible.
2. In 1992, East German wages reached 62 per cent of the West German wage level (Brenke, 2001); meanwhile they have converged to about 80 per cent (Ragnitz, 2010).
3. Data collected from online statistics of the Bundesfinanzministerium and Deutscher Bundestag (2001).
4. Bonds and equities, as well as bank credits.
5. Hoffmann and Schnabl (2011) argue that asymmetric interest rate cuts – i.e. larger interest rate cuts during the crisis than interest rate increases during the recovery – have hidden the cost of crisis resolution and have contributed to a fall of the global interest rate level towards zero.

REFERENCES

Brenke, Karl (2001), 'Löhne in Ostdeutschland – Anpassung an das westdeutsche Niveau erst auf lange Sicht möglich', DIW Wochenbericht, No. 24/01.
Bundesfinanzministerium (2010), 'Bund/Länder – Finanzbeziehungen auf der Grundlage der Finanzverfassung', Ausgabe 2009 (Berlin).
Deutscher Bundestag (2001), 'Entwurf eines Gesetzes über verfassungskonkretisierende allgemeine Maßstäbe für die Verteilung des Umsatzsteueraufkommens, für den Finanzausgleich unter den Ländern sowie für die Gewährung von Bundesergänzungszuweisungen', Drucksache, No. 14/6577.
European Commission (1990), 'One market, one money: an evaluation of the potential benefits and costs of forming an economic and monetary union', European Economy, No. 44.
European Commission (2010), 'Surveillance of intra-euro-area competitiveness and imbalances', European Economy, No. 1/2010.
Freitag, Stephan and Gunther Schnabl (2011), 'Reverse causality in global and intra-European imbalances', Global Financial Markets Working Paper 25.
G20 (2011), 'The Cannes Action Plan for growth and jobs', Communiqué of the

G20 Meeting, 4 November 2011, Cannes. Available at http://www.g20.org/ Documents2011/11/Cannes%20Action%20plan%204%20November%202011. pdf.

Gros, Daniel (2010), 'The long shadow of the fall of the wall', VOX Column. Available at http://www.voxeu.org/index.php?q=node/5191.

Hoffmann, Andreas and Gunther Schnabl (2011), 'A vicious cycle of manias, crashes and asymmetric policy responses', *The World Economy*, **34**(3), 382–403.

Koedijk, Kees G. and Clemens J.M. Kool (1992), 'Tail estimates of East European exchange rates', *Journal of Business & Economic Statistics*, **10**(1), 83–96.

McKinnon, Ronald (1963), 'Optimum currency areas', *American Economic Review*, **53**, 717–25.

McKinnon, Ronald (2004), 'Optimum currency areas and key currencies: Mundell I versus Mundell II', *Journal of Common Market Studies*, **42**(4), 689–715.

Mundell, Robert (1961), 'A theory of optimum currency areas', *American Economic Review*, **51**(4), 657–65.

Mundell, Robert (1973a), 'A plan for a European currency', in H. Johnson and A. Swoboda (eds), *The Economics of Common Currencies*, London: Allen and Unwin, pp. 143–72.

Mundell, Robert (1973b), 'Uncommon arguments for common currencies', in H. Johnson, and A. Swoboda (eds), *The Economics of Common Currencies*, London: Allen and Unwin, pp. 114–32.

Ragnitz, Joachim (2010), 'Strukturelle Ursachen des Einkommensrückstands Ostdeutschlands', Ifo Dresden Berichtet, No. 2/2010, 17–23.

Sinn, Hans-Werner (2010), 'The financial crisis: the way forward', *CESifo Forum*, **11**(3), 12–19.

Tietmeyer, Hans (2000), 'Die 1:1-Umstellung der Ost-Mark war problematisch', Speech at Die deutsch-deutsche Währungsunion – Zehn Jahre danach.

Zemanek, Holger (2010a), 'Competitiveness within the euro area: the problem that still needs to be solved', *Economic Affairs*, **30**(4), 42–7.

Zemanek, Holger (2010b), 'Asymmetric international risk sharing in the euro area', mimeo.

Zemanek, Holger, Ansgar Belke and Gunther Schnabl (2010), 'Current account balances and structural adjustment in the euro area', *International Economics and Economic Policy*, **7**(1), 83–127.

PART III

Competitiveness and trade

8. Why do trade negotiations take so long?

Christoph Moser and Andrew K. Rose[1]

There is widespread agreement among economists that trade liberalization is best conducted at the multilateral level. Indeed, facilitating multilateral negotiations is one of the primary objectives of the World Trade Organization (WTO), as it was with its predecessor the General Agreement on Tariffs and Trade (GATT). By way of contrast, regional trade agreements (RTAs) may create some trade, but they also have the potential to harmfully divert it.

Still, the global approach to multilateral trade liberalization seems moribund. The Doha Round sponsored by the WTO 'celebrated' its tenth birthday in 2011, with no end in sight. Table 8.1 shows that the duration of GATT/WTO trade liberalization rounds – the length of time between the start of negotiations and their completion – has grown consistently with the number of participants. The 23 participants of the first (Geneva) round of GATT negotiations took only six months to conclude a deal that reduced 45 000 tariffs. But there are now over 150 members of the WTO, a number that makes negotiations considerably more difficult. Moreover, membership in the WTO has continued to grow since the completion of the last (Uruguay) round, notably with the accession of countries like China (in late 2001) and the approval of Russia's WTO membership (in 2011).

It may be problematic to generalize from the small number of observations on the duration of global (GATT/WTO) rounds of trade talks. Still, we have a large number of observations on regional trade negotiations. Since those are likely to be similar in nature to their GATT/WTO analogues, we study the determinants of the duration of RTA negotiations in this chapter. We are motivated by the question: what effect does the complexity of trade negotiations have on the duration of those negotiations? We proxy complexity with two measures: (a) the number of countries participating in the negotiation; and (b) the regional diversity of those countries. We find that negotiations do indeed take significantly longer when they involve more countries, especially if the countries are spread across different regions. Thus it seems reasonable to us that one appeal

European integration in a global economy

Table 8.1   Duration of GATT/WTO rounds

Round	Initiated	Completed	Participants	Duration (months)
Geneva	Apr. 1947	Oct. 1947	23	6
Annecy	Apr. 1949	Aug. 1949	13	4
Torquay	Sep. 1950	Apr. 1951	38	7
Geneva II	Jan. 1955	May 1956	26	16
Dillon	Sep. 1960	Jul. 1962	26	22
Kennedy	May 1964	Jun. 1967	62	37
Tokyo	Sep. 1973	Nov. 1979	102	74
Uruguay	Sep. 1986	Apr. 1994	123	91
Doha	Nov. 2001		153	>123

Reference:
http://www.wto.org/gatt_docs/English/SULPDF/91030141.pdf
http://www.wto.org/english/thewto_e/whatis_e/tif_e/fact4_e.htm

Source: Authors' calculations, available online at http://faculty.haas.berkeley.edu/arose/ON1111.zip.

of RTAs is the fact that they represent a feasible, if imperfect, route to greater trade integration. While all this is economically sensible, it still leaves us feeling depressed about the feasibility of the current Doha and future WTO rounds.

1.   METHODOLOGY AND DATA

We estimate a standard Cox proportional hazards model that links the duration of RTA trade negotiations to a number of determinants (Cox, 1972; Cleves et al., 2004) provide a reference. This model assumes that the hazard takes the form:

$$h(t) = h_o(t)\exp(\Sigma_i \beta_i x_i) \tag{8.1}$$

where the baseline hazard $h_o(t)$ is not directly estimated, xs are regressors, and the coefficients $\{\beta\}$ are estimated semi-parametrically. We estimate our models using the Efron method to handle ties, clustering our standard errors by RTA, and report our results in coefficients rather than in hazard ratios.

   Our data sample includes 88 RTAs from 1988 to 2009; Moser and Rose (2011) provide more details. We consider all RTAs that have been

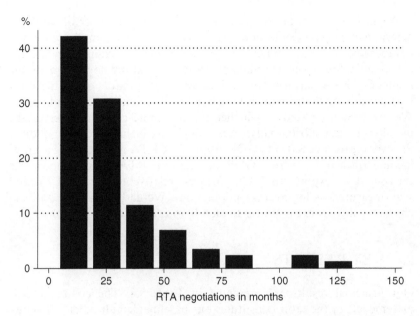

Source: Authors' calculations, available online at http://faculty.haas.berkeley.edu/arose/
ON1111.zip.

Figure 8.1   Histogram – duration of RTA negotiations

signed and reported to the WTO. The universe of RTAs is drawn from the
'Regional Trade Agreement Information System' (RTA-IS) database of
the World Trade Organization (WTO), available at http://rtais.wto.org.[2]

A central component of our data set and identification strategy consists
of a unique set of dates. We consider two important dates: (a) the day
when it was announced that negotiations on a RTA would commence at
some future date (which we dub 'Start'), and (b) the day that agreement
on the RTA was actually reached ('Deal').[3, 4] The gap between these two
dates constitutes the duration of the trade negotiation, used to construct
our hazard rate.[5] We identify the exact announcement dates through a
full-text analysis on LexisNexis, where we mainly focus on international
newswires, press releases and well-established newspapers published in
English.[6] Announcements of RTAs are usually made by prominent policy
makers such as the president, prime minister, or the minister of finance,
economics, or the trade minister of the country, and often precede official
signature dates (as reported by the WTO) by several weeks or months.[7]
While RTA negotiations in our sample last on average for 28 months,
Figure 8.1 displays considerable heterogeneity in their duration.

We link the duration of trade negotiations to a number of potential determinants (xs). Negotiations are likely to be more complicated as the number and regional diversity of members rises. Accordingly, we include as potential duration determinants both the natural logarithm of the number of RTA partners, and a dummy variable that is one if the RTA partners are drawn from more than one WTO region, and zero otherwise. We are also interested in whether the economic characteristics of the members matter substantially.[8] Accordingly, we include the natural log of the average openness (trade/GDP ratio) of the RTA members, log average income (measured as real GDP per capita), RTA export-importance (measured as exports to RTA partners, relative to RTA GDP), and size (measured as log average population). We gather data on national characteristics from the World Bank's *World Development Indicators*.

2. KEY RESULTS

Our principal results are presented in Table 8.2. The column at the extreme left of the table constitutes our baseline default model. It shows the coefficient effects for the four variables that prove to be robust determinants of the length of RTA negotiations.

Negotiations tend to be more protracted for more RTA members at the negotiation table ('Log number of RTA members'). Since we tabulate our results as coefficients, the negative sign indicates that the length of negotiations rises with the number of countries involved in RTA negotiations. This effect is significant from both the statistical and economic perspectives; trade negotiations are clearly more difficult with more countries sitting at the table. Regional diversity also seems to slow down the process significantly; our dummy variable for RTAs involving members for more than one country also has a large effect on duration.[9] We consider both of these results intuitive and sensible. Said differently, bilateral agreements between neighbours take less time to be hammered out, an unsurprising result.

We illustrate these key results in Figures 8.2 and 8.3, which show a number of different survival functions for the length of RTA negotiations. The graphs are based on our default specification in Table 8.2, with other control variables held at their average values. Figure 8.2 shows clearly that bilateral negotiations are much more likely to be concluded than multilateral ones. Similarly, Figure 8.3 makes it clear that negotiations are much more protracted for RTAs that span regions compared with intra-region negotiations.

Our default results in Table 8.2 also demonstrate slightly weaker results

Table 8.2   Baseline – determinants of duration of RTA negotiations

Model	Default	Exports within RTA	RTA's population	RTA's income divergence	Full model
Log number of RTA partners	−0.642**	−0.639**	−0.650**	−0.672**	−0.715**
	(0.13)	(0.14)	(0.15)	(0.14)	(0.17)
Cross-regional RTA	−0.687**	−0.707*	−0.666**	−0.739**	−0.714*
	(0.22)	(0.28)	(0.25)	(0.24)	(0.28)
RTA's log trade/GDP	0.585*	0.590*	0.598*	0.613**	0.675*
	(0.24)	(0.24)	(0.27)	(0.24)	(0.28)
RTA's log real GDP p/c	0.245*	0.246*	0.253*	0.246*	0.276*
	(0.12)	(0.12)	(0.13)	(0.12)	(0.13)
RTA's exports to RTA partners/GDP		−0.262			−0.310
		(1.93)			(1.97)
RTA's log population			0.021		0.075
			(0.11)		(0.12)
RTA's IQR of log real GDP p/c				−0.069	−0.103
				(0.10)	(0.10)
Number of observations	296	296	296	296	296
Log-likelihood	−297.5	−297.5	−297.4	−297.3	−297.1

Notes: Each column is estimated via a Cox proportional hazards model. Estimates based on 88 RTAs from 1988 to 2009 (see Moser and Rose, 2011, for details on data set). Survival time regressions employ the **RTA** negotiation duration in days as dependent variable. The results are shown as coefficients, not hazard ratios. Hence negative coefficients indicate longer negotiations relative to the baseline. *Log number of RTA partners* refers to number of signatories of RTA (in logarithm). Dummy variable *Cross-regional RTA* is one for RTAs with members from different regions. The variables *RTA's log trade/GDP, RTA's log real GDP p/c, RTA's exports to RTA partners/GDP and RTA's log population* refer to the RTA's average. *RTA's IQR of log real GDP p/c* measures interquartile range of income within RTA. Coefficients significantly different from zero marked at [0.10] 0.05 (0.01) with [one circle] one (two) asterisk(s).

Source: Authors' calculations, available online at http://faculty.haas.berkeley.edu/arose/ON1111.zip.

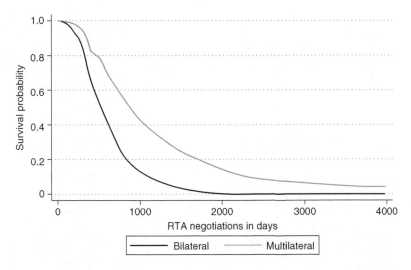

Note: Multilateral based on avg. log number of RTA members for multilateral RTAs.

Source: Authors' calculations, available online at http://faculty.haas.berkeley.edu/arose/ON1111.zip.

Figure 8.2   Survival functions for RTA negotiations

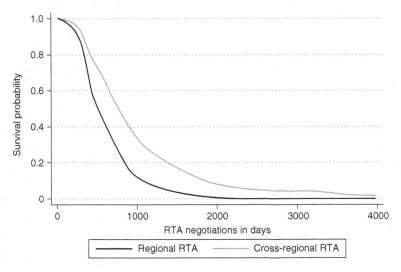

Source: Authors' calculations, available online at http://faculty.haas.berkeley.edu/arose/ON1111.zip.

Figure 8.3   Survival functions for RTA negotiations

for two other effects of interest to us: openness and income. In particular, we find that RTA partners that are more open to trade and richer tend to conclude their negotiations more quickly.

We have performed two standard specification tests for the Cox model: the link and Schoenfeld-residual tests. Reassuringly, neither test indicates any misspecification.

Our default results are presented at the extreme left of Table 8.2; the remainder of it provides some sensitivity analysis. Of special interest is the role of intra-RTA exports (measured relative to GDP), which we include as a potential determinant in another column of Table 8.2. Surprisingly, we estimate a non-result: higher export-to-GDP ratios within the RTA do not appear to speed up negotiations. The same is true of the effect of RTA size (measured as population), and intra-RTA income divergence; neither has a measurable effect on the duration of negotiations.

Extra sensitivity analysis is provided in Tables 8.3 to 8.5. In each table, we tabulate our default baseline estimate at the extreme left of the table, and then add additional factors, both one by one and together. Table 8.3 adds a dummy variable that indicates whether both goods and services are covered by the RTA (rather than just goods alone), as well as two measures of the financial depth of the economy. Table 8.4 focuses on whether the USA or the EU/EC plays special roles in the length of RTA negotiations; Table 8.5 focuses on non-linear interactive effects. The bottom line from these sensitivity checks is clear: our results appear to be robust.

3.   SUMMARY AND CONCLUSION

In this chapter, we have empirically modelled the duration of trade negotiations; that is, the length of time between the start of trade talks and their conclusion. Since the world has experienced only eight rounds of global trade talks through the GATT/WTO mechanism, we use data from 88 regional trade agreements between 1988 and 2009. We estimate a plain-vanilla semi-parametric Cox proportional hazards model and find four intuitive results. Trade negotiations are more protracted when there are more countries at the negotiation table, and when the countries are not from the same region. Negotiations between more open and richer countries are also finished more quickly.

Our results lead us to be pessimistic about the prospects for future global trade talks. The membership of the WTO continues to grow as the few remaining outsider countries (like Russia) join. As the number of participants and the diversity of their preferences grow, it becomes increasingly difficult to imagine a successful conclusion to the Doha Round, let alone

Table 8.3 *Extra controls – determinants of duration of RTA negotiations*

Model	Default	Coverage of RTA	RTA's listed firms	RTA's stock market	Full model
Log number of RTA partners	−0.642**	−0.605**	−0.747**	−0.757**	−0.717**
	(0.13)	(0.14)	(0.18)	(0.15)	(0.18)
Cross-regional RTA	−0.687**	−0.648*	−0.802**	−0.731**	−0.674*
	(0.22)	(0.22)	(0.27)	(0.23)	(0.28)
RTA's log trade/GDP	0.585*	0.537*	0.573*	0.799**	0.760*
	(0.24)	(0.25)	(0.25)	(0.27)	(0.32)
RTA's log real GDP p/c	0.245*	0.213°	0.259*	0.298*	0.257*
	(0.12)	(0.12)	(0.12)	(0.12)	(0.12)
Goods & services included		0.217			−0.296
		(0.28)			(0.28)
RTA's log number of listed firms			−0.154		0.005
			(0.18)		(0.25)
RTA's log national stocks/GDP				−0.224	−0.252
				(0.14)	(0.20)
Number of observations	296	296	296	296	296
Log-likelihood	−297.5	−297.2	−297.1	−296.3	−295.8

Notes: As for Table 8.2. Dummy variable *Cross-regional RTA [Goods & Services included]* is one for **RTA**s with members from different regions [**RTA**s covering goods and services – and not only goods]. The variables *RTA's log trade/GDP*, *RTA's log real GDP p/c*, *RTA's log number of listed firms* and *RTA's log national stocks/GDP* refer to the **RTA**'s average. Coefficients significantly different from zero marked at [0.10] 0.05 (0.01) with [one circle] one (two) asterisk(s).

Source: Authors' calculations, available online at http://faculty.haas.berkeley.edu/arose/ON1111.zip.

Table 8.4   RTAs, the EU and the USA – determinants of duration of RTA negotiations

Model	Default	RTA involved	EU/EC involved	USA involved	Full model
Log number of RTA partners	-0.642**	-0.497**	-0.775**	-0.608**	-0.504
	(0.13)	(0.19)	(0.26)	(0.13)	(0.37)
Cross-regional RTA	-0.687**	-0.556*	-0.688**	-0.675**	-0.547*
	(0.22)	(0.24)	(0.22)	(0.23)	(0.27)
RTA's log trade/GDP	0.585*	0.603*	0.616*	0.704*	0.747*
	(0.24)	(0.24)	(0.26)	(0.28)	(0.31)
RTA's log real GDP p/c	0.245*	0.246*	0.242*	0.204°	0.200°
	(0.12)	(0.12)	(0.12)	(0.12)	(0.12)
One party RTA		-0.430			-0.413
		(0.33)			(0.37)
EU/EC part of RTA			0.388		0.107
			(0.52)		(0.61)
USA part of RTA				0.431	0.479
				(0.32)	(0.33)
Number of observations	296	296	296	296	296
Log-likelihood	-297.5	-296.5	-297.2	-296.9	-295.9

Notes: As for Table 8.2. Dummy variables *One party RTA, EU/EC part of RTA* and *USA-part of RTA* is one for RTAs with another RTA, EU/EC or USA involved. The variables *RTA's log trade/GDP* and *RTA's log real GDP p/c* refer to the **RTA**'s average. Coefficients significantly different from zero marked at [0.10] 0.05 (0.01) with [one circle] one (two) asterisk(s).

Source: Authors' calculations, available online at http://faculty.haas.berkeley.edu/arose/ON1111.zip.

Table 8.5 *Bilateral RTAs and non-linearities*

Model	Default	Interaction	Bilateral RTA	Bilateral RTA	Full model
Log number of RTA partners	-0.642**	-0.644**	-0.531°	-0.528*	-0.674°
	(0.13)	(0.17)	(0.32)	(0.23)	(0.39)
Cross-regional RTA	-0.687**	-0.695**	-0.670**		
	(0.22)	(0.35)	(0.23)		
RTA's log trade/GDP	0.585*	0.585*	0.582*	0.537*	0.546*
	(0.24)	(0.24)	(0.24)	(0.26)	(0.25)
RTA's log real GDP p/c	0.245*	0.245*	0.246*	0.219°	0.217°
	(0.12)	(0.12)	(0.12)	(0.11)	(0.11)
Cross-regional RTA* Log number of RTA partners		0.005			
		(0.21)			
Bilateral RTA			0.217	1.032**	0.840*
			(0.60)	(0.27)	(0.42)
Cross-regional RTA* Bilateral RTA					0.282
					(0.47)
Number of observations	296	296	296	296	296
Log-likelihood	-297.5	-297.5	-297.4	-299.0	-298.8

Notes: As for Table 8.2. Dummy variable *Bilateral RTA* is one for a bilateral RTA. Furthermore, interaction terms between cross-regional RTA and *log number of RTA partners* and bilateral are added in column (2) and (5), respectively. The variables *RTA's log trade/GDP* and *RTA's log real GDP p/c* refer to the RTA's average. Coefficients significantly different from zero marked at [0.10] 0.05 (0.01) with [one circle] one (two) asterisk(s).

Source: Authors' calculations, available online at http://faculty.haas.berkeley.edu/arose/ON1111.zip.

future liberalization rounds engineered under the auspices of the WTO. While multilateral liberalization has many advantages over regional trade liberalization, feasibility does not appear to be among them.

NOTES

1. The authors thank Christoph Trebesch for his guidance.
2. These are listed in the RTA-IS under 'List of all RTAs in force' as well as those that have been signed but are not yet in force (listed in the RTA-IS under 'List of early announcements').
3. If the countries officially decide to conduct some sort of 'pilot study' together, this announcement is defined as the official start of negotiations, so long as *de facto* negotiations are not conditional on the success of the pilot study.
4. In the case of entry into the European Community/European Union, we define a 'deal' as the European Commission's announcement to officially recommend the accession of a new member. While the European Council technically decides to accept this recommendation, the Council has never yet rejected a positive recommendation.
5. Note that the samples of this chapter and Moser and Rose (2011) diverge because for some RTAs the start date of the negotiations could not be determined by the full-text research.
6. The full-text research via LexisNexis (LexisNexis Academic) was performed between October and December 2009, at the Haas Business School and between December 2009 and March 2010 at ETH Zurich. The full-text research typically starts with the key words 'free trade' or 'trade agreement' and the two respective country names. We restrict ourselves to dates before the respective RTA went into force.
7. One of the reasons for a gap between the official announcement and the signature ceremony is 'legal scrubbing' since it usually takes some time to transform the political will of a general agreement into a contract. (We are not aware of any cases where an agreement has not been followed by the formal signing of a RTA.) A number of RTAs have been signed but not yet ratified; these RTAs are not yet in force (prominent examples would be the US–Korea and US–Colombia RTAs).
8. Political factors might also play a role in determining the duration of RTA negotiations. We leave this for future research.
9. The WTO distinguishes between eleven regions and we use their classification.

REFERENCES

Cleves, Mario, Roberto Gutierrez, William Gould and Yulia Marchenko (2004), *An Introduction to Survival Analysis Using STATA*, College Station, TX: Stata Press.

Cox, D.R. (1972), 'Regression models and life-tables', *Journal of the Royal Statistical Society*, Series B, **34**, 187–220.

Moser, Christoph and Andrew K. Rose (2011), 'Who benefits from regional trade agreements? The view from the stock market', NBER Working Paper No. 17,415 and CEPR Discussion Paper No. 8566.

9. Global trade, regional trade and emerging Europe

Loukas Stemitsiotis and Willem J. Kooi[1]

Global trade fell during the global economic and financial crisis at a pace unseen since the 1930s. While trade adjusted mostly in volume terms in the countries mainly exporting manufactured goods, commodity exporters experienced a sharp drop in their terms of trade. In both cases, demand came under pressure because of the synchronized fall in export value on top of a sharp drop in the value of assets.

The fall in demand was a major factor behind the fall in world trade. Still, the fall in aggregate demand alone appears insufficient to explain the size and steepness of the fall in world trade. As a matter of fact, the elasticity of trade to gross domestic product (GDP) was the highest in the post-World War II period. Other explanatory factors are therefore needed. One of these is the specific effect the financial crisis had on trade in capital goods, a category that has a relatively large share in traded goods. This is the composition effect. While manufacturing has a high share in traded goods, it is also a sector that is vulnerable to the (non-)availability of finance for its working capital because of an increasingly high degree of vertical specialization in world production. The segmentation of the production chain is likely to have made this chain more reliant on external finance, more vulnerable to volatility in financial markets including exchange rate volatility, and may have increased its total need of financing for working capital. Also, trade finance was probably a contributing factor,[2] even if it is hard to determine whether demand or supply factors prevailed in the decline in trade finance.

The strong and sudden fall in world trade could easily have tempted governments into mercantilist policies, thus enhancing the chance of a replay of the Great Depression. And indeed, as noted by the World Trade Organization (WTO),[3] some countries did succumb to the temptation. Major players in the world trade system, however, broadly resisted the temptation. Their opposition to domestic forces for shielding local producers was supported by (1) the credibility of the WTO as an independent arbiter and defender of open markets, (2) the significant positive momentum of global trade integration in particular by the emerging economies, (3) the overall strong commitment by major advanced economies to free trade,[4] and (4) internationally segmented production chains.

Resisting protectionism was a prerequisite for global trade to rebound as the world economy recovered. In turn, the rebound of world trade also reinforced the recovery of world economic growth. Global trade reached pre-crisis levels in mid-2010, two years after the initial decline. However, when considering the relationship between trade and GDP, the trade to GDP ratio is still below its long-term level; it could need one or two more years to reach pre-crisis levels. Just as demand composition effects aggravated the income elasticity of world trade during the crisis, in the recovery these effects' reversal appears to have helped exports. An important share of the recovery in imports can be explained by the high import intensity of exports, and the implied reactivation of production chains. The increased availability of trade finance, also made possible by the G20 trade finance initiative, has supported the recovery of world trade.

TRADE DEVELOPMENTS IN THREE EMERGING REGIONS

The decline in world trade was not only without precedent in terms of size and pace, but also in terms of synchronization. According to Araúja and Martins (2009), the synchronization was even the distinguishing feature of the trade decline that started in October 2008. In order to perform their high-frequency analysis, however, the authors have to resort to a database that only reports data on a set of 23 OECD countries. To get a better idea of how the trade collapse worked out in the emerging market economies, we analyse the trade developments in three of the most prominent regions of emerging economies. These regions are emerging Europe,[5] Mercosur and ASEAN.

Emerging Europe, Mercosur and ASEAN represent the most integrated regions among emerging economies on their respective continents. Emerging Europe stands out as many economies of this group are part of an advanced economic region, the European Union (EU). This gives these economies unrestrained access to the EU's internal market. Japan is the most proximate developed market for ASEAN economies, while goods from Mercosur have to travel the largest distance to the nearest developed markets. However, ASEAN is mostly associated with dynamic economic developments in its own member states and in China. Even if the largest advanced trading partner of Mercosur is the EU, in recent years emerging market economies have become increasingly important and have

Table 9.1   Developments in exports during the recent crisis and recovery (annual percentage change in value)

	Intra-regional (%)		Extra-regional (%)	
	2008–09	2009–10	2008–09	2009–10
CESEE	−26.9	16.9	−21.7	14.7
Mercosur	−21.4	35.3	−23.1	30.3
ASEAN	−20.9	31.9	−16.2	28.3

Source: Authors' calculations on the basis of IMF Direction of Trade Statistics, Reuters Ecowin.

Table 9.2   Developments in imports during the recent crisis and recovery

	Intra-regional (%)		Extra-regional (%)	
	2008–09	2009–10	2008–09	2009–10
CESEE	−27.5	15.7	−29.9	14.1
Mercosur	−24.9	35.4	−28.4	45.8
ASEAN	−22.8	30.4	−21.9	30.1

Source: Authors' calculations on the basis of IMF Direction of Trade Statistics, Reuters Ecowin.

been responsible for a large share of its dynamism in trade. In contrast to ASEAN and most of emerging Europe, Mercosur's dynamism in trade in the years preceding the crisis relied more on demand for raw materials and less on manufactured goods.

Exports

How the crisis and recovery played out in the three regions of interest is shown in Table 9.1. In the table as well as in the discussion henceforth, we use IMF Direction of Trade Statistics data. Contrary to the discussion above, which was based on developments in volume terms, we now switch to value terms. An important consequence is that commodities become more volatile because of the inclusion of the price effect, which is the dominant adjustment channel for trade in commodities. To understand the resilience of regional trade compared to global trade, Table 9.1 splits the decline in trade in an intra-regional part and an extra-regional part for the three regions. Table 9.2 makes the same distinction for the developments in imports.

All three regions saw a fall in intra-regional exports by over 20 per cent with emerging Europe's exports declining the most. In both ASEAN and emerging Europe, the value of exports to countries outside the region fell almost a quarter less than within the region. In Mercosur, extra-regional exports actually fell slightly more than intra-regional exports. Intra-regional exports in Mercosur have had an advantage over extra-regional exports because of the higher share of manufacturing goods. The adjustment in manufacturing exports comes mostly through volume and was not as large as the adjustment in Mercosur's exports of commodities, which suffered from both a sharp decline in commodity prices and disappointing harvests. As a consequence, the value of extra-regional exports with a larger share of commodity exports fell more than the value of intra-regional exports with a relatively large share of manufacturing exports.

Since the bottom of the crisis, export growth of emerging Europe seems to have broadly followed the pattern of advanced economies and, in particular, that of the EU. Emerging Europe has, thus, not benefited from the global recovery as much as other emerging economies. Throughout the crisis and the recovery, Mercosur is the region that has seen its intra-regional exports of goods gain share relative to extra-regional exports. Indeed, over this period, Mercosur has taken important steps towards further regional integration through the establishment of a customs union. Regional integration in terms of goods exports fell slightly in ASEAN and emerging Europe from 2008 to 2010.

Imports

An impressive import recovery in both Mercosur and ASEAN meant that imports from within and outside the region were back at or above the level of 2008 as early as 2010. For emerging Europe, the level of imports in 2010 was still 16.1 per cent below the pre-crisis level in the case of intra-regional imports and 20.0 per cent in the case of extra-regional imports. In emerging Europe, just as in Mercosur, extra-regional imports also fell slightly more during the crisis whereas in ASEAN imports from both categories fell at a similar pace. An important source of the difference is, again, the composition of the import basket. Mercosur is a net importer of oil and oil-related products, for which the prices have greatly fluctuated throughout the crisis and recovery. However, a major share of the intermediate products in Mercosur is imported from other Mercosur countries. In the case of ASEAN and emerging Europe, the supply chains extend mostly beyond the regions' boundaries: China, Korea and Japan in the case of ASEAN, and Western Europe in the case of emerging Europe. The effect of the fall in (intermediate) manufacturing imports was, thus, spread more evenly between intra- and extra-regional imports.

In this section we have analysed how the trade dynamics in the past turbulent years differed between the regions because of different forms and degrees of regional integration. In the following section we deepen this analysis by focusing on the role of China and Europe throughout the crisis, the recovery and the future.

CHINA AND THE EU AS GROWTH POLES FOR EMERGING EUROPE, ASEAN AND MERCOSUR

China and the EU are major players and partners in international trade. China and the EU are not only major trade and investment partners with respect to each other but also with respect to the three above-mentioned regions of emerging economies. China has become a major trade partner as well as an engine of growth for both the EU and emerging economies. Still, notwithstanding recent increases in domestic consumption and imports, China's growth model is still mostly associated with exports and domestic investment.

Although the share of exports to China in total exports has increased in all three emerging regions, the main beneficiaries have been ASEAN and Mercosur (see Figure 9.1). In the case of Mercosur this is mostly related to an increased demand for its commodities, whereas ASEAN's manufacturing sector has had a relatively strong export performance.

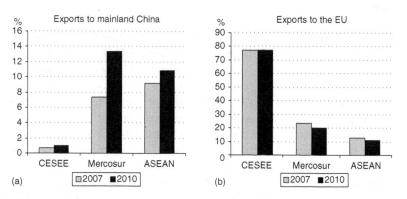

Note: Please note the different scales of the two panels.

Source: Reuters Ecowin.

Figure 9.1   Exports to mainland China and the EU

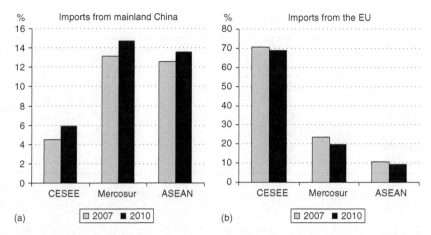

Note: Please note the different scales of the two panels.

Source: Reuters Ecowin.

Figure 9.2   Imports from mainland China and the EU

Notwithstanding the increased exports to China and its proximity, the share of China in exports from ASEAN is roughly on a par with Europe's share, according to IMF data. For Mercosur, the EU is still a more important export destination by a margin of several percentage points. In the case of emerging Europe, the EU is by far the most important export destination.

ASEAN countries import relatively more from China than from the EU whereas the EU has a slightly bigger share in the imports of Mercosur and a much bigger share in the imports of emerging Europe (see Figure 9.2). Imports from China nearly doubled in value between 2007 and 2010 for Mercosur, while they increased less rapidly in emerging Europe and ASEAN.

As a consequence of the respective developments in imports and exports, the net contribution of trade with China and the EU to growth has differed between the three regions. Table 9.3 shows estimates of the net exports' contribution to economic growth in the three regions between 2008 and 2010. The net contribution to growth of trade with the EU has clearly been positive for emerging Europe over this period. The economies of emerging Europe benefited from trade particularly strongly in the crisis year 2009. This is an indication that trade with the EU has worked as a shock absorber for emerging Europe during the crisis.

Trade's contributions to growth have been more muted for other

Table 9.3　Estimates of net exports' contribution to GDP growth (%)

Contribution to growth in:	Trading partner	2008	2009	2010	Total, 2008–10
Emerging Europe	EU	−0.3	3.4	0.6	3.8
	China	−0.5	0.5	−0.7	−0.7
ASEAN	EU	−0.4	−0.6	0.8	−0.2
	China	−0.6	0.5	0.0	0.0
Mercosur	EU	−0.1	−0.3	−0.2	−0.6
	China	−0.3	0.5	−0.1	0.1

Source:　Authors' calculations on the basis of IMF data, Reuters Ecowin.

regions and for both trade with China and with the EU in 2009 and also in 2008 and 2010. Such a lower contribution of trade to growth is in line with the benefits of increased trade occurring through the years.

It is worth noting that the three regions have sizeable surpluses on their trade balance with the EU. The trade balance with China has been either sizeably negative in the case of emerging Europe (an accumulated –7.2 per cent of GDP over 2008–10), significantly negative in the case of ASEAN (–3.6 per cent), or somewhat negative in the case of Mercosur (–0.7 per cent).

All in all, trade relations with China are important for all three emerging regions; however, the EU is still more important for these regions in particular when it comes to exports and its contribution to growth.

Of the three regions, emerging Europe is likely to receive the most competition from China in the future and benefit relatively less from its consumer market. In contrast to ASEAN countries, it is less likely that emerging European countries benefit from an integration into the supply chain. At the same time, with China moving up the quality ladder, emerging Europe will have to increasingly confront competition from China in its market. ASEAN countries become integrated into the supply chain even if they have to compete for their position on the highest rungs of the value-added ladder.[6] As primarily a commodity exporter, Mercosur stands out and will benefit from the need for raw materials in China.

CONCLUSIONS

Emerging Europe's trade is closely related to the EU market. This has benefited emerging Europe in two ways: it has helped upgrading of production structures; and it has provided support to growth through net exports. As expected, emerging Europe's trade is closely related to EU GDP growth, the internal market and EU trade policy.

Over the past 20 years, the emerging economies of Europe have significantly increased their openness ratio, have undertaken major structural reforms, and have increasingly specialized in medium- to high-technology products. They have managed to increase substantially their world market share despite the real effective exchange rate appreciation that they have faced over the same period. The region can be expected to remain the emerging part of Europe in the future as there is still high potential for growth.

However, emerging Europe is now facing new challenges. The above analysis demonstrated that, compared to Mercosur and ASEAN, it stands to benefit least from the emergence of East Asia and, in particular, China as a global trading power. It will neither benefit as much from increased demand for raw materials as Mercosur nor from the incorporation into the supply chain that is associated with the dynamism in East Asia. Rather, it will have to face increasing competition in the medium-tech to high-tech traded goods from East Asia. The main challenge will, therefore, be to continue structural reforms, to further attract FDI, to further upscale exports and to further diversify trading partners. Through its large internal market with a transparent and solid institutional framework, the EU will continue to be a relatively stable base for trade expansion by emerging European countries.

NOTES

1. Statistical support by Catrin Ericson is gratefully acknowledged.
2. For instance, Marc Auboin (2009) points out that the global market for trade finance (credit and insurance) represented approximately 80 per cent of trade value in 2008.
3. See WTO (2011a).
4. See, for instance, WTO (2011b).
5. When referring to emerging Europe, we mean the countries in Central, Eastern and South-Eastern Europe. At times, because of limited information on the broader set of countries, we limit emerging Europe to the Central and Eastern European countries that are part of the EU.
6. Pula and Santabárbara (2011).

REFERENCES

Araújá, S. and J. Martins (2009), 'The great synchronisation: what do high-frequency statistics tell us about the trade collapse?', VoxEU, 8 July.

Auboin, Marc (2009), 'Trade finance: G20 and follow-up', VoxEU, 5 June 2009.
Pula, G. and D. Santabárbara (2011), 'Is China climbing up the quality ladder? Estimating cross-country differences in product quality using Eurostat's Comext trade database', ECB Working Paper No. 1310, March.
WTO (2011a), *Report on G-20 Trade Measures*, October.
WTO (2011b), *Trade Policy Review of the European Union*, July.

10. Competition in the EU-15 market: CESEE, China and Russia

Christian Schitter, Maria Silgoner, Katharina Steiner and Julia Wörz[1]

Producing exportable products for the most highly industrialized markets has shaped many emerging economies' growth paths since World War II. With the fall of the central planning system in the late 1980s and early 1990s, the countries of Central, Eastern and South-Eastern Europe (CESEE[2]) embarked on such a growth path. Their exports have mainly targeted the Western European countries, the EU-15,[3] which have since become highly contested, even in times of strong world market growth. Thus the question of competitiveness has become crucial, above all in the face of an expected decline in world demand for imports. Therefore we investigate the competitiveness of CESEE – compared with that of China and Russia – in terms of their 'ability to sell', that is, their exports to the EU-15 market. How did the exports from CESEE, China and Russia perform in the EU-15 market from 1995 to 2010? What has driven the growth of exports of the three regions to the EU-15? Were these exports complementary or did they crowd each other out?

While there is ample literature[4] on the trade competitiveness and comparative advantages of these three regions, we provide a direct comparison of their export performance in the EU-15 market. Our assessment is based on export volumes and the number of trade links at the very disaggregated six-digit Harmonized System (HS) level. That is to say, when we speak of China's exports to the EU-15, we are actually using EU imports from China (based on Eurostat's COMEXT database) as our data source and so on. Working with the mirror trade flow ensures that the data are fully comparable across all three regions of interest. Specifically, we analyse export market shares, decompose export growth along two different lines and analyse the number of trade links to find evidence of crowding out at the product level.

Our study is structured as follows. In Section 1 we describe the regions' regional and sectoral composition of export market shares. Section 2 analyses the revealed comparative advantages of exports according to product categories. Section 3 investigates the sources of export growth by decomposing it into the intensive and extensive margin. Evidence for possible crowding out by analysing the number of trade links is shown in Section 4. Section 5 concludes.

1. ARE CHINA, CESEE AND RUSSIA FISHING IN THE SAME POOL?

Since the mid-1990s, CESEE and China particularly have intensified their global trade integration, as shown by Figure 10.1. Above all in the CESEE countries, trade growth has by far outpaced domestic income growth since 1995. Consequently, trade integration has increased substantially and steadily, with only a short interruption in the course of the global financial crisis (Figure 10.1). China's openness developed from less than 20 per cent in 1995 to 35 per cent before the start of the global financial crisis. While exports suffered substantially in 2009, GDP continued to grow at 9 per cent, so that openness declined dramatically to less than 25 per cent. In CESEE the decline was less pronounced in 2009.

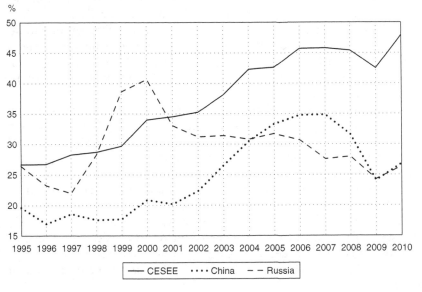

Sources: IMF, OECD.

Figure 10.1   Openness in terms of total exports to GDP

% of total exports

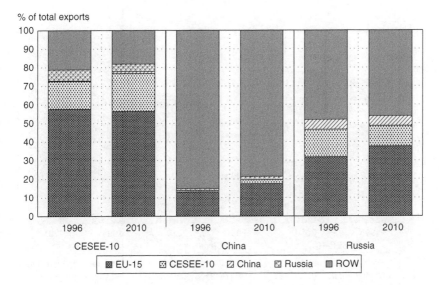

Source: UN Comtrade, authors' calculations.

Figure 10.2   Regional composition of exports

The pattern of Russia's trade integration differs substantially. Openness peaked at around 40 per cent in the years 1999 and 2000, following the Russian currency crisis when the depreciation of the ruble fuelled export growth while the economy dropped into recession. The following decade was characterized by extraordinarily high economic growth: between 2000 and 2007 GDP grew by 7 per cent on average. As growth was mainly driven by domestic rather than external demand – the ruble gained 30 per cent against the US dollar between 2002 and 2008 – openness decreased steadily. In 2010, the openness of both Russia and China corresponded roughly to that of the EU-15. Overall, the CESEE region shows a much higher degree of openness than China and Russia.

Figure 10.2 reveals the regional composition of exports and confirms that the regional trade focus of the CESEE countries lies on Western Europe. From 1996 to 2010 the share of total exports from CESEE countries going to the EU-15 remained roughly stable at 57 per cent. Over the period, intra-regional trade within the CESEE region recovered from the transformational shock and expanded from 16 per cent to 21 per cent, mostly at the expense of exports to Russia and the Commonwealth of Independent States. Exports to China increased slightly but remained negligible.

China's export focus shifted from Asian countries towards European

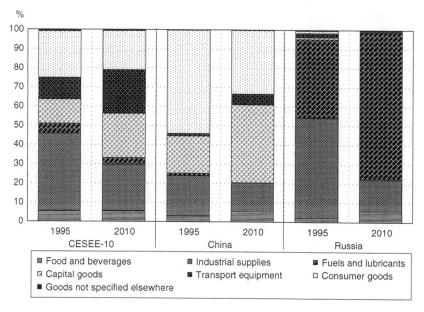

Source: COMEXT.

Figure 10.3   Share of product category in total exports to the EU-15

countries and the rest of the world. The importance of the USA as an export destination remained constant. For Russia the chart shows a clear reorientation of trade away from the CIS and CESEE region and towards the EU-15 and the rest of the world. The fact that the CESEE countries' export share to the EU-15 remained roughly stable while that of China and Russia expanded markedly is a first indication that the emergence of these global players in the EU-15 market might become a restraining factor for CESEE's exports.

To establish more closely whether the three regions under consideration are actually 'fishing in the same pool' of products in the European market, we decompose total exports to the EU-15 according to end-use categories, also referred to as broad economic categories (BEC).[5] Figure 10.3 shows that, over the last 15 years, both China and the countries in CESEE markedly expanded exports of capital goods and transport equipment (relative to their total exports to the EU-15). In the same period, exports of consumer goods and industrial supplies lost importance in the regions' portfolio of exported goods. This similarity in trade patterns may indicate that China has become an important competitor for the CESEE region.

Russian exports to the EU-15, by contrast, are heavily dominated by commodities and industrial supplies. More specifically, the increase of oil and gas prices over recent years, to a large extent driven by rising demand from fast-growing emerging economies, led to a further increase of the share of fuel and lubricant exports in total exports to the EU-15. This indicates that Russia has indirectly benefited from the catching-up process in other emerging markets such as China via rising oil and gas prices, while its role as a trade competitor to China and the CESEE countries in the EU-15 market appears to be extremely limited.

Overall, the EU-15 has been the traditional export destination for the CESEE region, reaching more than 55 per cent of total CESEE exports in 2010. Although less than 20 per cent of China's exports were targeted towards the EU-15, we recognize the increasing similarity in the development of trade patterns of CESEE and China according to product categories. In other terms, China has increasingly become a competitor for CESEE exports to the EU-15, particularly in the field of transportation equipment and capital goods. Russia's export pattern is different and increasingly dominated by exports of fuels and lubricants.

2.   WHAT DO MARKET SHARES TELL US ABOUT THE REGIONS' COMPETITIVENESS?

Balassa (1965) argued that comparative advantages, the basic source of trade according to classical trade theory, cannot be observed. However, they manifest themselves in export market shares, which can then be used to 'reveal' comparative advantages. The relative over- or under-representation of a specific exporter on a certain export market allows us to draw conclusions with respect to this exporter's competitive strength or weakness. A country can, for example, be assumed to have a global comparative advantage in producing cars if the country is over-represented in the global car market or, alternatively, if cars are over-represented within the country's export portfolio.

We use a measure of revealed comparative advantage (RCA), which calculates the relative representation of a region's exports in one product category compared to the average representation of that product category in total trade of the sample as a whole, including CESEE, China and Russia, with the EU-15 where

$$RCA_{ki} = (X_{ki}/X_{ni})/(X_{kr}/X_{nr}) \tag{10.1}$$

with X_{ki} representing total exports of product k and region i. Subscript n refers to all products and subscript r denotes all regions of the sample (see

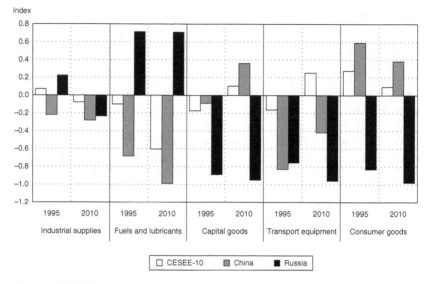

Source: COMEXT, authors' calculations.

Figure 10.4 *Revealed symmetric comparative advantage in selected broad economic categories (BEC) of goods*

Vollrath, 1991). As the index varies from zero to one for product categories in which a region has a revealed comparative disadvantage and from one to infinity for product categories where countries do have a RCA, it is asymmetric, which has an impact on the distribution of the RCA. We therefore apply the revealed symmetric comparative advantage (RSCA) following Fertö and Soós (2006) with

$$RSCA_{ki} = (RCA_{ki}-1)/(RCA_{ki}+1) \qquad (10.2)$$

where changes in the value below unity have the same weight as changes above unity (Dalum et al., 1998). Figure 10.4 shows the RSCA in the EU-15 export market for selected broad economic categories (BEC) of goods.

CESEE is the only region in the sample that has developed a revealed comparative advantage in exporting transportation equipment since 1998. It even expanded further during the crisis period. This pattern corresponds to the increasing export share of these goods in total CESEE exports to the EU-15 market (see Figure 10.3). Although China also recorded rising exports of transportation equipment, it could not develop a revealed comparative advantage in this product category in the EU-15 market *vis-à-vis* the other regions of the sample. Both regions gained a comparative advantage in exports of capital goods – with CESEE following China in 2004. However, they recorded a declining RSCA index for consumer goods. The latter is also reflected in decreasing market shares of this product category in total exports to the EU-15 market by region (see Figure 10.3). For industrial supplies, the RSCA even turned negative in 2002.

Russia competes in different product categories, such as minerals, pearls and metals. However, the number of product categories showing a positive RSCA index even declined over the period. For example, Russia lost competitiveness in leather production as well as in wood and pulp products, which is also reflected by decreasing market shares of related product categories in total exports. Overall the results presented in this section indicate that both CESEE and China are increasingly fishing in the same pool of product categories where their exports exhibit revealed comparative advantages *vis-à-vis* each other in the EU-15 market.

3. AN ANALYSIS OF THE SOURCES OF EXPORT GROWTH: NEW VERSUS INTENSIFIED TRADE LINKS

Ultimately, the 'ability to sell' on which we focus in this analysis is also reflected in the absolute dynamics of exports. Export growth can essentially arise from two sources: first, by exchanging higher values along existing trade linkages, that is, trading more of the same products with the same trading partners; and second, by developing new trade relationships, that is, either by selling new products to traditional trading partners or by entering a new geographical market. The decomposition into the intensive and extensive margins identifies these two effects and gives interesting insights into the durability and orientation of trade integration. Developments in each of these margins allow us to draw conclusions on the form of competition between exporters. Was it mainly the establishment of new trade relationships or the intensification of existing trade that fostered the growth of exports of CESEE, China and Russia to the EU-15?

We use highly disaggregated data at the six-digit HS level to identify changes in the individual trade relationships with the EU-15 over time. A trade relationship is defined as exports of a specific product a from country or region b to the EU-15 export market (whereby we distinguish between individual importing countries within the EU-15) in year c. We can then decompose export growth to the EU-15 into three parts: export growth of products that are continuously traded; additional exports arising from new trade relationships (new products); and export losses due to the discontinuation of trade flows.

We define the 'extensive margin' of trade as the difference between the value of newly established trade links and the value of trade flows that have disappeared, measured as a share of total export gains. It is thus a measure of trade diversification within the EU-15 export market, in terms of exchanged products. The 'intensive margin', on the other hand, is defined as the change in the value of continuous trade connections as a share of total export growth. By definition the extensive and intensive margin sum to one.[6]

In line with the majority of previous papers with comparable methodology, the contribution of the extensive margin to export growth is small and remains under normal conditions mostly below 5 per cent on a yearly basis. The first section in Figure 10.5 presents the average contribution of the extensive margin to total export growth from 1996 to 2009. It shows that the major part of trade growth comes from deepening trade linkages rather than from exploring new markets. This is surprising given that Hummels and Klenow (2005) find that larger and richer countries have a more diversified set of export goods so that a catching-up process should affect the extensive margin. Similarly Imbs and Wacziarg (2003) find that catching-up countries initially tend to diversify their production portfolio and only start to specialize once they reach a higher level of development. Yearly data on the Chinese extensive margin somewhat confirm this finding as the extensive margin showed a tendency to decline between 1995 and 2008. However, its contribution remained small compared to the intensive margin and even slightly declined over time. This is in line with Amiti and Freund (2008), who find a clear dominance of the intensive margin for China's world trade growth: a small number of products accounts for the major part of trade growth of China. Cheptea et al. (2010) make the same observation, but conclude that China's export diversification was already accomplished in 1994: China's product diversity in exports to the USA is comparable to the German pattern. In Russia, the average contribution of the extensive margin to export growth was slightly negative (−0.7 per cent) over 1996 to 2009. While Russia succeeded in fostering new trade relationships until the early 2000s, the net contribution of new trade to export growth turned negative in 2002.

CESEE's slightly higher average contribution of the extensive margin to total export growth over 1996 to 2009 than that of China is mainly driven by the years 2003 to 2005. The second section of Figure 10.5 reveals that at the time of EU accession of eight Central and Eastern European (CEE)

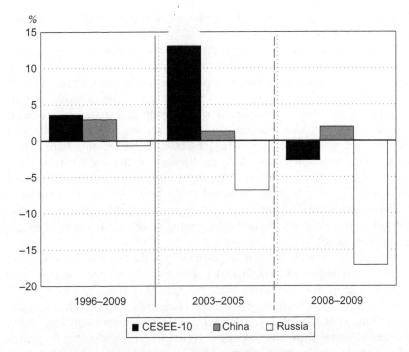

Note: Percentages for 1996 to 2009 and 2003 to 2005 represent averages over time. As major revisions of the HS classification of goods in 2002 and 2007 cause breaks in the time series, with products being moved into other or new categories, the average contribution of the extensive margin to export growth excludes the values for 2001 to 2002 and 2006 to 2007.

Source: COMEXT, authors' calculations.

Figure 10.5   *Contribution of the extensive margin to total export growth (selected periods of interest)*

countries in May 2004, many new trade relationships were established, which resulted in an extensive margin of 13 per cent for the CESEE region on average over 2003 to 2005. Although trade in manufactures between CEE and the EU-15 became tariff-free as early as 1998 as a result of the Europe Agreements, the elimination of substantial non-tariff barriers to trade and the liberalization of trade in agricultural products inside the EU led to the formation of many new trade relationships over the following two years. Subsequently, the contribution of CESEE's extensive margin to export growth to the EU-15 turned negative for two years, pointing to some market adjustment as more trade relationships were lost than newly established. For China, the contribution of the extensive margin remained below 5 per cent at the time of EU Eastern enlargement while its contribution was negative for Russia.

Figure 10.5 also shows the evolution of the extensive margin during the global economic crisis when trade contracted substantially in all countries. The general decline in exports makes the interpretation of the results more difficult: the negative contribution of the extensive margin in CESEE and Russia indicates that this trade contraction was entirely driven by the intensive margin: trade relationships diminished but were hardly ever severed permanently. Russia was the region where export losses were most pronounced, again because of the sudden reversal in energy prices. Here, the contribution of the extensive margin to total export growth was highest compared to the other regions. In contrast to CESEE and Russia, China lost many trade relationships during the crisis period as the extensive margin contributed to the contraction in export growth to the EU-15.

Overall we observe that – in line with most of the existing literature – the largest contribution to trade growth comes from the intensive margin, that is, from a deepening of existing trade linkages. However, one has to bear in mind that focusing on both products and countries could result in a higher contribution of the extensive margin to total export growth. The results presented above show that accession to the EU resulted in the formation of new trade relationships between CESEE and EU-15 over 2004 to 2005, although at low volume. With a delay of one year, these new trade links and a deepening of traditional trade relationships started to pay off for trade growth, despite some market adjustment that led to the loss of trade links. In general, the global financial crisis temporarily hit trade but did not permanently destroy trade links. This is true for CESEE and Russia, while many Chinese trade relationships to the EU-15 were lost on net.

4.   CROWDING OUT AT THE PRODUCT LEVEL

Finally, we use the information for each individual exporter about the number of new, lost, existing or non-existing trade links to establish at the product level whether our exporters of interest are indeed 'fishing in the same pool'. For this exercise we move away from trading volume and look at the number of trade links. We combine the information for pairs of trading partners and focus on a comparison of CESEE with China on the one hand and CESEE with Russia on the other. Country pairs that have a high number of simultaneous trade links in many categories are close competitors while countries with fewer common links can be assumed to export complementary goods; that is, there is less intense

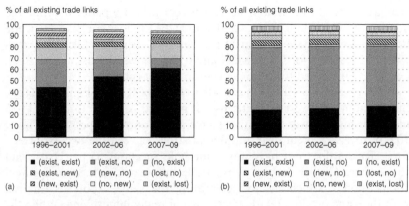

Source: Authors' calculations.

Figure 10.6   Comparison of CESEE–China (a) and CESEE–Russia (b) trade relationships (selection, omitted category pairs add up to 100%)

competition between them, notwithstanding a potentially high level of mutual dependence – as in the case of raw materials.

We are particularly interested in cases where CESEE has an existing trade link and one of the competitors (China or Russia) is entering the market. Another interesting case is given by combinations where the trade link with CESEE vanishes and China or Russia establishes a new trade link. Such cases can be interpreted as evidence of cut-throat competition from China or Russia for CESEE. Figure 10.6 shows a selection of the most interesting combinations of trade links for the two pairs of exporters – CESEE–China (Figure 10.6(a), left panel) and CESEE–Russia (Figure 10.6(b), right panel) – ordered by decreasing importance. Each combination is calculated as a fraction of all existing trade links by at least one exporter in one of three distinct time periods: 1996–2001, 2002–06 and 2007–10.[7] There is a great deal of overlap when comparing CESEE and China's trade links with EU-15 partners. Figure 10.6(a) is clearly dominated by cases where both exporters have existing trade links. The fraction of existing trade links where the two exporting regions are in direct competition has risen from 44 per cent to over 60 per cent over the observation period. This increase has arisen from both China establishing trade links where CESEE has already been active (exist, new) as well as CESEE entering into Chinese markets (new, exist). Interestingly, the latter is becoming more important lately. It is clearly visible that the number of trade links where CESEE was active and China showed no market presence (exist, no) has declined over time from 25 per cent to just 9 per cent, while the number of cases where China is active and CESEE does not have any trade links (no, exist) has risen from 11 per cent to 13 per cent. Likewise, cases where CESEE has lost a trade link and China shows an existing link (lost, exist) have increased from 1.6 per cent to 2.5 per cent.

When comparing CESEE's exports to those of Russia (Figure 10.6(b)), the fraction of overlap in terms of products offered to the EU-15 market is much lower and rather stable at just above 25 per cent. Figure 10.6(b) reveals a great deal of differentiation between the two exporters. First, Russia does not have any trade links in about 55 per cent of all cases where CESEE has an active trade link (exist, no). Second, direct competition – which means penetrating the same export destination with the same product (exist, exist) – is not really intensifying. While the number of newly established trade links by Russia with a direct overlap with CESEE's active trade links (exist, new) amounted to roughly 4.5–5 per cent of all cases on average in each year, the average number of cases where Russia lost a trade link and CESEE remained active (exist, lost) also totalled about 4 per cent. In other words, Russia repeatedly attempted to enter into CESEE's existing trade links, but was unable to retain these trade links over longer periods. In contrast, China entered CESEE's existing trade links on a more sustainable basis, thus creating increased competitive pressure for CESEE economies.

It is also interesting to observe that, in sharp contrast to the significant share of CESEE trade links with the EU-15 where Russia is not active (*c.* 55 per cent in each year on average), Russian trade links where CESEE countries are not active account for only about 2 per cent to 1.5 per cent of all cases at all times. This underlines the greater diversification of CESEE exports to the EU-15 as compared to Russia's export structure.

5.   SUMMARY AND CONCLUSIONS

CESEE, China and Russia have shown impressive export growth dynamics since the mid-1990s. In particular, exports to advanced economies played a major role in boosting domestic growth. Trade integration with the EU-15 strongly intensified over the period 1995 to 2010 with only a few temporary drawbacks for Russia. While CESEE has played the dominant role in the EU-15 market in terms of export market shares since 1995, it has recently been challenged by China. A shift in Chinese export destinations from Asian towards European countries and the rest of the world can be identified. These developments might indicate fierce competition in the EU-15 market and also affect the trade patterns of

CESEE countries. In face of such developments and an expected decline in world demand for imports, the question of competitiveness is crucial. Therefore we ask whether the Chinese and Russian trade expansion to the European market has partially come at the expense of CESEE export growth.

We analyse standard output measures of competitiveness and decompose trade growth along the intensive and extensive margin to find indications of whether growing exports from the three regions to the EU-15 market resulted from establishing new trade relationships or intensifying existing ones. The results showed that we got the first guess wrong: Chinese export growth in the EU-15 market did not mainly result from the establishment of new trade relationships. Growth along the extensive margin was rather limited when looking at yearly changes in volume. In general, the largest contribution to trade growth resulted from the intensification of already existing trade links for all three regions. However, EU accession by eight countries in 2004 has clearly created several new trade links with high trading volumes. For the CESEE countries, the extensive margin of trade was notably higher around the time of accession, while it shrank to almost zero for China in those years. This one-off effect caused CESEE to exhibit a greater extensive margin of trade over the observation period, although China continually created new trade relationships over the entire period. Nevertheless, the intensive margin of trade remains the dominant source of trade growth for all export regions. Even during the crisis period the reduction in trade volumes rather than the termination of trade relationships accounted for the sharp contraction of export growth in CESEE and Russia. Losses for Russia along the intensive margin were most pronounced, related to the rapid decline in world energy prices. While contracting volumes of existing trade links also accounted for most of the trade collapse in the case of China, the extensive margin played an aggravating role here. In other words, unlike CESEE and Russia, China experienced a net loss of trade relationships in its exports to the EU-15 during the crisis.

Further analysing the number of trade relationships at the detailed product level, we also observe that the extent of overlap in terms of exported products and destinations is rising steadily between China and CESEE. China is rapidly entering product categories where CESEE countries are already active and vice versa. This implies intensified competition in the same products on the same markets. Recently, China has increasingly entered CESEE markets, whereby a market is defined in terms of a specific product to a specific destination country. On the other hand, there is less and falling evidence that CESEE countries are entering into China's trade relationships. In total, the fraction of product codes where both exporters are active in the EU-15 market has continually risen and has reached more than 60 per cent of all trade links at the HS six-digit level by at least one partner by 2010. In contrast, Russia continues to be serving the EU-15 market with highly distinct products; the share of overlapping trade links between Russia and CESEE is rather stable and had reached only 28 per cent by the end of our observation period. Thus China and CESEE are increasingly 'fishing in the same pool' on the EU-15 market, while there is considerably more differentiation between Russia and CESEE economies. While there is considerable evidence for rising competition between China and CESEE, there is to date only weak evidence that CESEE exports have been crowded out of the European market by Chinese exporters. The number of cases where CESEE has lost a trade link while China maintains a relationship is still small, but has risen from 1.6 to 2.5 per cent.

Summing up, future export growth to the EU-15 market will crucially depend on two aspects for all three regions compared, but especially for CESEE and China: first, it is necessary to target demand for exactly those products in which the respective exporting region is highly competitive taking into account the growth prospects in the respective market segments; second, as import demand for certain products, such as vehicles, may well decline over the long run, structural change and constant quality improvements will be crucial. The increasing overlap in products and markets served generates additional pressure to strengthen a region's position in existing trade relationships and/or establish new trade relationships in different product segments.

NOTES

1. The authors would like to thank Angelika Knollmayer and Andreas Nader for research assistance, Peter Backé, the participants of an internal OeNB research seminar, the ECB Expert Meeting on 'Assessing Competitiveness' and the CEEI 2011 for valuable comments and suggestions. The opinions expressed by the authors do not necessarily reflect the official viewpoint of the OeNB or the Eurosystem. Opinions expressed in this chapter are not those of Commerzbank, but solely those of the authors.
2. CESEE refers to Bulgaria, the Czech Republic, Estonia, Hungary, Latvia, Lithuania, Poland, Romania, the Slovak Republic and Slovenia. If Croatia is added to the group of countries, it is explicitly referred to in the text.
3. Austria, Belgium, Denmark, Finland, France, Germany, Greece, Ireland, Italy, Luxembourg, Netherlands, Portugal, Spain, Sweden, UK. This selection implies that we have no overlap between exporters including new EU member states in the CESEE region and importers in Western Europe.
4. For further research see e.g. Amiti and Freund (2008), Imbs and Wacziarg (2003), Benkovskis and Rimgailaite (2010).
5. The United Nations has classified international trade by seven broad economic categories (BEC) according to end-use categories: (1) food and beverages; (2) industrial supplies

not elsewhere specified; (3) fuels and lubricants; (4) capital goods; (5) transport equipment; (6) consumer goods not elsewhere specified; and (7) goods not elsewhere specified.
6. The results are highly sensitive to the definition of the extensive margin. Other papers focus on the number of trade relationships rather than on export volumes, use a different level of data disaggregation and country sample or apply a different definition of the extensive margin without subtracting lost trade links (e.g. see Besedeš and Prusa, 2011; Amiti and Freund, 2008; Imbs and Wacziarg, 2003). Because of these methodological differences, the results of the relative size of the extensive margins may deviate substantially from our results.
7. These subsamples avoid deviations that could arise from the reclassification to the HS system in the years 2002 and 2007.

REFERENCES

Amiti, M. and C. Freund (2008), 'An anatomy of China's export growth', mimeo, 31 January.
Balassa, B. (1965), 'Trade liberalization and "revealed" comparative advantage', *Manchester School of Economic and Social Studies*, **33**(2), 99–123.
Benkovskis, K. and R. Rimgailaite (2010), 'The quality and variety of exports from new EU member states: evidence from very disaggregated data', Latvijas Banka Working Paper, 2/2010.
Besedeš, T. and T.J. Prusa (2011), 'The role of extensive and intensive margins and export growth', *Journal of Development Economics*, **96**(2), 371–9.
Cheptea, A., L. Fontagné and S. Zignago (2010), 'European export performance', CEPII Working Paper 2010-12, Centre d'Études Prospectives et d'Informations Internationales.
Dalum, B., K. Laursen and G. Villumsen (1998), 'Structural change in OECD export specialization patterns: de-specialization and stickiness', *International Review of Applied Economics*, **12**(3), 423–43.
Fertö, I. and K.A. Soós (2006), 'Trade specialisation in the European Union and in European former communist countries', INDEUNIS Paper, February.
Hummels, D. and P.J. Klenow (2005), 'The variety and quality of a nation's exports', *The American Economic Review*, **95**(3), 704–23.
Imbs, J. and R. Wacziarg (2003), 'Stages of diversification', *The American Economic Review*, **93**(1), 63–86.
Vollrath, T.L. (1991), 'A theoretical evaluation of alternative trade intensity measures of revealed comparative advantage', *Weltwirtschaftliches Archiv*, **127**, 265–80.

11. Opportunities and challenges – the impact of Chinese competition on Hungarian manufacturing

Ágnes Csermely, Péter Harasztosi and Gábor Pellényi

The rapid development of China is reshaping the dynamics of the global economy and has contributed to significant restructuring in both emerging and developed economies. As a result, traditional manufacturing exporting countries are facing a complex situation. Some companies and sectors can take advantage of new growth opportunities, while others are facing severe competitive threats. Gains arise in terms of additional exports to and growth opportunities within China, and cost savings from utilizing Chinese supply chains, contributing to enhanced competitiveness. But these gains are partially mitigated by the loss of domestic and traditional export markets to Chinese competitors.

In this chapter we investigate the impact of China's rise from different angles. On the positive side, Hungary has benefited from growing Chinese demand for capital equipment. Hungary specializes in supplying parts and appliances for large capital-equipment-exporting countries, first and foremost for Germany. On the other hand, China has fuelled spectacular growth in commodity prices. Although Hungary is a net exporter of agricultural products, the benefits from rising agricultural prices were more than offset by the deterioration in the terms of trade, due to oil and other commodity price hikes. We apply a GVAR (global vector auto regressive) methodology to quantify these effects. The results illustrate the intensifying trade linkages with China and confirm that stronger trade brings net gains in terms of output. On the other hand, the impact of growing Chinese demand on global inflation is more intense in Hungary than in the developed countries. This can be explained by lower energy efficiency of production, but it also highlights that inflation expectations are less firmly anchored in Hungary.

While the intensified trade relationships with China deliver net gains for Hungary on the aggregate level, the traditional exporting sectors are confronted with severe competitive challenges from Chinese suppliers on both domestic and traditional export markets. In the second part of the chapter, we study how the Hungarian manufacturing sector has responded to the increasing import competition from China. We use plant-level manufacturing data for the period 1992–2008. We follow the approach of Bernard et al. (2006), who estimate the impact of import penetration from low-wage countries in the US manufacturing industries in two dimensions. First, we analyse whether import competition from China and other low-wage economies has caused downsizing in manufacturing. In particular, we focus on employment growth and the probability of exiting. Second, we analyse whether plants have been able to adjust to Chinese competition by changing their output mix or increasing productivity growth and capital intensity.

The empirical results are mixed. We were not able to identify a typical response by manufacturing firms to increased Chinese competition. Exporting firms exhibit two distinct adjustment patterns. Low-tech, low-skill industries shrank rapidly when Chinese competitors started to penetrate their traditional markets. On the other hand, more skill-intensive sectors were successful in boosting the capital intensity and productivity of their operations. As a result, turnover increased rapidly in the successfully adjusting sectors, but these industries were not able to absorb the people released from the shrinking companies. Improving employment possibilities for low-skilled workers has become a crucial social problem in Hungary.

1.   THE IMPACT OF CHINA ON AGGREGATE OUTPUT AND PRICES

This section looks into the transmission of macroeconomic shocks from China to the rest of the world. Analysing the international transmission of macroeconomic disturbances is not a straightforward exercise. Individual economies are interconnected through various channels, for example trade, financial and institutional linkages. Country-specific events can spread rapidly through these various channels. Modelling this transmission requires a tool that can reasonably describe both economic developments within countries, and the most relevant transmission channels across countries.

The global VAR (GVAR) model introduced by Pesaran et al. (2004) is ideally suited for this task. It consists of several country-specific vector autoregressive (VAR) models, which incorporate domestic and foreign variables for each country. For each country, the foreign variables are constructed as weighted averages of all other countries' respective variables. The weights represent the international linkages; they are usually derived from bilateral trade flows.

GVAR models have recently been used to analyse the transmission of various (real, financial or monetary) shocks across countries and regions. The most relevant paper for our topic is by Cesa-Bianchi et al. (2011). They assess the changing role of China for Latin American business cycles from the 1980s. We extend their analysis – in a simplified GVAR model – to Central and Eastern European economies.

Our model includes 30 countries that account for about 90 per cent of global GDP. The euro area is modelled as a single region. We also include four Central Eastern European economies (the Czech Republic, Hungary, Poland and the Slovak Republic) in the model. Each country-specific VAR includes two domestic variables (GDP and inflation) as well as three foreign variables (foreign GDP, inflation and the oil price). When estimating country-specific VAR models, we use time-varying trade weights to construct the foreign variables. The estimation sample spans the 1995–2010 period.

The GVAR is aggregated from the country-specific VAR models using weights for one specific year. By changing the reference year we can identify the changing role of Chinese shocks in the world economy. We calculate generalized impulse response functions (GIRFs) of key variables to shocks of Chinese GDP to capture demand shocks originating from China. GIRFs should be used with the caveat that they do not have a direct economic interpretation, because the VAR residuals can be contemporaneously correlated across countries. Reassuringly, statistical tests indicate that this correlation is low.

First, we estimated the reaction of global GDP growth to a 1 per cent shock of Chinese GDP. The impulse responses of three advanced economies and three developing-country groups are summarized in Figure 11.1. We did not find significantly different patterns between the Hungarian and the average Central European impulse responses, so only the regional results are presented here. Two impulse responses are reported for each region: one is calculated from the GVAR using the trade weights of 2000 and the other is calculated with the 2008 weights. The difference between the two impulse responses highlights the growing importance of China for the world economy through increasing trade linkages.

Chinese GDP shocks have the strongest impact on neighbouring Asian economies. Latin America is also strongly influenced by Chinese developments, which could be a consequence of China's hunger for raw materials. The USA and the euro area are less affected by China; the weakest impact appears in Central Eastern Europe. However, taking into account the

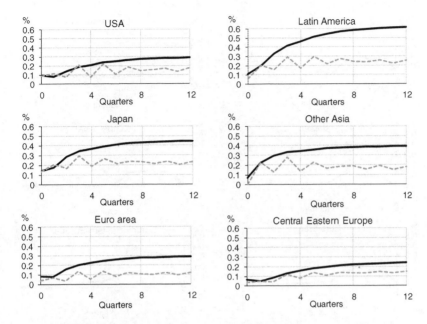

Note: Dashed line = GVAR with 2000 weights; solid line = GVAR with 2008 weights.

Figure 11.1   *Impact of a 1 per cent shock to Chinese GDP on global GDP (generalized impulse response functions)*

geographical distance between China and Central Eastern Europe, the 0.1–0.2 percentage point GDP response is not negligible.

The importance of China has grown over time for all economies. Between 2000 and 2008 the trade integration of China proceeded to such an extent that the medium-term impact of Chinese GDP shocks doubled throughout the world.

The impulse responses of global inflation are presented in Figure 11.2. These effects arise mostly as a result of China's demand for commodities including oil: a Chinese GDP shock raises the oil price significantly. The impact on global consumer prices is generally moderate, though, not exceeding 0.1 percentage points in the first year and fading to zero in the second year. However, the impact on Central Eastern European inflation appears particularly strong, reaching as much as 0.4 percentage points. This is explained by the fact that the share of energy is relatively large in the consumption baskets of the region's economies.

Finally, based on the results presented above, we try to assess the role of China in the global recovery in 2009–10. As the world economy headed

European integration in a global economy

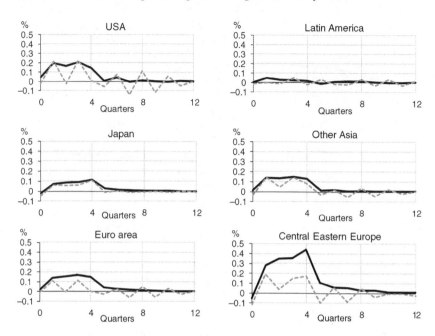

Note: Dashed line = GVAR with 2000 weights; solid line = GVAR with 2008 weights.

Figure 11.2   Impact of a 1 per cent shock to Chinese GDP on global inflation (generalized impulse response functions)

towards recession, the Chinese government launched a sizeable stimulus package to support domestic growth. Dreger and Zhang (2011) estimate that the stimulus amounted to 3.1 per cent of Chinese GDP in 2009 and a further 2.7 per cent in 2010. We used the GVAR with the 2008 weights to assess the impact of the stimulus package on global GDP and inflation (Table 11.1).

Chinese GDP growth was boosted by over 2 percentage points on average in 2009–10. Recovery in the rest of the world received considerable support from China. Most advanced and developing economies grew 0.5–1 percentage points faster as a result of the Chinese stimulus. Even Central Eastern Europe received on average 0.4 percentage points growth momentum. The support for global growth did not come without side-effects, though. The GVAR model suggests that the Chinese stimulus raised oil prices by as much as US$20, contributing to rising inflationary pressures in 2010–11. Central Eastern Europe is particularly affected by rising oil prices. Inflation in the region may have risen by 1 percentage point in 2010 due to this factor.

Table 11.1   Impact of Chinese stimulus measures in 2009–10 on global GDP growth and inflation (percentage points)

	GDP growth			Inflation		
	2009	2010	2011	2009	2010	2011
USA	0.4	0.7	0.4	0.5	0.6	0.1
Latin America	0.8	1.5	0.9	0.1	0.1	0.0
Japan	0.7	1.1	0.6	0.2	0.3	0.1
China	2.0	2.5	0.9	0.5	0.5	0.1
Rest of Asia	0.7	1.0	0.4	0.3	0.4	0.1
Euro area	0.4	0.7	0.4	0.4	0.5	0.2
Central Eastern Europe	0.3	0.5	0.4	0.7	1.1	0.5

2.   SECTORAL ADJUSTMENT TO INTENSIFYING CHINESE COMPETITION

China has become one of the most important import trade partners for Hungary since the mid-1990s. The increased exposure to Chinese trade affects Hungarian manufacturers in two respects.

First, Chinese products compete with Hungarian ones. The intensity of competition is often measured by import penetration, the share of imports in total consumption. In general, Hungary's import penetration is relatively high and shows an increasing tendency over time. The average import penetration of the manufacturing industries over the 1999–2006 period is 40–45 per cent. Machinery and Apparel and Textiles exhibit the highest import penetration, above 80 and 60 per cent respectively. The share of Chinese imports is significantly lower, at 2–4 per cent on average (see Figure 11.3). Some sectors exhibited a more dynamic increase in Chinese import penetration: in the Electrical machinery sector Chinese import competition rose from 4 to 12 per cent from 1999 to 2002, while it increased from 3 to 20 per cent in the Radio and Television sector.

Second, manufacturing firms can use Chinese products as input for production. While Hungarian manufacturing production has a high import content, at 70–80 per cent of the production value on average, the share of Chinese imported inputs is increasing, but is still rather low, at less than 4 per cent. There are only two sectors where Chinese imports are prominent: Office Machinery and Radio and Television. In these sectors over 20 per cent of imported inputs originated in China. In other sectors the share of Chinese imports is much smaller, but increasing rapidly.

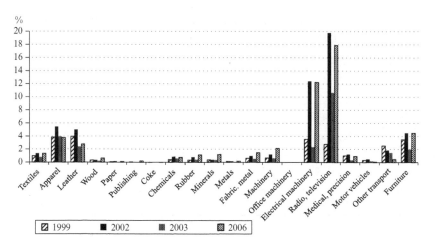

Figure 11.3   Share of Chinese imports in the consumption of sector output, 1999–2006

3. FIRM-LEVEL RESPONSES

To quantify how the increased Chinese trade exposure affects firm performance and the behaviour of Hungarian manufacturing firms we follow the approach of Bernard et al. (2006). They investigate firm-level responses in the USA to increased exposure to trade with low-wage countries. Motivated by the Hecksher–Ohlin trade framework, which suggests a decrease in the wages in the labour-intensive sectors in the USA, they look into employment growth and plant survival responses. Looking at the 1972–97 period, they find that plant survival and growth are lower in industries with high trade exposure to low-wage countries. Within those industries, capital-intensive plants outperform labour-intensive plants. In addition, they show that firms react with their product mix and eventually change to sectors less exposed to low-wage country competition. Drawing on Bernard et al. (2006), Álvarez and Opazo (2011) address the issue of how import competition from China has affected relative wages in the Chilean manufacturing industry. Looking at the 1996–2005 period, they find that increasing imports from China have depressed relative wages in sectors with higher Chinese import penetration. The competition affects the firms of the Apparel, Footwear and Pottery manufacturing industries, especially smaller firms.

We investigate the effect of Chinese exposure from two angles: (i) Chinese products as competitors in domestic markets, measured by industry-level import penetration; and (ii) Chinese products as imported inputs, measured as the ratio of Chinese imports to total material input used by the sector. The measures formally are:

$$Import\ penetration_{st} = \frac{Imports^{China}_{s(product)t}}{Imports^{World}_{s(product)t} + Output^{Home}_{s(product)t} - Exports^{World}_{s(product)t}}$$

$$Import\ share_{st} = \frac{Imports^{China}_{s(input)t}}{Materials_{st}}$$

To investigate firm responses to changes in Chinese import exposure, we relate outcome variables to exposure variables, either import penetration or import share, and firm characteristics. For firm i:

$$Outcome_{it} = f(X_{it}, Exposure_{st}, V_{st}) \qquad (11.1)$$

We investigate several outcome variables: *average wage, employment, productivity, firm exit.* Except for firm exit, where we use a logistic function for f, we take f to be linear. The set of individual characteristics (X) includes size, labour productivity, a foreign ownership dummy and exporter/importer status indicators. The set of sector-specific characteristics (V) includes industry size and concentration measures in terms of employment and value added. Regressions also include time dummies and firm fixed effects.[1]

Our expectations about the results are in line with Bernard et al. (2006). We expect that increased competition from a low-wage country will reduce relative wages in more exposed sectors, make firms downsize and increase the probability of exit. We expect increased Chinese outsourcing to be productivity-enhancing by decreasing material input costs.

For the analysis, we use data from multiple sources. The first is a firm-level database provided by the National Tax and Customs Office (NAV, formerly APEH). It contains balance-sheet information on double-entry book-keeping companies subject to corporate taxation. The data are available from 1992 to 2008; the firms are categorized according to four-digit TEAOR'03 industry classification. The firm-level database is augmented with two data sets with sectoral-level commodity trade information collected by the Central Statistical Office (CSO). The first provides country-sector-level import values, where sectoral categories are determined by the producing sector. Partner countries are defined on the basis of the country of origin for 1999–2002, and on the basis of the sending country until

Table 11.2   Results from Chinese trade exposure regression on wages in
              Hungary

Dependent variable: average wages	1999–2002	2003–07
Import penetration	−0.31***	−0.16
Import share	−0.03**	−0.35**

Note: *** 1 %, ** 5% significance level.

2006. The second trade data set categorizes product imports by the sectoral classification of the importing firm from 1998 to 2003. It uses country
of origin classification until 2003.[2]

Carrying out regressions defined by the general equation (11.1) reveals
that there is no typical response of firms facing increased Chinese exposure. We found statistically significant results only in the case of wages,
where increasing exposure has a significant negative effect on relative
wages. The results reported in Table 11.2 imply that if exposure to Chinese
imports increases by 1 percentage point, the relative wages in the affected
sectors decrease by 0.35 per cent at most. This outcome is in line with our
expectations and with the inference of Álvarez and Opazo (2011) for the
Chilean manufacturing industry.

4. DIFFERENT ADJUSTMENT PATTERNS IN MANUFACTURING SECTORS EXPOSED TO INCREASED CHINESE COMPETITION

A possible explanation for the lack of a general adjustment pattern among
firms facing competitive threats from China might be that firms responded
in diverse ways to the challenges arising. We can illustrate these strategies from sector-level information. As we can see from Figure 11.4, in
2001, China's WTO entry coincided with a turnaround in the prosperity
of sectors relying on low-skilled labour. At the same time, the Hungarian
electrical devices sector has been doing better on both export and domestic
markets. As Chinese trade slowly shifted towards more skill- and capital-
intensive products, these sectors were also exposed to stronger competition.[3] Enhanced productivity and increased capital intensity constituted
the most important adjustment margins. They employed more skilled
labour and relied on outsourcing. Consequently, the growing turnover did
not result in higher employment in these sectors (see Figure 11.5).

Finally, we investigate why the low-skill sectors were so unsuccessful

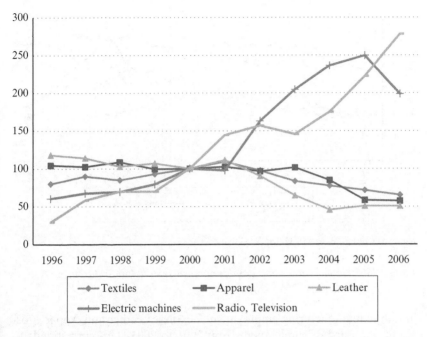

Note: Data based on APEH firm-level panel.

*Figure 11.4   Real export value added in selected manufacturing sectors,
2000 = 100*

in adjusting to the new challenges that arose after China's WTO entry. Hungary's low-tech sectors might have become more competitive by cutting relative wages. However, wages in the low-tech sectors did not increase more slowly than wages in high-tech, high-skill sectors during the 1992–2007 period (see Figure 11.5). One reason for this was a sizeable increase in minimum wages in 2000–01, coinciding with the intensification of Chinese trade. The almost twofold increase in the minimum wage did not allow downward wage adjustments in the low-tech sectors. The small room for adjustment in wages is shown by the Kaitz index,[4] which has been higher in Hungary than in Poland, Slovakia, Romania or the Czech Republic since 2001.

Most firms either increased the share of part-time workers or down-sized (see Kertesi and Köllő 2003, for details). The measures affected the low-tech manufacturing more severely, as these sectors had the most workers employed at the minimum wage. The adjustments resulted in a sharp decrease in employment in the low-tech industry sectors, resulting

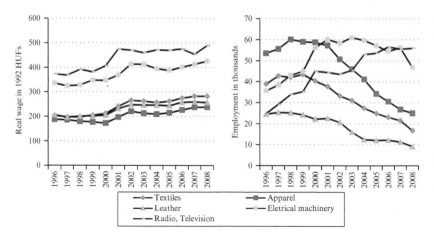

Note: Data based on APEH firm-level panel.

Figure 11.5   *Real wages and employment in selected manufacturing
                sectors, 1996–2008*

in falling manufacturing employment. Textiles, Leather and Apparel lost
about one-third of employment from 2001 to 2003. This corresponds to
about 20 000 jobs in Apparel, the biggest sector. Eventually, smaller and
less productive firms left the sectors, triggering within-sector reallocation.

5.   CONCLUSIONS

In this chapter we investigated the impact of China's rise on Hungarian
manufacturing from different angles. Based on a GVAR analysis, we
found that the aggregate impact of growing Chinese demand is positive
for Hungary, while the traditional exporting sectors are confronted with
severe competitive challenges from Chinese suppliers. The more skill-
intensive sectors adjusted successfully by increasing labour productivity
and using the cost advantages of outsourcing to low-cost economies.
On the other hand, low-skill industries lost significant market share and
underwent a significant downsizing under the increased competitive
pressure from China.

Downsizing resulted in sustained employment problems among low-
skilled workers. Although there was a high-growth period between 2005
and 2007, the manufacturing sector in Hungary was less successful in
reintegrating workers with low skills than the manufacturing industries of
other CEE countries. Hence the acceleration of technological changes put

an increasing burden on the low-skilled workforce. Improving the employment chances for the low-skilled and raising the educational attainment of society are the most important challenges facing Hungary due to the changing global trade patterns.

Another policy challenge revealed by our analysis was the strong reaction of domestic inflation to higher commodity prices triggered by increasing Chinese demand. This can be explained by the lower energy efficiency of production, but it also highlights that inflation expectations are less firmly anchored in Hungary.

NOTES

1. We used Moulton's correction to control for any bias that may result from regressing with an aggregate explanatory variable, and also controlled for the selection bias of exit.
2. Hungary's EU accession introduced methodological changes to the import statistics, which make data comparisons before and after accession misleading. The changes affect the definition of the import partner country, which was based on the product's country of origin before accession, but on the sending country afterwards. This modification changes the relative importance of countries whose products reach Hungary via third countries, for example countries at a remote distance from Hungary. Data for 2003, for which statistics are available in both methodologies, provide insights into the magnitude of the problem. Defined as a country of origin, China is the third most important trading partner and as such is responsible for 6.9 per cent of the overall import volume. When defined as the sending country, China's share in the import volume drops to 2.2 per cent. Consequently, China falls back into eleventh place in the ranking of the trading partners.
3. Chinese exports are changing gradually from more labour-intensive to more capital-intensive. While there is solid evidence for the shift, the current debate in the international trade literature shows some uncertainty about the quality of these capital-intensive products. On the one hand, Chinese exports are just low-quality replicas of the products of advanced economies (Xu, 2010). On the other hand, with the increased involvement in global production chains, China exports more and more high-tech, IT and electronic products (Rodrik, 2006; Schott, 2008). Pula and Santabárbara (2011) also provide evidence on the increasing quality and sophistication of Chinese exports.
4. The Kaitz index shows the relationship between average and minimum wages. The higher the Kaitz index, the smaller the distance between the minimum and average wages.

REFERENCES

Álvarez, Roberto and Luis Opazo (2011), 'Effects of Chinese imports on relative wages: microevidence from Chile', *Scandinavian Journal of Economics*, **113**(2), 342–63.
Bernard, Andrew B., J. Bradford Jensen and Peter K. Schott (2006), 'Survival of the best fit: exposure to low-wage countries and the (uneven) growth of U.S. manufacturing plants', *Journal of International Economics*, **68**(1), 219–37.
Cesa-Bianchi, A., M.H. Pesaran, A. Rebucci and T.T. Xu (2011), 'China's

emergence in the world economy and business cycles in Latin America', IZA Discussion Paper No. 5889, Forschungsinstitut zur Zukunft der Arbeit.

Dreger, C. and Y. Zhang (2011), 'The Chinese impact on GDP growth and inflation of industrial countries', DIW Discussion Paper No. 1151, Deutsches Institut für Wirtschaftsforschung.

Kertesi, Gábor and János Köllő (2003), 'The employment effects of nearly doubling the minimum wage – the case of Hungary', Budapest Working Papers on the Labour Market 0306, Institute of Economics, Hungarian Academy of Sciences.

Pesaran, M. H., T. Schuermann and S.M. Weiner (2004), 'Modeling regional interdependencies using a global error-correcting macroeconometric model', *Journal of Business and Economic Statistics*, **22**(2), 129–62.

Pula, Gábor and Daniel Santabárbara (2011), 'Is China climbing up the quality ladder? Estimating cross country differences in product quality using Eurostat's COMEXT trade database', Working Paper Series 1310, European Central Bank.

Rodrik, Dani (2006), 'What's so special about China's exports?', CEPR Discussion Papers 5484.

Schott, Peter K. (2008), 'The relative sophistication of Chinese exports', *Economic Policy*, CEPR, CES, MSH, **23**(53), 5–49.

Xu, Bin (2010), 'The sophistication of exports: is China special?', *China Economic Review*, **21**(3), 482–93.

PART IV

On the sustainability of current growth strategies

12. Economic problems facing the next Russian president

Sergey Aleksashenko

Although many Russian politicians may believe that Russia is not really part of Europe and definitely not part of the integration process, nevertheless, Russia is connected to Europe. For example, in 1990 it was possible to exchange the Soviet ruble, which was not in short supply in the Soviet Union, in Vienna. In 1992, when the Soviet Union collapsed, Finland experienced perhaps the most severe recession because of the collapse of trade with the Soviet Union, because of problems with bilateral clearing and so on. So Russia will definitely influence what is going on in Europe, and the next Russian president will face some of the problems that will affect Europe in general.

Although the Russian presidential elections are scheduled for March 2012, the outcome seems to be clear to everyone – Vladimir Putin will be announced as the winner and in early May he will take his place in the Kremlin. His aim will be to stay there for six or twelve years or maybe even more, but, unlike his first term in the Kremlin, the 2010s will be much more difficult for him, with the economy no longer booming after the transformation of the 1990s and no longer recovering from the severe financial crisis of 1998. Rather, he will face many problems that he has not had to deal with before: slow after-crisis recovery, the demographic trap, growing dependence on oil, a lack of investment, a weak financial system and, finally, the need for political change.

The 2008–09 crisis was a severe experience for Russia. The deep recession during the global crisis resulted in minus 10.5 per cent in GDP from peak to bottom. At the time of writing, many Russian politicians believe that the crisis is over. Of course, if overcoming the crisis is tantamount to passing over the bottom point, that happened sometime in spring 2009; but if the crisis is deemed to have been overcome once the economy reaches the pre-crisis maximum, that will occur in Russia in early 2012. If we say that the crisis will not have been overcome until the Russian economy returns to the trend line, this moment may be some time away because the Russian economy has not been growing very fast after the

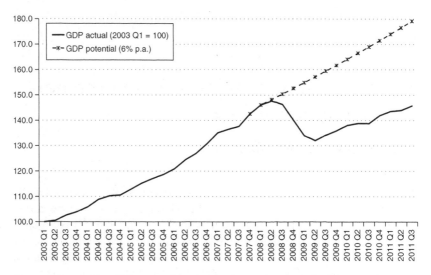

Source: Rosstat, http://gks.ru/wps/wcm/connect/rosstat/rosstatsite/main/account/#.

Figure 12.1   Slow after-crisis recovery

crisis. According to Rosstat data, output has been growing between 3.5 and 4.5 per cent on average, and, what is more important, the recovery is not stable. The Russian economy may grow for two quarters but then halt for one quarter, and may then grow again and stop again. And this is really worrying, as it would imply that the economy has lost its momentum (see Figure 12.1).

One of the most severe problems for Russia, maybe not for the next presidency but for the coming couple of decades, is the demographic trap (see Figure 12.2). According to different estimates, the Russian population is going to decline, and rather fast. Some experts say that the population may decline by 10 per cent, some more pessimistic forecasts say by 20 per cent in 30 years. But within this declining population there is another trend: the growing ratio of the number of people at pension age to the number of those at working age. And that creates a double shortage: a shortage of population and a shortage of labour force. The Russian economy has never faced this problem before, and currently it is on the brink. This process should start around 2013 or 2014 and it will be visible in the overall shortage of labour resources in the economy as well as in the increasing pension burden for the federal budget. Up to now, Russian politicians have believed that it is possible to solve this problem by inviting labour from the Central Asian countries. But, on the one hand, the speed of decline of the Russian labour force will increase and the Central Asian

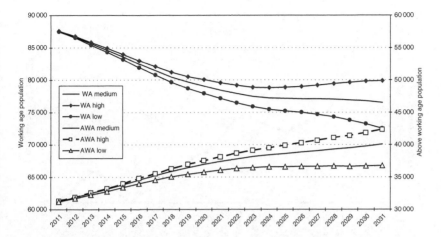

Source: Rosstat, http://gks.ru/wps/wcm/connect/rosstat/rosstatsite/main/population/demography/#.

Figure 12.2　Demographic forecast for Russia ('000s)

republics have no such amount of labour to supply to Russia. On the other hand, the educational and professional quality of the labour force from Central Asia is low. Moreover, the supply of labour resources from Central Asia does not solve the demographic problem itself and does not solve the problem of the pension burden.

After the 2008–09 crisis, the dependence of the Russian economy on oil and gas has increased. At the time of writing, more than 85 per cent of proceeds from Russian exports are from the sale of raw materials and primary commodities, while exports of oil, gas and refineries represent 67 per cent of overall exports. In fact, we may say that Russia has just one commodity for export. And that is very dangerous for balance of payments stability because the price of oil is volatile and so the export proceeds will be volatile.

At first glance, Russia has an enormously strong current account and trade balance, standing at somewhere between 8 and 12 per cent of GDP in the 2000s (see Figure 12.3). But if we exclude oil, gas and refineries, we see that the deficit of the trade balance is growing rather fast. Moreover, it was huge in mid-2008, and after the crisis it took only a couple of years to reach the same level. This means that the Russian balance of payments is not only dependent on oil but is increasingly so.

The level of oil dependence for the balance of payments is evident from Figure 12.4. The dotted line – the oil price on the left-hand scale – indicates when the current account of the Russian balance of payments is neutral,

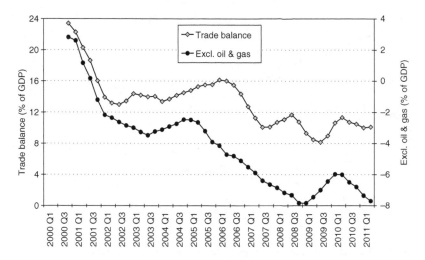

Source: Bank of Russia, http://www.cbr.ru/statistics/print.aspx?file=credit_statistics/trade.htm&pid=svs&sid=vt.

Figure 12.3   Oil dependence: balance of payments

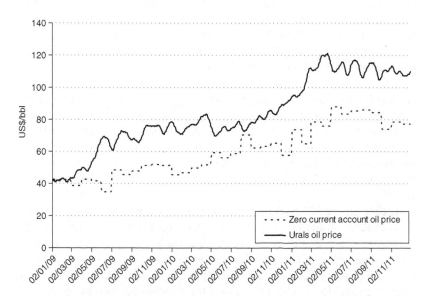

Source: Bank of Russia, Development Center's estimates, http://www.dcenter.ru/pdf/2012/NewKGB_16.pdf.

Figure 12.4   Current account neutral price for oil

that is, equal to zero. Russia historically lived with a positive current account. There was not one quarter in Russian history after 1991 when Russia had a negative current account. It occurred for a month, maximum for two months, but never in a quarter. Moreover, as soon as the Russian current account was below 1 percentage point of GDP, Russia faced a devaluation of the ruble. And we see that once again in 2011. Today the solid line and the dotted line – the oil price and the current account neutral price for oil – are not very close to one another. But the oil price is not growing, while imports to Russia were growing in the first eight months of 2011 at a rate of 35 to 37 per cent compared to the previous year. Moreover, no one can assure Russian economists and politicians that the oil price will grow forever, which means that the potential instability of the balance of payments is a very important factor for the coming years. Moreover, the Russian balance of payments may become unstable even when the current account is rather positive, as happened in the third quarter of 2011 when a small, not very significant capital outflow resulted in a 10 per cent devaluation of the Russian ruble as financial conditions on international markets tightened.

The Russian Central Bank today allows the free floating of the ruble, but in a situation where the balance of payments is not stable, the instability and volatility of the exchange rate may pose a big problem for many sectors of the Russian economy.

As well as the balance of payments, the Russian budget is significantly dependent on the oil price. Russia has a very specific taxation system for oil revenues, where 85 to 87 per cent of the increase in the oil price goes to the federal budget, but the budget is suffering mostly from the decline in the oil price: as the oil price declines by $1 the Russian budget loses 85 to 87 cents. But, on the other hand, that is why the Russian oil industry and the Russian real sector are not very strongly affected by the changes in the oil price.

Currently, slightly more than 50 per cent of revenues of the federal budget are linked to the oil price, that is, export tariffs for oil, refineries and gas or natural resources tax for oil and gas. And if revenues of the federal budget account excludes oil and gas revenues, we see – the solid line in Figure 12.5 – that the deficit of the federal budget has increased from 3 to 4 per cent before the crisis to a level of approximately 10 per cent in 2010 and 8 per cent in 2011.

Moreover, the Russian oil industry will face a serious problem in the coming years. It needs to develop new oil fields in the east and in the north that are more expensive than current oil fields. But the current tax system does not leave oil companies enough financial resources for such investment. This means that the Russian government has an option either to

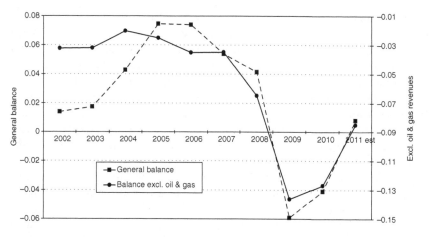

Source: Economic Expert Group, http://www.eeg.ru/pages/186.

Figure 12.5   Russian federal budget balance (% of GDP)

keep the current tax burden and to face the decline in oil production or to give more money to the oil sector to keep production stable but to lose oil revenues in the federal budget.

No economy can grow without investment, and Russia – despite all the efforts of the federal government – cannot increase the investment level above 21 to 22 per cent of GDP, while in major fast-growing developing countries the share of investment is 25 to 30 per cent of GDP. Moreover, after the 2008–09 crisis investments in Russia have become more and more concentrated in the raw materials sector and in the public sector and state-controlled infrastructural monopolies. As is evident from Figure 12.6, the share of investment by the public sector and of state monopolies (railways, pipelines and power grids) in the overall increase in investment exceeds 50 per cent, which means that investment is more and more government-driven. The other two sectors – private and 'quasi-private investment' – represent investment in commodities, the export-oriented sector, and all other sectors. The declining share of the last sector reflects the deterioration of the investment climate in the country. From 2003 to 2007 the share of private investment in the increase of investment was approximately half (49 per cent), in 2010 it fell to 9 per cent and in 2011 it was somewhat better at 16 per cent. Economic growth in Russia cannot rely on government-driven budget investments because many of them are non-productive. For example, in 2010, 10 per cent of federal budget investments were dedicated to the programme for the development of Vladivostok, where the summit of the APEC (Asian-Pacific Economic Cooperation) region will take place in 2012.

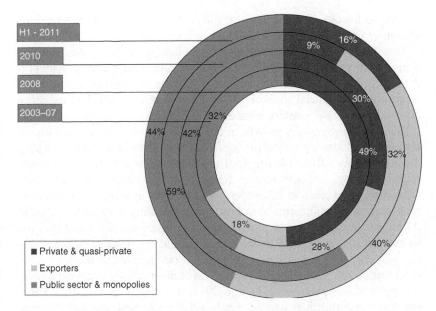

H1 - 2011

2010

2008

2003–07

9% 16%

30%

49% 32%

32%

44% 42%

59%

18%

28% 40%

■ Private & quasi-private
■ Exporters
■ Public sector & monopolies

Source: Development Center, http://www.dcenter.ru/news_main/NEP_2011-Q3_present.
pdf.

Figure 12.6   Lack of investment

One more crucial problem that Russia will face in the coming decade
is the weak financial system. The Russian financial system is not very big:
it is below 4 per cent of GDP, but in the crisis of 2008–09 the banking
system suffered mostly from the unhedged foreign exchange exposure that
exceeded 30 per cent of its capital, lack of liquidity and non-controlled
credit risk. As a result, the Russian authorities have implemented a huge
programme of support for the Russian financial system, which may be
compared to the maximum level of support to the banking system in the
developed countries. None of the emerging economies/G20 members
has realized any banking system support programme except Russia.
Liquidity support to the banking system exceeded 11 per cent of GDP,
while the capital injection in different forms, such as subordinated credits
and subsidies from the budget, exceeded 5 per cent of GDP. That is the
price that Russia paid for the rather poor quality of its banking supervision. But unfortunately the lessons from the banking crisis and from the
financial crisis have not been learned properly by the Russian authorities,
and in 2010 and 2011 another two big banking bankruptcies took place –
Mezhprombank and Bank of Moscow – and the government once again

needed to inject a huge amount of public funds to support the banking system or to repay banking losses.

The quality of the financial sector, the adequacy of financial regulation and supervision are crucial factors for economic stability. Russia is dependent on foreign financing and is looking to borrow money from international financial markets while its financial system has to be an adequate and reliable intermediator.

Sustainable economic growth in Russia, unfortunately, is not only an economic but also a political problem. Many experts agree that the crucial issue for today's Russia is the poor investment climate. Its improvement requires serious political reform because Russia needs fair courts, law enforcement, protection of property rights, fight against corruption and racketeering, opening the economy and welcoming foreign investment. All those are not economic problems, but political problems and they are so evident that even the Russian president and the Russian prime minister, whoever they are, will say, 'We need a better investment climate, we need fair courts', but they do nothing. Moreover, the political campaign, the election campaign of 2011 and 2012, has clearly demonstrated that the Russian authorities are not ready yet for any real political changes. The civil protests that emerged in the winter of 2011–12 may have demonstrated that many Russians are not ready to accept the political climate as it is and are looking for changes that will shift the iceberg. But no one can be sure of that.

Nevertheless, when Vladimir Putin returns to his office in the Kremlin he will face a much more difficult economic situation than 11 or 12 years ago. Russia is facing serious economic challenges that are connected with political problems. Many experts, including me, argue that Russia cannot achieve sustainable and stable economic growth unless the political problems are solved, or unless a political transformation occurs.

Unfortunately, Vladimir Putin has never before demonstrated readiness to liberalize the political regime of Russia and has never trusted economic incentives and private initiatives, but only the state-controlled economy. His economic policy in the last ten years led to visible positive results based on the growing oil price alone. The coming years will be different and the economic situation in Russia by 2020 will mostly depend not on oil price but on political will.

13. Is the catching-up process in Central and Eastern Europe sustainable?

Anders Åslund

This chapter focuses on where the ten countries that joined the European Union (EU) in 2004 or 2007 stand on the road to convergence after the financial crisis of 2008–09.[1]

The countries under review here – from north to south – are Estonia, Latvia, Lithuania, Poland, the Czech Republic, Slovakia, Hungary, Slovenia, Romania and Bulgaria; together we call them Central and Eastern Europe (CEE) – all came out of the financial crisis quite well within about two years. This chapter investigates their fiscal sustainability and likely growth path and finds them set to continue the process of European convergence, though at a somewhat lower pace than before 2008.

The first section of this chapter – which deals with the purely economic side of the crisis, leaving aside politics and political economy analysis – reviews the resolution of the financial crisis. The second section investigates what crisis resolution meant for competitiveness and future growth, compared with the PIGS economies – Portugal, Italy, Greece and Spain, the weakest and least developed part of the EU at the time of crisis. Finally, we conclude what this might mean for the future convergence of the ten new eastern members of the EU with the old members. The main conclusion is that the three Baltic countries have undertaken sweeping structural changes and are likely to achieve among the highest growth rates within the EU for the foreseeable future. But also the other CEE countries have carried out sensible changes and are likely to see their continued economic convergence with the EU, although Hungary is an exception.

Since our interest in this chapter is the effects of policy in each country, not the impact on the regional economy as a whole, all averages are unweighted. The statistics used are primarily from Eurostat and the IMF *World Economic Outlook* databases.

CRISIS RESOLUTION

The great positive surprise is that the financial crisis in the region abated and all countries returned to economic growth within two years, thanks to decisive and successful crisis resolution measures. As these measures were forceful and radical, they are well worth studying. Among the CEE crisis countries, the Baltic countries were the ones that adopted the most radical cures. Hence we shall focus on them, since they offer the starkest case studies, although Hungary, Bulgaria and Romania undertook substantial changes as well. Their cures have several characteristic features, although they were not shared by all.

As the extent of the financial disaster became evident, the first question was whether international financial assistance was needed or not. In spite of the tremendous economic shocks and prior imbalances, only Hungary, Latvia and Romania required IMF standby programmes; in addition, the European Commission, the World Bank and Latvia's neighbours contributed substantially. The reasons are illustrative. Latvia suffered the collapse of its biggest domestically owned bank, Parex Bank. In Hungary a government bond auction failed in October 2008, while a multitude of partial causes rather than a specific reason brought trouble to Romania. Estonia and Bulgaria could hold their own thanks to multi-year fiscal surpluses. The biggest surprise was that Lithuania was able to manage without international financial support.

Several countries, including Lithuania, Latvia, Hungary and Romania, changed governments as the crisis started to bite, and the new governments were invariably bent on dealing with the financial crisis head on. These government changes were facilitated by the parliamentary system with coalition governments, which quickly adopted radical crisis programmes and budgets for 2009. The approach was quite far-reaching, as the crisis demanded. But as the economic decline proceeded, even more radical measures became necessary, so supplementary budgets with further cuts were adopted in the second quarter of 2009.

Surprisingly, none of the four countries with pegged exchange rates – Latvia, Lithuania, Estonia and Bulgaria – devalued. In a small and open economy with heavy euroization, devaluation would have offered little relief. The main argument for devaluation would have been to boost exports, but these countries stayed competitive and could hardly have expanded their exports faster than they did. Devaluation would have bankrupted many banks and enterprises, but the collapse of the Latvian Parex Bank was the only significant bank bankruptcy. Another problem avoided was a sharp rise in foreign indebtedness. Moreover, devaluation would have boosted inflation, as many prices are internationally set.

Instead, Latvia, Lithuania, Estonia and Bulgaria pursued 'internal devaluation', cutting wages and public expenditures, which rendered their cost levels competitive and allowed them to turn their large current account deficits swiftly into substantial surpluses. A corollary is that depreciation is a much over-advertised cure in current macroeconomic discourse. Regardless of exchange rate policy, monetary policy and bank regulation, no small open economy can safeguard itself against sudden capital inflows and outflows. In fact, no country changed its exchange rate policy, suggesting that exchange rate policy might be less essential than commonly thought.

Especially the three Baltic countries, but also Bulgaria, Hungary and Romania, undertook sweeping fiscal adjustments in early 2009, which were remarkable in three respects: they were radical, they were highly front-loaded, and they consisted of three-quarters of expenditure cuts rather than revenue measures. If policies had not changed, the IMF assessed that in 2009 Latvia would have reached budget deficits of 18 per cent of GDP, Lithuania 16 per cent and Estonia more than 10 per cent of GDP. Therefore these countries undertook in that very year gross fiscal adjustments of 13.9 per cent of GDP in Latvia, 8.8 per cent of GDP in Estonia, and 8.0 per cent of GDP in Lithuania (Purfield and Rosenberg, 2010, pp. 17–18).

Large cuts in public expenditure facilitated beneficial structural reforms. The most popular reforms were cuts in the state apparatus. All did that, but Latvia went the furthest, cutting the number of state agencies by half, the number of public servants by 30 per cent, and average public wages by 26 per cent, while prohibiting double earnings by public servants. The ministers set an example by accepting salary cuts of 35 per cent (Åslund and Dombrovskis, 2011). Lithuania cut public wages by 20 per cent.

A hard and unpopular measure was to cut wages throughout the economy. In general, wage cuts were smaller in the private sector than in the public sector. By the end of 2009, average earnings had fallen from the peak by 11 per cent in Latvia, 9 per cent in Lithuania and 6.5 per cent in Estonia (Purfield and Rosenberg, 2010, p. 24).

Social benefit expenditures had risen excessively throughout the region during the boom years 2005–08. Now, the governments had little choice but to trim sickness, disability, maternity and pension benefits, often in a progressive fashion to safeguard the most vulnerable. At the same time, eligibility requirements were tightened. Education and health care reforms are proceeding, but more gradually. Financing is being tied to output and quality rather than to institutions and moved from real estate to qualified professional services. In health care, financing has been transferred from hospitals to primary care. Latvia closed down many schools with too few students. Lithuania launched a substantial higher education reform, tying state financing to students, so that institutions of higher education are competing to attract the best students and have obtained incentives both to economize on resources and to raise quality.

Most of the CEE countries have reasonable business environments, but virtually all of them undertook substantial reform to improve conditions further during the financial crisis. The easiest reform was market deregulation. The Baltic countries had largely liberalized their markets for goods, services and capital, making further advances with the guidance of the World Bank index for ease of doing business.

Several countries also carried out substantial liberalization of their labour markets, removing restrictions on flexible work arrangements. Moreover, unemployment fell fast from high peaks, for example, from 20.7 per cent in Latvia in the first quarter of 2010 to 14.4 per cent in the third quarter of 2011. Most governments have established substantial job support programmes with EU funds. The two goals of increasing employment and social safety have been reasonably balanced.

The single big failure during the crisis was the reversal of pension reform measures. Public pensions have expanded at the expense of private pension schemes and their share of GDP has risen, as dictated by equity concerns and fiscal necessity. Pension cuts in Latvia, Romania and Lithuania were revoked by their respective constitutional courts. The country that advanced most with entitlement reform during the crisis was Hungary, which even decided to raise the retirement age in the midst of the crisis. Governments need to proceed with pension reform, restoring the funding of the second, private pillar of the pension system. In June 2011, the Lithuanian parliament legislated a gradual increase of the retirement age to 65 for both men and women, to render the public pension system financially sustainable. This has to be done throughout the region.

While the total tax burden increased marginally, the structure of the tax system changed considerably. In all six crisis countries, taxes moved from labour and corporate profits to consumption, while tax bases were broadened. Many countries raised excise taxes and eliminated loopholes in the value-added tax (VAT). The worst-hit crisis countries, Latvia, Lithuania, Hungary and Romania, were forced to hike their VAT by a few per cent. Property taxes were increased in a few countries, notably Latvia and Romania, but the Romanian Constitutional Court aborted the Romanian property tax.

The flat personal income tax stays popular. When the crisis hit, six of the ten countries had flat income taxes, ranging from 10 per cent in Bulgaria to 23 per cent in Latvia. Now their number has expanded to eight as the Czech Republic introduced a flat income tax of 15 per cent in

2008, and the Hungarian government adopted one of 16 per cent in 2011. In general, personal taxes have gradually been reduced. Lithuania did so most radically, slashing its flat personal income taxes from 33 per cent in 2006 to 15 per cent at present. Corporate profit taxes are similarly low, and the number of taxes is small. This tax structure offers people and entrepreneurship improved incentives for work.

The CEE countries have greatly benefited from larger EU funds, which they realized had not been fully utilized. Especially Latvia and Lithuania have sharply raised their absorption of such grants from 3–4 per cent of GDP to 6–7 per cent of GDP. Not least, several governments established substantial job support programmes with EU funds. However, Bulgaria and Romania have had serious problems accessing EU funds, being unable to fulfil all the EU requirements.

OUTCOMES

We are interested in two kinds of outcomes. First, have the CEE economies got their macroeconomic situation under control? Second, have they developed conditions for a return to high economic growth so that they can pursue economic convergence with the old EU-15?

Throughout the region, swift economic adjustment took place from the end of 2008. The East European current account crisis that erupted in the fourth quarter of 2008 was settled in the middle of 2010, when all countries had returned to economic growth. The region as a whole lost two to three years of economic growth, which was sad but no catastrophe, considering the excellent growth the region enjoyed from 2000 until 2008. In 2010, only Romania did not grow, while the Latvian economy stagnated on balance. In 2011, all the CEE countries were set to grow significantly (Figure 13.1).

Seldom has the world seen such rapid changes in the current account. The swing was most pronounced in Latvia, which went from a current account deficit of 13 per cent of GDP in 2008 to a surplus of 9.4 per cent in 2009 – no less than 22 per cent of GDP in one single year. Estonia and Lithuania also shifted from big deficits to significant surpluses, while most other countries ended up close to balance. Only Bulgaria maintained a large current account deficit of 9.5 per cent of GDP, but it was financed by continued large foreign direct investment. By 2010, no CEE country had a current account deficit above 4.5 per cent of GDP, and the countries worst hit by the crisis displayed surpluses. Greece and Portugal, by contrast, had current account deficits of 10 per cent of GDP (Figure 13.2).

Inflation that had hit double digits in the Baltic states and Bulgaria in 2008 fell sharply in the deflationary climate of the global recession because

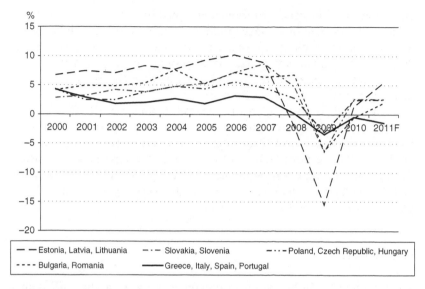

Source: International Monetary Fund, World Economic Outlook Database, September 2011 (accessed 31 October 2011).

Figure 13.1   GDP growth, 2000–2011

of minimal credit issuance. In the Baltic countries, the change was most extreme. Credit had expanded by about 50 per cent a year in 2006 and 2007, but it started shrinking in 2009, resulting in 1 per cent deflation in Latvia in 2009. In 2010 and 2011, most countries had moderate inflation of about 3 per cent (Figure 13.3). These countries have finally been able to get price developments under control. Yet no country, apart from Latvia, showed deflation for any year.

Budget deficits were limited in 2007 but increased because of the crisis, yet not as much as in Western Europe. The average unweighted budget deficit of the CEE-10 rose from 2.8 per cent of GDP in 2008 to 6.6 per cent of GDP in 2009, and it contracted minimally to 5.6 per cent of GDP in 2010. Most countries are intent on reducing their budget deficits to 3 per cent of GDP by 2012. This stands in stark contrast with the PIGS economies (Portugal, Italy, Greece and Spain), where budget deficits swelled to 10.6 per cent of GDP in 2009 and stayed at 8.6 per cent of GDP in 2010 (Figure 13.4).

Public expenditures rose as a share of GDP. Before the crisis, the EU-15 had average public expenditures of 46–47 per cent of GDP. Central Europe had almost as high public expenditures, but the average was

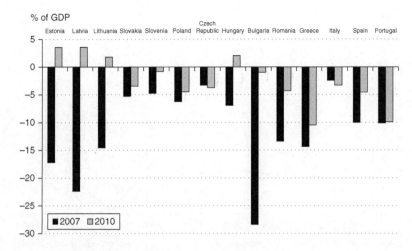

Source: International Monetary Fund, World Economic Outlook Database, September 2011 (accessed 31 October 2011).

Figure 13.2   Current account balance, 2007 and 2010

boosted by Hungary. The three Baltic states saw their public expenditures rise as a share of GDP from 35 per cent in 2007 to 45 per cent in 2009, while Central Europe experienced a marginal rise to 46 per cent of GDP. Bulgaria and Romania reported far lower public expenditures, peaking at 38 per cent of GDP in 2010 (Figure 13.5). In the crisis year of 2009, public expenditure as a share of GDP rose sharply because of contracting GDP, rising pension costs and other social costs related to rising unemployment. Still, the East Europeans largely abstained from state aid, so common in Western Europe during the crisis.

Based on these criteria, we can claim that the CEE countries, with the exception of Hungary, have overcome the macroeconomic crisis. They have sound economic growth, although much lower than before the crisis. The current account is reasonably close to balance. Budget deficits are moderate and set to fall further. Only Hungary has a public debt that exceeds the Maastricht limit of 60 per cent of GDP, while most CEE countries have public debts of about 40 per cent of GDP. The only really worrisome feature is that public expenditure has risen far too high. In Central Europe and the Baltics, public expenditure as a share of GDP has risen to 45–46 per cent, and it needs to be brought down to about 35 per cent of GDP to allow for sound economic growth (Sachs and Warner, 1996; Tanzi and Schuknecht, 2000). Fortunately, most CEE governments have such ambitions.

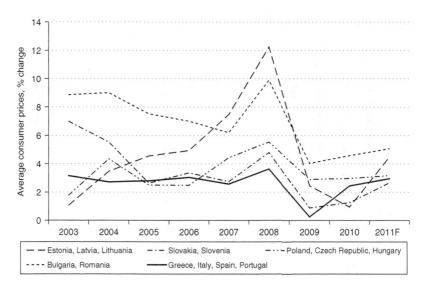

Source: International Monetary Fund, World Economic Outlook Database, September 2011 (accessed 31 October 2011).

Figure 13.3   Inflation, 2003–11

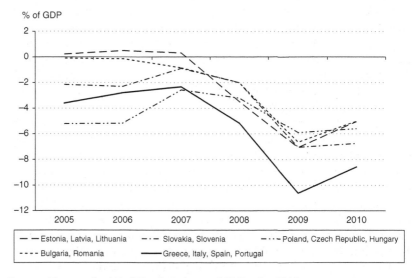

Source: Eurostat Statistical Database (accessed 31 October 2011).

Figure 13.4   Budget deficit, 2005–10

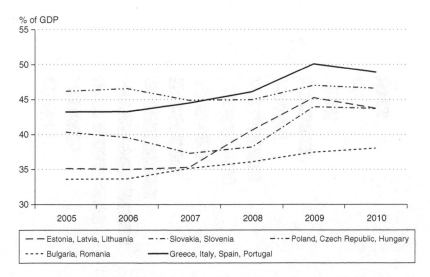

% of GDP

Source: International Monetary Fund, World Economic Outlook Database, September 2011 (accessed 31 October 2011).

Figure 13.5   Public expenditure as a share of GDP, 2005–10

Our second query is whether conditions have been created for high future economic growth. By and large, the CEE countries had already advanced further in structural reforms than other countries at their level of economic development, which was a reason for their fast economic growth (excepting only Hungary because of too large public debt and still the highest public expenditures).

A first measure of the potential for structural reform is a nation's ranking on the World Bank Ease of Doing Business index. Among the CEE countries, Latvia has taken the lead, advancing to no. 21 among 183 countries, while Estonia ranks no. 24 and Lithuania no. 27. Since Latvia and Lithuania rank about no. 50 in the world in terms of GDP per capita in purchasing power parities, this indicates substantial capacity of further growth. Romania is doing the worst, ranking no. 72, but Italy ranks no. 87 and Greece no. 100 (Figure 13.6). Typical recent reform measures have been to make it simpler to register property, resolve insolvency, pay taxes, start a business and enforce a contract.

As a consequence of improving business conditions, corruption is abating. Transparency International's Corruption Perception index offers a similar ranking, but it reflects the greater inertia of corruption than of deregulation. It ranks Bulgaria and Romania as poorly as Greece and

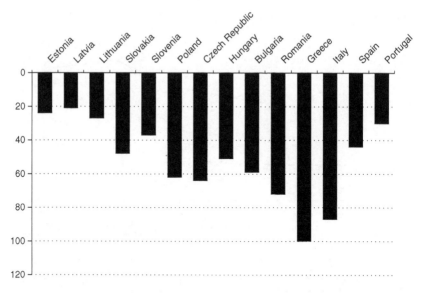

Note: Lower score indicates greater ease of doing business.

Source: World Bank and the IFC, *Doing Business Report, 2012* (accessed 31 October 2011).

Figure 13.6   Ease-of-doing-business ranking, 2012

Italy (Figure 13.7), although the former two do much better on the Ease of Doing Business index.

The large structural adjustments have had a considerable, but varied, impact on real unit labour costs, which have been brought down both by nominal wage cuts and various forms of rationalization. Real unit labour costs have fallen in no less than six of the ten CEE states, most of all in Latvia, where they fell by 16.4 per cent from 2008 to 2011, followed by Romania (–11.7 per cent), Lithuania (–9.5 per cent) and Hungary (– 9.1 per cent) (Figure 13.8). Naturally, this means greatly improved competitiveness of these countries.

The real effective exchange rate (REER, deflated with unit labour cost) offers quite a revealing composite picture. The overall message is that nominal or internal devaluation can work, but labour costs must be checked either way. The differences from 2008 to 2010 are amazingly large. Two countries stand out, Latvia and Poland, whose REER fell by 17 and 12 per cent, respectively. Also Hungary, Lithuania and Estonia saw significant falls. By contrast, in Bulgaria, Slovakia and Slovenia – one

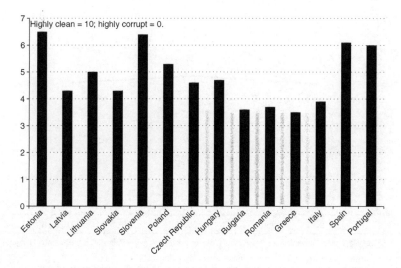

Note: Highly clean = 10; highly corrupt = 0.

Source: Transparency International, Corruption Perceptions Index 2010 (accessed 31 October 2011).

Figure 13.7 Corruption Perceptions Index, 2010

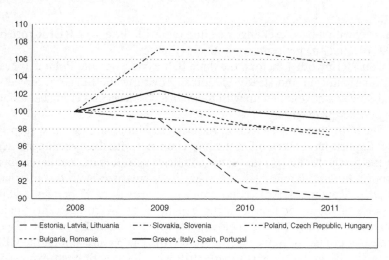

Note: Index: 2008 = 100

Source: Eurostat Statistical Database (accessed 31 October 2011).

Figure 13.8 Real unit labour cost, 2008–11

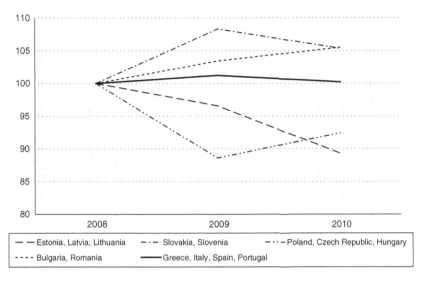

Note: Index: 2008 = 100, ULC

Source: Eurostat Statistical Database (accessed 31 October 2011).

Figure 13.9   Real effective exchange rate, 2008–10

country with a fixed exchange rate and two with the euro – REER rose by 109, 105 and 105 per cent, respectively (Figure 13.9).

Considering other factors, the three Baltic countries and Poland appear set for significant and steady economic growth, while Bulgaria, Slovakia and Slovenia have ended up with too high a cost level and Hungary suffers from other problems.

The most impressive effects of the crisis resolution are the most surprising. Exports have taken off in the four countries with fixed exchange rates. In the first half of 2011, the Baltic countries and Bulgaria increased their exports by a stunning 29–42 per cent in comparison with the first half of 2010. Romania fared second best with a growth of 27 per cent, while exports of the other five countries expanded by 14–20 per cent. Spain, Portugal and Italy all saw their exports grow at a similar rate of 15 per cent, like Poland or Slovenia (Figure 13.10). The picture among the CEE countries is similar if we compare 2010 with 2009, with great expansion and similar differences between the CEE countries. Export expansion led the recovery of output in all countries and it was driven by a similarly rapid increase in manufacturing.

This result is surprising and prompts one major conclusion:

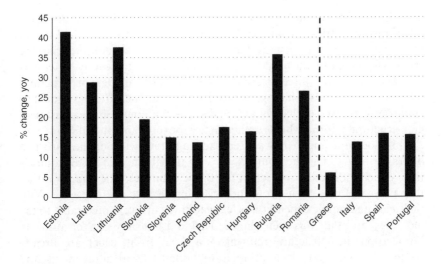

Source: Eurostat Statistical Database (accessed 31 October 2011).

Figure 13.10   Total exports, per cent increase 2010–11 (first half of year, yoy)

depreciation is neither necessary nor beneficial for kickstarting exports, contrary to conventional wisdom. Paradoxically, the country with the largest real effective exchange rate decline – Poland – experienced the smallest export expansion.

A priori, this conclusion appears illogical. Depreciation should reduce export prices, and with normal price elasticity exports should increase. Such reasoning, however, is incomplete. The choice was not between depreciation and a stable real exchange rate, but between nominal or internal devaluation. As argued above, the countries with fixed exchange rates undertook far greater structural adjustments than those with floating exchange rates. Nominal devaluation saved Poland, Hungary and the Czech Republic from the need to undertake more radical structural reforms.

Similarly, Slovakia and Slovenia, which enjoyed ample liquidity thanks to being members of the euro area, did not face the same pressure to carry out major structural reforms and wage cuts, as the countries with currency boards that had to defend their fixed exchange rates with little access to liquidity. This reasoning boils down to János Kornai's (1980) old argument about the impact of hard budget constraints. Export expansion was proportionate to the contraction of domestic demand, which was the greatest in the Baltic countries and Bulgaria.

The countries that have reached the highest export growth and GDP growth are Estonia and Lithuania, followed by Latvia, while the three other crisis countries – Romania, Hungary and Bulgaria – have had slower recoveries. The first three were the leaders in structural reform during the crisis, which appears the most likely reason for their significantly better performance. The latter three focused more on austerity and less on structural reforms, which seems to have generated less growth. The pattern is clear. The countries with fixed exchange rates undertook both more fiscal adjustment and structural reform, which resulted in faster export and output growth.

This does not imply that a fixed exchange rate without the euro is a desirable policy. On the contrary, it was the absence of ECB liquidity that rendered the crisis so deep in the Baltic countries. The point is rather that they exploited their profound crisis in the best possible way. With their elevated public expenditures, expenditure cuts were preferable to tax increases, and that was their choice. They did not only opt for austerity but also pursued structural reforms on a broad front, which are already paying off. The sad observation is that major fiscal adjustments and reforms rarely occur without being prompted by a major crisis (Drazen and Grilli, 1993). Estonia was so determined to join the euro area that it managed to do so as early as January 2011, and Latvia and Lithuania are firmly determined to do so in 2014, while Bulgaria's entry date has been somewhat delayed by the crisis.

Among the CEE countries, a clear pattern is present. The biggest countries – Poland, Romania, the Czech Republic and Hungary – have opted for floating exchange rates and inflation targeting, while the six smaller economies have adopted fixed exchange rates or the euro. Similarly, the four big countries have had larger budget deficits on average during the last decade than the six smaller ones. Clearly, we are seeing different choices depending on the size of the economy, and they seem rational. Inflation targeting appears to have worked well in Poland and the Czech Republic, while it does not make much sense in very small and open economies, notably like the Baltics, which can hardly shield themselves from excessive capital inflows with any exchange rate and monetary policy. Since the small nations perceive more external dangers, they manage to maintain greater fiscal discipline than the more confident larger countries.

The existence of an IMF standby programme does not appear important in itself. Latvia carried out substantial reforms under an IMF programme, while Hungary and Romania did much less. The explanation is that the IMF is favourable to structural reforms, but it does not necessarily demand them, whereas its conditions on fiscal and monetary policies are strict.

For future growth, investment in human and physical capital is vital. Given the level of development, an investment ratio in the order of

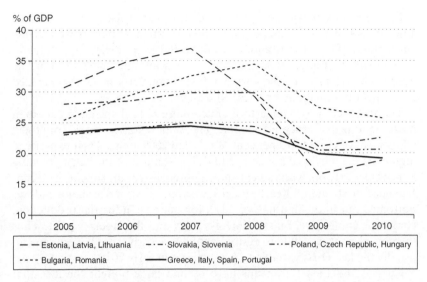

% of GDP

Source: International Monetary Fund, World Economic Outlook Database, September 2011 (accessed 31 October 2011).

Figure 13.11   Investment as a share of GDP, 2005–10

25 per cent of GDP or slightly more would appear appropriate. At the peak of the boom, investment ratios were if anything too high, ranging from 23.5 per cent of GDP in Hungary to 40 per cent of GDP in Latvia. These ratios plummeted during the crisis from 37 per cent of GDP in the Baltics in 2007 to 16.5 per cent of GDP in 2009. Yet, with economic recovery investment is resurging, and seems likely to converge around 25 per cent of GDP in the near future (Figure 13.11). Investment will probably be sufficient to sustain substantial growth.

CONCLUSIONS: FIXED EXCHANGE RATES BROUGHT MORE ADJUSTMENT AND ECONOMIC CONVERGENCE LIKELY TO CONTINUE

When discussing CEE during the global financial crisis, it is important to remember that only six of these ten countries experienced severe crises, namely the three Baltic countries, Hungary, Romania and Bulgaria. Slovakia and Slovenia were shielded through euro area membership, and Poland and the Czech Republic escaped most of the crisis through large depreciations. Two major conclusions emerge.

First, fixed exchange rates prompted the greatest fiscal and structural adjustments because neither devaluation nor external liquidity were viable alternatives. The crisis resolutions of the Baltic countries and Bulgaria have proven that internal devaluation is a possible and viable option. The fixed exchange rates of the currency board countries have not impeded adjustment but facilitated radical adjustment.

The Baltic countries undertook much more radical spending cuts than most economists considered possible. The Baltic countries carried out fiscal adjustment of close to 10 per cent of GDP in 2009 alone. Their experience highlights the universal advantage of doing as much of the belt-tightening as possible early on, with radical and comprehensive adjustment. As a consequence of strong and early fiscal measures, most performance indexes bottomed out in the first half of 2009, for example industrial production, consumer confidence, market interest rates and the stock market. Thus the government was able to restore confidence early on. Unemployment, usually the last crisis variable to peak, did so in early 2010.

Central and East Europeans have by and large bought the idea that it is better to cut expenditures than to raise taxes. Three-quarters of the early fiscal adjustment in the Baltics came through public expenditure cuts rather than tax hikes. Large selective cuts facilitate beneficial structural reforms. They not only reduce the capacity of public services but also often improve the quality of public services through reforms of administration, health care and education. Alesina and Ardagna (2009) offer substantial statistical evidence for the thesis that 'fiscal adjustments . . . based upon spending cuts and no tax increases are more likely to reduce deficits and debt over GDP ratios than those based upon tax increases'. In 2011, the three Baltic countries belong to the fastest-expanding economies in Europe with a likely growth of 5–6 per cent. None of them suffered more than two years of output contraction. Their growth is driven by exports.

Second, the crisis forced all countries to trim their public sectors and improve their already well-functioning economic systems, rendering them even more competitive. The Baltics stand out for several wise choices. They acted fast with large, early adjustments. They chose to cut their elevated expenditures rather than raise taxes. They used austerity measures to implement structural reforms on a broad scale that are likely to promote economic growth.

With regard to exchange rate regimes, our observations confirm the current state of economics. On the one hand, the role of the exchange rate regime seems to have been overstated. Obstfeld and Rogoff (2001, p. 373) pointed out 'the exceedingly weak relationship between the exchange rate and virtually any macroeconomic aggregates'. Other policies are simply more important. On the other hand, Rose (2011, p. 663) noted: 'Very small

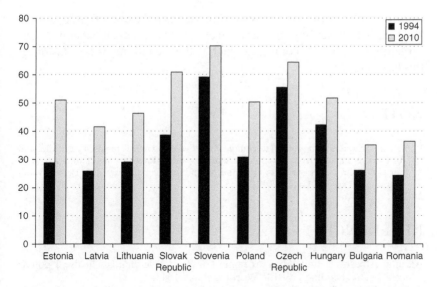

Source: World Bank, World Development Indicators (accessed 3 November 2011).

Figure 13.12   European convergence (GDP in PPP as a percentage of EU)

countries tend to fix', especially for countries with less than 2.5 million, which includes Estonia and Latvia, and Lithuania is only slightly larger.

Most factors point to renewed, elevated, sustainable economic growth for most of the region, with the possible exception of Hungary and Slovenia that have undertaken less reform. Overall growth will be constrained by less credit expansion because of deleveraging and slow economic growth in Western Europe, the dominant export market of CEE. Free market policies are not in danger, nor are democracy or social peace.

After a decade of very high economic growth, these countries encountered their first serious recession, but they took it on the chin. At the outset of the crisis it appeared as if the big issue to resolve was the exchange rate and monetary regime, but in the end no country changed its exchange rate regime, suggesting that it was neither crucial nor necessary. There is no reason to suspect that these countries have got stuck in any middle-income trap (Eichengreen et al., 2011). They have competitive economic systems and are likely to undertake sufficient investment in human and physical capital.

Before the crisis, all the CEE countries evidenced substantial economic convergence with the old EU-15, and they do so also after the crisis (Figure 13.12). The three Baltic countries have undertaken sweeping structural changes and are likely to achieve among the highest growth rates within the EU for the foreseeable future. But also the other CEE countries have carried out sensible changes and are likely to see their economic convergence with the EU continue, which is the second major conclusion of this chapter.

NOTE

1. For this chapter, I am grateful to Natalia Aivazova for excellent research assistance and for useful comments from the conference participants. Moreover, this chapter draws on our two recent books: Åslund (2010) and Åslund and Dombrovskis (2011). An overall source is Bakker and Gulde (2010).

REFERENCES

Alesina, Alberto F. and Silvia Ardagna (2009), 'Large changes in fiscal policy: taxes versus spending', NBER Working Paper 15438.
Åslund, Anders (2010), *The Last Shall Be the First: The East European Financial Crisis, 2008–10*, Washington, DC: Peterson Institute for International Economics.
Åslund, Anders and Valdis Dombrovskis (2011), *How Latvia Came out of the Financial Crisis*, Washington, DC: Peterson Institute for International Economics.
Bakker, Bas B. and Anne-Marie Gulde (2010), 'The credit boom in the EU new member states: bad luck or bad policies?', IMF Working Paper 10/213.
Drazen, Allen and Vittorio Grilli (1993), 'The benefit of crises for economic reforms', *American Economic Review*, **83**(3), 598–607.
Eichengreen, Donghyun Park and Kwanho Shin (2011), 'When fast growing economies slow down: international evidence and implications for China', NBER Working Paper No. 16919.
Kornai, János (1980), *Economics of Shortage*, Amsterdam: North-Holland.
Obstfeld, Maurice and Kenneth S. Rogoff (2001), 'The six major puzzles in international macroeconomics: is there a common cause?', in Ben S. Bernanke and Kenneth S. Rogoff (eds), *NBER Macroeconomics Annual 2000*, Cambridge, MA: MIT Press, pp. 339–90.
Purfield, Catriona and Christoph Rosenberg (2010), 'Adjustment under a currency peg: Estonia, Latvia and Lithuania during the global financial crisis 2008–9', IMF Working Paper 10/213.
Rose, Andrew (2011), 'Exchange rate regimes in the modern era: fixed, floating, and flaky', *Journal of Economic Literature*, **49**(3), 652–72.
Sachs, Jeffrey D. and Andrew Warner (1996), 'Achieving rapid growth in the transition economies of Central Europe', Harvard Institute for International Development Discussion Paper no. 544.
Tanzi, Vito and Ludger Schuknecht (2000), *Public Spending in the 20th Century*, Cambridge: Cambridge University Press.

14. Short-term outlook and long-term convergence in China, Russia and Eastern Europe

Jean-Luc Schneider

This chapter presents the author's views as of late November 2011 on how global economic developments may affect growth in the short term and, in the longer term, the growth strategy in China, Russia and the Eastern European countries, a rather heterogeneous group of countries that for ease of reference will be called 'transition countries' in what follows.

1. THE OECD ECONOMIC OUTLOOK AT END NOVEMBER 2011

Forecasting economic developments is especially difficult in times of high uncertainty. The volatility observed in equity and bond markets since the summer of 2011 is exceptional and reflects a situation seen by market participants as prone to accidents. Concerns about possible accidents relate mostly to the euro area, where they range from the disorderly default of sovereign borrowers, to the contagion of sovereign debt stress to core countries, to tensions and disruptions in the financial sector, and perhaps even to the break-up of the currency area. But not all possible negative events are located in the euro area, as concerns have also emerged about a political deadlock in the USA over fiscal policy, or about the possible hard landing of some large emerging economies and associated risks to their financial sectors.

Given the exceptional level and range of uncertainty, the only way to make quantitative projections at this juncture is to assume that none of these negative events occurs. Thus the OECD has constructed a baseline scenario that may not be the most likely but that is workable, and that assumes that business and consumer confidence worsens in late 2011/early 2012, before recovering only very gradually, as economic agents observe that none of the risks initially envisaged has materialized.

148

European integration in a global economy

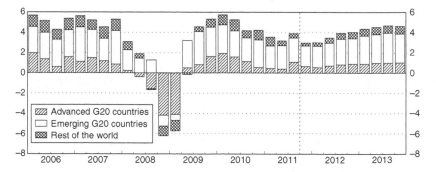

Note: Annualized quarterly rates, percentage points. Calculated using moving nominal GDP weights, based on national GDP at purchasing power parities.

Source: OECD, *Economic Outlook*, No. 90, November 2011.

Figure 14.1 OECD growth projections (as of November 2011) under a 'no-event' scenario

The quantitative projection resulting from this assumption should be seen as a baseline around which risk is clearly tilted to the downside, rather than an optimistic forecast. It can also be interpreted as a 'muddling-through' scenario, in which countries avoid the worst, without taking sufficient measures to re-establish confidence immediately. Hence the actual economic outcome may even outperform the baseline scenario.

Keeping these qualifications in mind, the baseline projection can be described as bleak (see Figure 14.1). It features a sharp slowdown in world trade and a slowdown in growth in almost all countries in late 2011/early 2012. Quarter-on-quarter annualized growth rates are expected to be markedly below trend during those two quarters, by about 1 to 1½ per cent of GDP in the OECD area as well as in most member countries. Japan is an exception, because the reconstruction after the disasters of spring 2011 will temporarily boost growth, but it is almost the only one. In Europe, this scenario involves a mild recession, defined as two quarters of negative growth, and only a gradual recovery toward potential growth, with the individual country profiles varying, not least as a function of fiscal policy.

Unemployment will go up and remain elevated during 2012 and 2013, as the output gap will become more negative in the short term and will not close by much subsequently. Against this background and assuming that oil and commodity prices remain at their current level, inflation will gradually go down in 2012 and 2013, but deflation should not become a threat as long as the current strong anchoring of inflation expectations is preserved.

2.   THE OUTLOOK FOR TRANSITION ECONOMIES

Where do transition countries situate themselves against this global background? In the baseline scenario, most economies, including China and Russia, are projected to feature the same growth profile as the aggregate OECD, namely a marked slowdown at the end of 2011, followed by gradual re-acceleration over 2012. Translated into annual growth numbers, this means a year-on-year growth rate in 2012 that is significantly below that of 2011 and a 2013 annual growth rate back toward trend growth. But, of course, in most transition countries the slowdown starts from higher growth rates than in G7 countries.

However, there are many differences within the set of transition countries, both in terms of their initial situation and in terms of the challenges they face.

Starting with China, we observed high growth in 2010 after the stimulus policies, so that the output gap was null or already positive in early 2011, and the slowdown is somewhat welcome, as it reduces the risk of overheating and inflationary pressures. At the same time domestic demand is still buoyant in spite of the global slowdown, which implies a reduction in the trade surplus, further amplified by the recent price and cost increases in China, which have already translated into a deceleration in the growth of China's market shares. All this contributes to reducing previous concerns about a hard landing, even if this risk cannot be completely dismissed. Immediate concerns about the rebalancing of demand are also somewhat alleviated, as it seems to be already happening, even if there is much more to do. At the same time, new concerns have emerged concerning the financial sector, about the amount of underperforming loans distributed during the stimulus period in 2009 and 2010 and the increase in the size of the little-regulated shadow banking sector.

Russia presents a very different picture, with a sustained growth momentum resulting primarily from energy prices remaining high in spite of the global slowdown, and from global food prices that have stabilized and stopped weighing on prices and real income. This has alleviated headline inflationary pressures, and so has a strong harvest in 2011. In addition, demand will be supported by the budget spending part of the energy bonanza in 2012. These various factors leave Russia in not so bad a situation, but also with its usual vulnerabilities. First, it remains overly vulnerable to changes in energy prices. Second, the fiscal deficit remains almost unchanged, once corrected for oil revenues, leaving only limited scope for fiscal action in case of negative shocks. And third, Russia is not immune to capital-market reversals and financial turmoil, as witnessed by the sharp capital outflows observed recently, which may complicate macroeconomic policy considerably.

As for Central and Eastern European countries, they differ markedly. Without going into details, their heterogeneity can be illustrated by two extreme cases. One is Poland, which showed strong growth through the crisis, even if about to slow, and one of the very rare positive output gaps in the OECD in 2011, so that the expected slowdown will not even be so unwelcome. Here, the immediate challenge is mostly to avoid complacency and to keep the momentum for reform, so that its relative position should not deteriorate. At the other extreme is Hungary, which is struggling with a host of interrelated problems, financial, fiscal and monetary, some of them cyclical, but many others more structural, and where the challenge is to strengthen the credibility and reliability of domestic policies, and to restore confidence as a prerequisite for a recovery in credit and investment.

With linkages to the global financial markets that are now strong and ever increasing, a common feature of transition countries is their growing vulnerability to developments in those markets and, more specifically today, to the consequences of the crisis that affects the euro area. This additional short-term challenge compounds with other difficulties related to the transition or the over-specialization in these countries.

The question is whether those short-term challenges may derail the convergence process. In the short term this is by no means certain, in the sense that we may see some 'bad convergence', in which growth would slow down in most or all countries, but with this slowdown being more pronounced or more durable in the richer economies than in the transition countries. This would repeat the pattern generally observed in 2008 and its aftermath.

However, the above-mentioned vulnerabilities and possible amplification mechanisms may counteract that bad convergence and turn it into an even worse divergence, that is, with some transition countries hit harder than other economies. For example, if a global downturn were to translate into a sharp fall in energy prices, Russia's lack of diversification would expose it to a severe demand shock. The fact that macroeconomic policies have allowed them to weather such shocks relatively well in the recent past is no guarantee for the future. Another, perhaps more worrying, concern is the situation of the financial sector in some transition countries, where tensions could be amplified by higher global risk aversion. This may at some point weigh on their spreads and on the cost of public debt in countries that have had less time to build fiscal credibility.

3. THE CONVERGENCE PROCESS BEYOND THE SHORT TERM

Turning to growth prospects beyond the short term, the question is whether the still-to-emerge post-crisis 'new normal' may involve slower convergence between the transition countries and the richer economies. One way to provide some insights into this controversial issue it is to try to identify the potential sources of future convergence and to assess whether and how much they may have been affected by the crisis.

In its annual *Going for Growth* exercise, the OECD analyses the gap between the GDP per capita in a given country and the average GDP per capita observed in the best-performing half of OECD member countries. This gap in GDP per capita is, in turn, decomposed into a gap in labour utilization and a gap in productivity, providing a metric for the catch-up potential of individual countries. This is done both for the 34 OECD members and for six large emerging economies (Brazil, China, India, Indonesia, Russia and South Africa).

Not unexpectedly, countries differ a great deal when considered through this metric. However, one general lesson concerning transition countries is that most of the gap is on the productivity side. Actually, in most transition countries (except in Slovakia), labour utilization is in line with or above what is observed in the average rich country, and this is also true in Russia and China (see Figures 14.2 and 14.3), leaving all of the catch-up to take place in productivity.

This allows reducing the question about convergence going forward to whether the future post-crisis conditions may weigh on the productivity catch-up of transition countries. At least in theory the answer is yes. This is due to the fact that one of the causes of the crisis was the underpricing of risk during the so-called Great Moderation, which involves that in the future 'new normal' world (that is, once the currently very accommodative monetary policies have normalized), the repricing of risk to a more adequate level will result in a marked increase in the cost of capital, by about 150 basis points or 8 per cent, according to OECD estimates. This increase in the relative cost of capital will reduce capital intensity, the accumulation of capital and productivity. But it does not need to affect convergence much, as the reduction is likely to be of a similar order of magnitude in transition countries and in richer countries, involving a downward-level shift in potential output by about 2 percentage points in most economies.

What may affect convergence more deeply is the fact that the increase in the cost of capital will result from a repricing of risk, and will therefore be higher for more risky investments. Risky innovative activities, but also

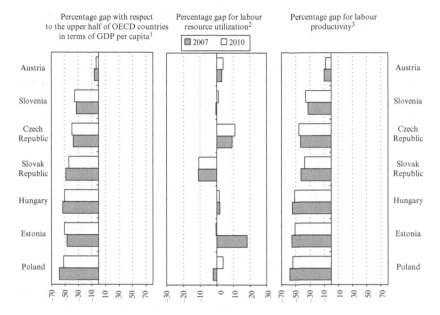

Notes:
1. Relative to the simple average of the highest 17 OECD countries in 2007 and 2010 in terms of GDP per capita, based on 2007 and 2010 purchasing power parities (PPPs). The sum of the percentage gap in labour resource utilization and labour productivity does not add up exactly to the GDP per capita gap since the decomposition is multiplicative.
2. Labour resource utilization is measured as total number of hours worked per capita.
3. Labour productivity is measured as GDP per hour worked.

Sources: OECD (2012), *Going for Growth*; OECD (2011), National Accounts database; OECD, *Economic Outlook*, No. 89: Statistics and Projections database and OECD, *Employment Outlook*.

Figure 14.2   Decomposition of the GDP/capita gap in Central and Eastern European OECD countries

investments in countries seen as generally more risky, will be hindered more, so that the part of the catching-up process that goes through higher capital intensity and higher R&D could be affected in the post-crisis 'new normal' world.

However, this theoretical slowdown in the convergence process could be partly or perhaps completely offset by structural reforms and the mobilization of new sources of growth. The potential for such reforms to unleash additional growth engines also exists in many of the richer countries, but it is smaller than in transition countries, which provides grounds for reasonable optimism about medium- and long-term convergence.

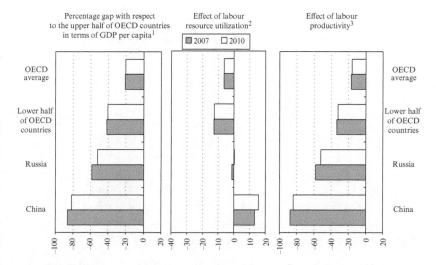

Notes:
1. Relative to the simple average of the highest 17 OECD countries in terms of GDP per capita, based on 2006 and 2009 purchasing power parities (PPPs) from the World Bank. The OECD average is based on a simple average of the 34 member countries. The sum of the percentage gap in labour resource utilization and labour productivity does not add up exactly to the GDP per capita gap since the decomposition is multiplicative.
2. Labour resource utilization is measured as employment per capita, based on KILM database estimates. In turn, employment per capita combines both the employment rate of the working-age population and the share of working-age individuals in the population. The latter reflects a demographic effect that may vary across countries and can be especially important for emerging countries in demographic transition.
3. Labour productivity is measured as GDP per employee.

Sources: OECD (2012), *Going for Growth*; World Bank (2011), *World Development Indicators* (WDI) and ILO (International Labour Organisation) (2011), *Key Indicators of the Labour Market* (KILM) databases.

Figure 14.3   Decomposition of the GDP/capita gap in China and Russia

At least three such potential sources of additional convergence can be mentioned. The first one concerns overall capital accumulation, which is not only driven by relative prices, as regulations and government intervention also matter. In this regard, the evidence is that transition countries are still in transition, in the sense that regulations and government interventions are still much heavier there than in the average OECD country (see Figure 14.4). This suggests that just reducing public ownership and government intervention toward the OECD average would allow private investment, capital intensity and productivity to increase

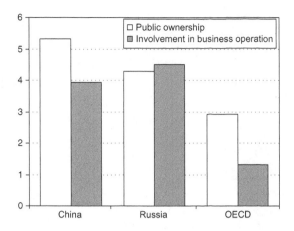

Note: Index scale of 0–6 from least to most restrictive.

Sources: OECD (2012), *Going for Growth*; OECD (2011), Product Market Regulation database.

Figure 14.4   State intervention in China and Russia

markedly, compared with a baseline scenario with no or few policy changes.

A second basis for reasonable optimism is that innovation and R&D can easily be encouraged more in transition countries. The generosity of tax incentives to invest in R&D can be measured in various ways (such as by the so-called B-index shown in Figure 14.5 for Russia and China) and it is empirically well correlated with business investment in innovation and eventually with productivity and growth. The fact that this index is low in many transition countries and is particularly low in Russia suggests that reforms could be envisaged that would have a high leverage on R&D and total factor productivity at a relatively low cost to the budget. Again the scope for such reforms is higher in transition countries, as is the fiscal room for manoeuvre in many of them.

Third, human capital is another source of productivity not yet fully tapped in many transition economies. Of course, upgrading the quality of human capital is a slow and largely endogenous process. But transition countries and China in particular are already catching up extremely fast, and this is likely to continue, providing a sustained momentum to productivity gains (see Figure 14.6).

To summarize on convergence prospects, short-term challenges and vulnerabilities do exist, and transition countries are not sheltered from global

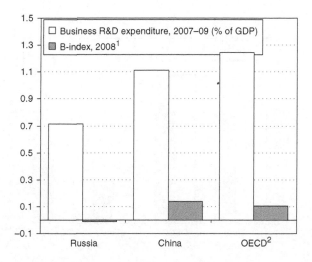

Notes:
1. Measures the generosity of tax incentives to invest in R&D, on the basis of the pre-
    tax income necessary to cover the initial cost of one dollar R&D spending and pay
    corporate taxes on one dollar of profit (B-index). A value of zero on the chart would
    mean that the tax concession for R&D spending is just sufficient to offset the impact of
    the corporate tax rate. Average of SMEs and large firms.
2. Excluding Estonia and Slovenia for the B-index.

Sources: OECD (2012), *Going for Growth*; OECD (2011), Main Science and Technology
Indicators database.

Figure 14.5   Business expenditures and the B-index

uncertainties and possible turmoil, especially if they were to affect their
financial sector. In the longer term, the convergence may also be affected
by the still-to-emerge conditions that will characterize the 'new normal'
and that may turn out less favourable than the (unsustainable) conditions
that prevailed during the Great Moderation.

But, on the other hand, and from an economic point of view, new long-
term sources of growth and convergence do not seem overly difficult to
mobilize in transition countries, and the scope for mobilizing them is probably larger than in many richer economies. These new sources of growth
would not require large changes in relative prices, nor necessarily involve
high fiscal costs, but they would involve pursuing and deepening a strong
structural reforms agenda. Even if the crisis and its legacy will only add to
the urgency of a more ambitious pro-growth reform agenda in transition
countries, the political difficulties attached to such an agenda should not
be underestimated. However, a final comforting observation is that, at

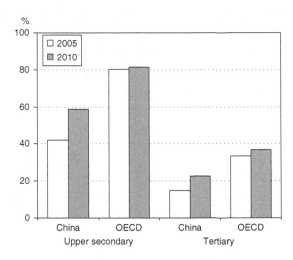

Note:　Graduation rate at upper-secondary level (first-time graduate) and graduation rate for single year of age at tertiary-type A level (first-time graduate). For upper-secondary education, average of OECD countries excluding Australia, Austria, Belgium, Estonia, France and the Netherlands; for tertiary education, average of OECD countries excluding Belgium, Chile, Estonia, France and Korea.

Sources:　OECD (2012), *Going for Growth*; OECD (2010), *Education at a Glance*; *China Statistical Yearbook* (2007).

Figure 14.6　Educational achievement in China and the OECD

least in OECD countries, and contrary to the view that economic down-turns may erode the political capital of governments and their appetite for structural measures, the crisis has indeed contributed to an acceleration of the pace of reforms in the recent past.

15. The impact of China and Russia on catching up in South-Eastern Europe

Altin Tanku

Globalization has been a key driving force behind economic development since the early 1990s, triggering significant changes in the world economy, most noticeably increasing production efficiency and lifting millions out of poverty. For Europe as a whole and above all for the economies of Central, Eastern and South-Eastern Europe (CESEE), the key defining element of this process has been the collapse of the socialist regimes that opened up eastern and western societies to each other for trade and investment. Developed Europe responded to these developments with investments and the promise of European economic and political integration. At the time of writing, most transition economies are actually enjoying full EU membership and working toward monetary union. The pace of progress has, however, not been the same throughout CESEE: the South-East European countries (SEE) are lagging behind.

In parallel, economic liberalization processes have changed the global economic landscape. Russia, around which almost all former socialist economies in CESEE used to gravitate, has itself become one of the transition economies and turned to fixing its own economic, political and social system after losing influence over its former partners. China embarked on a process of economic transformation since 1978 that has enabled it to become the second-largest economy worldwide and a major trade partner for the rest of the world. In addition, former poor economies are now powerful producers of commodities that used to employ the bulk of the labour force in developed economies.

Both China and Russia are relatively big economies that can affect the growth performance of other economies along several channels, most notably the trade channel. China's and Russia's export-led growth, based respectively on cheap labour and terms of trade, has given rise to huge international reserves, making them potential investors in the rest of the world's economy. There is empirical evidence that the Chinese growth momentum has spilled over to other countries' business cycle. China's growth in explaining output fluctuations in other countries has increased in recent decades and is now one of the key external variables explaining such fluctuations (Arora and Vamvakidis, 2010, p. 7). Several other works, including Autor et al. (2011), Rodrik (2011), Spence (2011) and Sachs (2011), have discussed these implications on the labour market, income redistribution, industrial development and so on.

This chapter essentially discusses whether and how the emergence of China and Russia has affected, and may continue to affect, the convergence capacity of the former transition economies. While the question is relevant for all CESEE countries, this chapter focuses on the SEE region, discussing the existing differences in economic and institutional developments between CEE and SEE. Developments in China and Russia, or globalization for that matter, are found to have potential direct and indirect effects on the economies of CESEE and their convergence. These effects will depend also on the ability of SEE economies to adjust and cooperate, in response to these changes in the global economy. The impact could go in both directions; moreover, SEE risks more than their CEE peers not only economically but also politically.

This conclusion follows a simple stock-taking analysis and discusses the probability of future events based on the economic theories of growth and of international trade, without making assumptions on the relative speed and successful implementation of the structural change of SEE compared to China and/or Russia.

The discussion is organized as follows: Section 1 looks at economic convergence and models of growth and trade in SEE versus Russia and China. Section 2 analyses how developments in the latter are affecting growth determinants in SEE directly and indirectly via their effects on the larger EU market. Section 3 concludes with the findings and recommendations for the SEE region.

1.   FORCES OF ECONOMIC DEVELOPMENT AND GLOBALIZATION

The parameters of the catching-up process are affected either by the ability of a country to increase its endowment of labour, physical or human capital, or increase its ability to improve technology, develop or maintain comparative advantages and trade globally. Any local or global development that affects one or more of these factors or their markets may affect the country's ability to catch up and the speed of this process. In the SEE area, the EU has been the engine of recovery and growth. Therefore the catching-up process of SEE would suffer if Russia and China were to steal EU markets and factors away from SEE. This section looks closely at the underlying growth models of CESEE, China and Russia, and highlights the defining trends that have contributed to their catching up from the point of view of growth and international trade theory. It basically answers the question: what drives EU trade and FDI with China, Russia and SEE? In what ways may the emergence of China and Russia affect SEE?

1.1 Economic Growth in CESEE: A Story of Structural Change, Capital Flows, Trade and Integration

The CESEE countries emerged as a separate group of interest after the fall of communism in Eastern Europe. As transition economies, they benefited from globalization within Europe, initially experiencing what is frequently referred to as automatic convergence: poor countries catching up with developed ones through factor redistribution and benefiting from trade, and capital and financial liberalization. CESEE offered relatively cheap factors of production and potential markets for western capital, technology and final products. All three flowed to the region in abundant quantities, thus fuelling productivity.

Later, structural reform, institution building and the ability to establish stable and functional democracies became the most important drivers for transition economies to benefit from, and catch up with, economic and political developments in the EU.

The CESEE model of growth depends exclusively on developments in the EU. Important industries, in particular manufacturing and chemicals industries, developed and became engines of growth and convergence for the transition economies according to the literature (Fidrmuc and Martin, 2011, provide a good summary). Trade and investment contributed to growth and to integration of western and eastern markets and industries. One could easily say that the EU and its integration process became the main, almost the exclusive, driving force in the transition countries in all aspects of life. It delivered on all its promises. All former transition economies have grown rapidly (see Figure 15.1) with impressive and steady growth rates, and many former transition countries are now full EU members.

However, progress has not been uniform across the transition economies. Figure 15.1 highlights three important facts. First, except for Kosovo and Albania, the CESEE countries boast higher living standards than China, while Russia is positioned in the middle. Second, the economies of CEE have been converging faster than their SEE peers. Third,

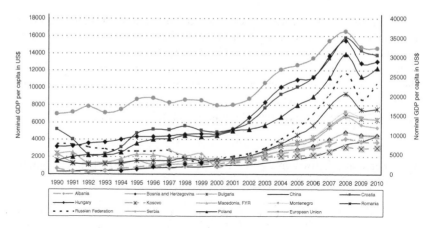

Source: Author's calculations based on World Bank and UNCTAD.

Figure 15.1   The speed of the catching-up process in CESEE and its partners

CEE has also faced larger volatility following the slowdown in Europe than SEE.

Figure 15.1 reflects the process of EU integration, which started with the Baltics and the Central European countries and is slowly spreading south, with the Western Balkans being the final destination. The SEE group of countries is lagging behind in terms of economic and political integration. The best performers are merely candidate countries. These economies have experienced fast economic growth and, like their successful peers, have relied heavily on EU economic and political support, but with less successful results.

1.2   Looking inside CESEE

CEE and SEE are different in many respects. For most countries of the SEE region the transition to free market and democratic societies either started later than in the rest of the former socialist economies or was temporary, interrupted at some point.[1] The history of early transition in SEE was defined by internal or external violent conflicts and other instances of political turmoil that are still haunting the region. In addition, the region differs from its CEE peers in size, demographics, infrastructure, institutional building, openness, as well as regional trade and regional cooperation. Exploring the determinants of FDI in CESEE, Kinoshita (2011) finds all these elements to be directly and positively related with FDI, in particular with FDI in tradable industries. The European Commission (2009) and the IMF (2011) analyse the growth patterns in emerging Europe against these differences and identify them as the main explanation for the poor performance of SEE relative to CEE in terms of overall productivity, competitiveness, speed of convergence and economic integration. Landesmann (2010) and Kinoshita (2011) also find substantial differences in the sectorial composition of FDI, export and productivity and competitiveness in CEE.

All these studies emphasize that CEE is getting most of the investments in the tradable sectors, while SEE is getting most of the investments in the non-tradable sectors, with a particularly high share of FDI in financial intermediation and in real estate. The outcome is a significant export share as a percentage of GDP in CEE, while having only a trivial effect in the SEE countries. What is more troublesome in the SEE countries is that the nature of FDI (in the non-tradable sectors) negatively affects the foreign sector of the SEE economies, increasing imports and widening the trade and current account deficits, while at the same time causing the domestic currency to appreciate, without the benefits of new technology and improving productivity.

The composition of FDI by partners reveals another important difference. Unlike the CEE economies, the SEE economies have relied heavily on FDI inflows from Italy and Greece, which are also the destination of their exports. This pattern is especially pronounced in the case of Albania, Serbia and Macedonia, where Greece and Italy provide around 60 per cent, 33 per cent and 16 per cent of total investments, respectively; Croatia received on average 13 per cent of its FDI from Italy. Other SEE sources of FDI are Austria, Germany, Slovenia, Bulgaria and Hungary. FDI comes mostly from privatization, and the size and nature of investments have not improved the competitiveness of these economies. Greenfield FDI generates mainly final consumption goods. This has prevented the SEE economies from moving up the value chain and integrating their production structures with developed Europe; this has constrained both the quantity and composition of exports, which are focused on final products in textiles and low-technology industries. Exports rely on geographical proximity to Europe and cheap unskilled labour, which makes them subject to competition because of the current composition of Chinese exports.

Intraregional trade in SEE is very low compared to CEE standards. Gravity models of trade suggest that trade with peers in SEE is below potential, while bilateral trade with EU partners is close to potential.[2] Cross-border FDI driven by past partnerships mainly within the states of former Yugoslavia are only emergent trends. Bosnia-Herzegovina and Kosovo represent the only significant cases of cross-border FDI, receiving on average around 7 per cent and 10 per cent of total FDI from Serbia and Albania respectively.[3] According to Fullani (2012), this pattern could be explained by the low trade complementarities between countries of the region,[4] resulting in low intra-industry trade, investments and regional factor redistribution. Anastasakis and Watson (2011) observe that this trivial cross-border integration acts as an obstacle to growth. Therefore the region can benefit hugely from the development of a more integrated regional market.

Schadler (2011) emphasizes remittances as another defining characteristic of SEE. SEE is several times more dependent on remittances (in per cent of total GDP) than CEE. All studies cited above find that remittances play an important role in consumption, savings and investments. They amount to 40 per cent of total exports and 8 per cent of total GDP and cover a substantial part of the region's trade deficit in goods and services.[5] The latter is particularly important in respect of Italy and Greece, accounting for about 30 and 15 per cent, respectively, of total remittances to SEE in 2008–09.[6]

Trade patterns are also affected by SEE's dependence on absorption-led growth models and abundant foreign financing as a defining element of growth sustainability. The degree of financial intermediation has increased substantially, exceeding the pace of GDP growth in all countries of the region, contributing to macro and financial vulnerabilities (Winkler, 2009). Financial difficulties of leading European financial groups that operate in the region, the economic difficulties of the EU partners and decreasing EU demand have slowed their catching up. For all these reasons the composition of trade and investment has generated significant trade and current account deficits in the pre-crisis period. Deficits remain a big problem for the region, as does their financing.[7] This model is not only different from the CEE model, but also from the Russian and Chinese models of growth.

1.3 Russia: An Endowment-based Model of Growth, Trade and Investment

Russia has experienced impressive economic results since the early 1990s. Income per capita puts Russia right in the middle of the pack of CESEE countries (see Figure 15.1): not quite as successful as the model of CEE but much better than SEE. The level of per capita income has increased by an impressive 15 percentage points since 2000 (Ghosh et al., 2009, p. 20). Globalization and the emergence of developing countries have improved the terms of trade for Russian exports and contributed to the fast accumulation of considerable wealth. Growth was also supported by a strong increase in consumption and investments, raising standards of living and reducing poverty. Yet for all this performance there is not much to be said for Russia's growth story: it is essentially built on growing exports of energy (oil and gas) and related products, depending on foreign demand and the global boom in commodity prices. Exports closely mirror developments in energy prices, causing considerable trade surpluses and therefore increases in domestic consumption, investment and foreign exchange reserves. Yet this has also encouraged double-digit inflation and currency appreciation in Russia.

The EU is Russia's main foreign investor. This position is driven largely by its strategic interest in the Russian economy, particularly Russian exports of energy. FDI generally started to grow in the 2006–07 period. Services, manufacturing and natural resources (mostly energy) are the main industries to benefit from FDI. This model makes the Russian economy particularly vulnerable to developments in the energy markets (prices and demand and capital flows). As global demand dropped during the crisis, Russia had to confront rapid depreciation and spend close to one-third of its international reserves to protect the ruble and support the economy.

Despite the stimulus and recovering commodity prices, the Russian economy has underperformed relative to the pre-crisis period. Growth rates and forecasts remain at around 4–5 per cent, in face of relatively high inflation. The Russian economy is vulnerable to foreign shocks, and its performance is more volatile than in the rest of the BRIC (Brazil, Russia, India and China). Together with problems in the banking system (a hint to the fact that Russia, like the rest of the former transition economies, has at least partially supported its growth via foreign financial funds), such problems are contributing to ongoing capital outflows.

The bulk of EU imports from Russia are mineral fuels, specifically oil, gas and coal. Russia is an important supplier of energy-related products for the EU, which explains its important position as the third-largest trading partner of the EU. This and the fact that the EU is the main FDI investor in Russia make it a strategic partner for the EU, accounting for 6 per cent of EU-27 exports and 11 per cent of EU-27 imports in 2010, according to Eurostat. EU trade with Russia grew continuously until 2008. Negative growth in trade in 2009 turned positive again in 2010; however, it has not recovered to pre-crisis levels. Germany is the largest exporter to and importer from Russia, with a respective share of 30 and 19 per cent. Unlike EU imports from Russia, EU exports to Russia are mainly manufactured goods, amounting to around 85 per cent of Russia's imports, mainly pharmaceuticals, motor cars, mobile phones and aircraft.[8]

1.4 China's Model of Growth and World Economy Globalization, Trade and Investment with the EU

China's model of growth and trade deserves a detailed narrative because it defines globalization at its best and in its most complete way. China has been growing impressively since the 1980s or so, following the implementation of market-friendly economic reforms and constrained liberalization.[9] The 'recipe' for China's miracle is the fast and sustainable growth in productivity that has resulted from factor (labour) redistribution. Special Economic Zones (SEZ), as first established in the southern regions with abundant cheap labour, are the centres of growth. Foreign capital and technology targeted SEZ, motivated by potential efficiency gains through low production and environmental costs as well as significant government spending in modern infrastructure; tax privileges and tariff exemptions; cheap financing; last but not least the opportunity to gain access to the huge domestic Chinese market and to increasingly affluent Chinese consumers. The liberalization and the demographic movements are supported by government export-led policies and undervalued domestic currency that most recently has changed to controlled appreciation. The strategy was effectively repeated in the successive periods, extending SEZ to inland provinces, and later to inward west provinces. All this was in response to potential negative effects resulting from increasing labour costs, addressing simultaneously foreign and domestic problems emerging from competitiveness, growth and social concerns. Despite its attractiveness and the interest of several EU multinational firms, the Chinese economy has not been a major destination of FDI (see Figure 15.2). According to Eurostat, Chinese FDI comprises only a fraction of total FDI flows to CEE, but exceeds total EU investments in SEE. On the other hand, the EU is the third-largest foreign direct investor in China with an average of around 20 per cent of total (global) FDI in recent years. This is much smaller than the corresponding figure for SEE (above 50 per cent, according to author's estimation based on Eurostat and UNCTAD data).

This model has seen most of the manufacturing jobs relocate from traditional producers to mainland China. China's exports moved up the value chain, growing from a centre of cheap labour-intensive manufacturing to a technology-intensive manufacturing economy. China thus increased its share as global exporter and recorded a high and significant trade surplus with the rest of the world. These foreign sector developments mixed with specific demographic issues[10] have resulted in a relatively high domestic saving rate and the accumulation of vast international reserves. This makes China the major financing source of several sovereign governments, in particular the US Treasury.

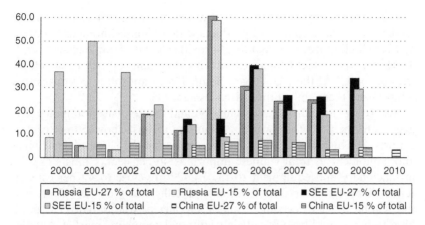

Source: Author's calculations based on *Eurostat* and UNCTAD.

Figure 15.2   EU share of foreign trade, SEE versus China and Russia

China's model represents a hybrid system: the state controls the economy through public ownership and influences factor distribution through direct interference and control.[11] Yet, despite this and the large size of the public sector, the markets shape the production of final goods and services and the distribution process. The Chinese model continues to evolve in response to domestic vulnerabilities and foreign developments. In this respect the latest economic policies highlight the emergence of three particular trends. First: the 'go-abroad' policy encourages Chinese firms to invest in foreign markets to meet China's growing need for foreign demand for Chinese products; the Chinese economy's growing demand for natural resources; and a better diversification of its investment portfolio. Second: new trends in industrial policy defined by the 'Foreign Investment Industrial Guidance Catalogue'.[12] Current and recent catalogues are encouraging FDI in the technology-intensive and high-end manufacturing industries, in favour of more traditional industries of the past, targeting EU and US high-tech companies. Promoting the services industry is another objective of the current catalogue, as is the coordinated development of different regions, aiming to achieve balanced growth and engage local resources in all regions. Third: fearing the dependence on the global economy, China wants to make the domestic economy a major driver of growth.

China became the main exporter of goods to the EU in 2005. In particular, China's exports to the EU-27 increased from a little more than US$35 billion in 1996 to more than US$395 billion in 2010. During the same period, Chinese exports expanded from low-technology base products of textiles, footwear and toys to products with a high technological content at a very high speed. Li et al. (2012) provide a good example of such trade developments. In fact China's exports are becoming a threat to the industries of the USA, the EU, Japan, South Korea and other countries that jumpstarted them almost three decades ago.

According to Eurostat, machinery and equipment dominates EU exports to the rest of the world, accounting for just above 50 per cent of exports in China and Russia. At the same time the share of machinery and equipment in total Chinese imports is 46 per cent. China's exports in machinery and equipment to the EU-27 are close to 42 per cent, as reported by Eurostat. The Economist Intelligence Unit (2011) predicts that China is set to become a major supplier of traditionally EU-made high-tech commodities not only in traditional competing markets but also in the European market itself.[13] Despite this fast expansion in high-tech content manufacturing and industries, China does not fit the traditional flying-geese model: it has been producing and exporting more of both traditional low-skill and high-tech products.

Fast growth, urbanization, trade and exchanges have indeed imposed cost and other pressures on factors of production, eroding the huge comparative advantage of the Chinese economy since 1979. However, average monthly wages are only US$130, which gives China a competitive advantage in the labour-intensive manufacturing and high-tech industries. This is true for Europe as much as it is for the rest of the global market. Most importantly, China had and still has a tremendous potential for liberalization and growth. Agriculture, services and other important sectors lag behind in productivity and contribution to final GDP relative to the rest of the world.[14] This economic and demographic-controlled fragmentation is the reason why theoretically China can still reap enormous productivity benefits from factor redistribution and liberalization. International trade theory and the current literature suggest that this can only happen at the expense of the rest of the world.

1.5 Potential Effects from Trade with Russia and China

The hypothesis of interest to this study is that the rise of China and Russia can and will affect the convergence of the SEE region because they are stealing markets for final goods and services and factors of production such as FDI. The above discussion highlights a few useful observations. The geographical location of the SEE economies, together with economic size, demographics, accumulated capital stocks and technology, seem to give China a large comparative advantage over the EU, CEE as well as SEE, where labour is not as abundant and more expensive at the same time. Russia is not a big exporter or importer in the region but has somehow sporadically invested in traditional SEE allies. In general the detailed analysis above suggests that until now the emergence of China and Russia has not posed a direct challenge to either SEE or CEE.

The underlying economic models and drivers of growth and trade are not natural competitors. The nature and motivation of FDI in SEE, China and Russia are of a very different kind. The fundamentals of trade and investment in Russia are driven by abundant natural resources of energy, while trade and FDI with China are driven mostly by the economies of scale that are available in the Chinese economy. SEE cannot provide substitutes for either model given the current state of affairs in terms of competitiveness, infrastructure, financing and market size. The size, origin and nature of EU investments in SEE show that the region has not been competing with China and Russia for EU FDI. The EU is an important trade partner for SEE as well as for Russia and China, but in different commodity and trade sectors. The emergence of China and Russia has not eroded trade in traditional SEE markets (commodities), judging from the share of EU trade with SEE relative to the share of EU trade with China and Russia (Figure 15.3). The relative shares suggest that trade has been almost stable in exports and increasing in EU imports. The bulk of trade with China and Russia is concentrated on particular groups that are not the traditional commodities of SEE exports.

Due to several factors, including economic cost, scale and risk, as well as political factors, SEE never actually succeeded in establishing itself as an important partner of the EU in the same way as CEE, Russia and China have done. The SEE model of political and economic development, and the level of regional cooperation, are the largest obstacles to SEE development. They impose far more stringent constraints on the development of the region than the rise of China and Russia. This notwithstanding, Chinese exports are already a threat to the SEE economies, and will continue to be.

Yet China and Russia might also have a positive impact on developments in SEE in the future. In fact foreign trade figures show that the emergence of China and Russia has coincided with growing trade exchanges of the region with both countries (Figure 15.4). In particular, Russia is interested in the region due to old partnerships. Unlike the CEE economies, some members of the SEE region, in particular Serbia (one of the biggest economies of the region), see Russia as a partner rather than a threat when past and current geopolitical developments are taken into account. Russia is one of the main sources of FDI in Serbia and Bosnia-Herzegovina, with 15 per cent of the total

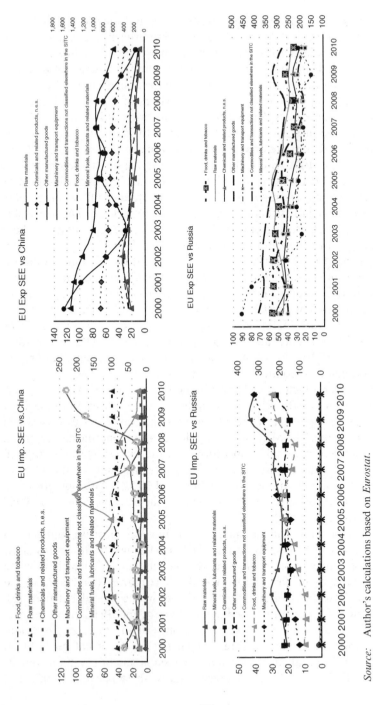

Source: Author's calculations based on *Eurostat.*

Figure 15.3 EU foreign trade with China versus Russia

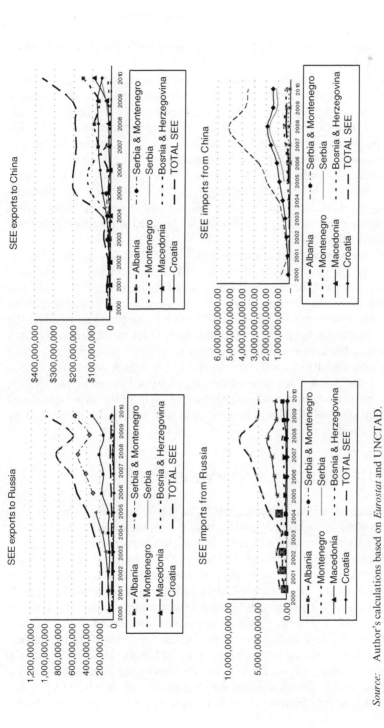

Source: Author's calculations based on *Eurostat* and UNCTAD.

Figure 15.4 SEE foreign trade with China versus Russia

in the 2005–10 period and 14 per cent of the total in the 2006–10 period, respectively.[15]

China is also showing a particular and growing interest in the SEE region. The Chinese model of growth, whether foreign or domestically focused, relies heavily on foreign resources of energy and minerals. In this respect China's expansion, especially toward European markets, holds an opportunity for the region as a whole, as it can exploit its natural resources of iron ore, copper and chromium and its geographical location as a potential shorter, faster, less expensive way to Europe. 'China's new Balkan strategy' by Poulain (2011) judges that China has a well-designed strategy for the SEE region, which is built around its natural resources and geographic location using a similar model designed and applied in the late 1970s and early 1980s.

Thus one can argue that the rise of China and Russia has not affected negatively the convergence of the CESEE countries. SEE in particular does not compete directly with China and Russia on the factor side and on trade flows. At the same time, the discussion above tells only half the story. The emergence of Russia and China has the potential to affect the region's catching up more profoundly in indirect ways. Given the high reliance of the economies of the region on the EU economy, any effect that China and Russia will have on the EU will spill over to the economies of the region. Developed Europe (Western Europe or the EU-17) is the main trade and financial partner as well as the most significant direct investor in SEE, at the same time it is potentially threatened by globalization.

2.   THE THIRD-COUNTRY EFFECT

Globalization is changing the world economy in many ways that go beyond stealing markets of goods, services and factors. Economic theory predicts that free trade will convert the global economy into an interlinked environment where developments in the emerging economies have a profound impact on the developed economies. If trade globalization were to continue, the theory of international trade of Samuelson (1948) shows that factor prices will be equalized among trading countries. In other words, if trade with China continues, the return on labour and capital in the rest of the world will in the long run converge respectively to the return on labour and capital in China. This means that the return on labour will adjust in a mutual simultaneous move toward the new sustainable global equilibrium. Supporters of free trade are quick to point out that benefits from free trade more than cover the losses.

Samuelson (2004) returns to this topic, pointing out that international trade is Pareto-improvement when compared to autarky, but might not be so if the analysis starts from an existing trade equilibrium. Free trade is not always beneficiary for the home economy when it occurs in the home exporting industries. The developed economies of Europe are not immune to these effects and to forces of globalization in general. These are overlooked themes in the convergence and the globalization debate. Unless equalization is achieved, jobs and capital will continue to flow toward China in response to its comparative advantages. This shift in comparative advantages is one of the factors that have given way to unemployment, indebtedness in private and/or public sector, and income inequality.[16] This is due to the fact that newly created jobs in more productive sectors are not sufficient to cover job losses in disappearing manufacturing industries. Several influential academics and business community members believe that globalization and the shift in comparative advantage means cheap labour competition from China and is one of the reasons for the current woes of the USA and Europe. The side effects of globalization or China's emergence include significant job losses, negative effects in labour income and increasing income inequality.

This literature is focused mostly on the US economy with very little (but growing) discussion about Europe along similar lines. Like Arora and Vamvakidis (2010), several authors observe that developed economies see their middle class as well as domestic demand and savings disappear. This relevance of international trade theory for future European developments is very important for SEE since the EU-17 is the biggest trade partner of the region, the biggest foreign direct investor and a source of abundant remittances. Last but most importantly for the moment, the EU and its integration process[17] is the leading anchor of economic, social and political development of SEE. A 'troubled Europe' means less European demand for SEE countries; fewer investments in productive industries; higher unemployment and fewer remittances. Rather than valuable economic hypothesis, these developments represent unpleasant facts of life in SEE. The economic crisis in Greece and Italy, along with rising unemployment, have reduced the demand for SEE exports and shrunk remittances.

Addressing financial stability issues with EU financial groups adds another potential implication. The European Bank Coordination Initiative, commonly known as the 'Vienna Initiative', provided a successful mechanism to prevent financial stability problems in CESEE in the aftermath of the financial crisis of 2008, as European banks pledged to maintain their commitment in the region. Now the support for this initiative is withering. Moreover, EBA's new regulation regarding capitalization and exposure of EU banks in the region has potential implications for SEE. Fulfilment of EBA's requirements will inevitably involve reduction of private or public sector financing, adding to the above-mentioned hardships.

Current economic problems (mostly due to the sovereign debt crisis that is plaguing Europe) have surprisingly transformed former investors into competitors for international institutional investors. Greece, Italy, Portugal and Spain offer brilliant opportunities of investment for China that can use their infrastructure as a gate to European expansion.[18] Before the 2008 crisis, scepticism toward Chinese investments and expensive non-tradable sectors in the EU gave SEE significant comparative advantages. Currently this advantage has disappeared as EU economies see Chinese reserves as potential solutions for their debt problems.

Last but most importantly, the EU and the integration process have been one of the leading anchors of political, social and economic reform in SEE. This anchor depends, first and foremost, on the ability of the European political and economic model to deliver higher standards of living on a sustainable basis. If the European public and leaders perceive the current hardships as direct or indirect outcomes of globalization, then the support for globalization in general and EU enlargement in particular will suffer a setback. Ironically the IMF *Economic Outlook* (October 2011) makes a reference which suggests that current troubles in the EU Southern members could be explained by a shift of traditional North–South trade and investment flows toward West–East investment flows and the resulting emergence of CEE. The debate over the future of the euro and the finger-pointing behaviour of EU members, on top of the 'old' enlargement fatigue, makes these more pressing issues for countries of SEE, which risk losing not only their partner but also their anchor. Moreover, it might put at risk its focus on the SEE region along with its economic and political support, respectively the very forces of unconditional and conditional convergence in SEE. At the current level of development and integration, without the EU or its economic and political attention, growth in SEE will stall altogether and might even reverse in the absence of a leading global economy.

3.   CONCLUDING REMARKS

This chapter analyses the effect that the economic emergence of China and Russia has on the catching up of the SEE economies. The analysis is focused on the models of growth and trade that have supported these economies since the early 1990s. The catching up of SEE is found to have depended almost exclusively on the EU. SEE in itself possesses neither the skills, nor the size and the infrastructure, nor the economic coordination to challenge or be challenged by either Russia or China, which depend on different models of growth than SEE. The main conclusion is that the emergence of China and Russia has been a Pareto-improvement for the economies of SEE, mostly because EU trade and FDI flows with China and Russia have not come at the expense of the SEE region. The economic size and scale offered by the economies of SEE has not, however, prevented it from benefiting from globalization trends in Europe and the rest of the world, increasing its exchanges with the euro zone as well as with Russia and China.

Globalization in SEE is praised for its positive effects, with poverty reduction and economic convergence of once-poor economies being the most important achievements. However, these developments have not been Pareto-improvements across the board. Recent developments in developed economies, at least some of them, provide evidence that convergence might be happening in both directions. Today's global economy resembles an endogenous system in which all economies, including the developed ones, respond to the trends of developments in China and Russia. In principle, any poor economy that gains a comparative advantage and is large enough has the potential to affect the ability of labour to earn more on a global scale but most of all in developed economies, in particular their traditional sectors, employment and income distribution. In a world where trade grows free of administratively imposed controls and capital and technology flow like water, demographics and size determine the potential for economic growth and welfare. Currently these two characteristics are the main advantages of developing economies including China and Russia. Whether these trends reflect permanent structural shifts or only temporary drifts from long-run equilibria will depend upon the ability of developed economies to adapt and find ways to respond to these challenges.

Understanding these trends and the error correction mechanisms of the global system becomes the imperative of SEE development. Global economic trends will have a significant impact on the model of growth and on the speed of reform and convergence for all small emerging economies. The EU is currently the anchor of SEE development. Any change in Europe, be it political, economic, social, demographic or moral, has and will have significant effects for the SEE countries, and their ability to establish models similar to those of their CEE peers. Currently, Europe is focused on finding a global optimal solution for its problems. While this search continues, impatient policy makers, analysts and suffering communities are pointing to several suboptimal but evident equilibria, which in general spell a setback in globalization and EU enlargement. On the other hand, due to their geographic location and abundant natural resources, the countries of the region can benefit from the emergence of China and Russia, which under current conditions bears the risk of leading to a growth model similar to Russia's. This model is credited by economic theory as a necessary (for survival) but not sufficient condition that guarantees sustainable economic convergence.

Given its location in the labour market, its economic size, its history, and the current political, economic and social developments in the region and in its main partners, SEE risks lagging behind global development trends; it risks disappearing from the radar of both developed and emerging economies. Therefore the SEE region must redefine itself in such a way that will make the entire region relevant to the global economy. The focus of economic policies must be to stay in the game, become relevant to both these development poles, and use smartly any opportunity that global developments bring their way. In order to succeed, the countries of the region must reinvent themselves and their marketing strategies, focusing on the potential of regional cooperation.

NOTES

1. Minchev et al. (2010) provide a detailed description of the current trends of economic, political and institutional development of the Western Balkan countries as well as of the past developments that define these current trends in the SEE region.
2. See Pllaha (2011) for a discussion of this topic.
3. Author's calculations based on national central banks' data.
4. This index shows the extent to which the exports of one country are compatible with the import patterns of another. In international trade, such an index is used to predict to a certain extent the success of a free trade agreement.
5. Author's calculation based on UNCTAD data.
6. Author's calculation based on Eurostat data.
7. Kaoudis et al. (2011) show that deficits were comfortably covered by the inflow of foreign capital either in the form of non-financial sector FDI or in the form of bank capital coming from parent banks to their local subsidiaries.
8. According to data reported by Eurostat in 'Partial recovery of trade in goods between EU-27 and Russia in 2010', Eurostat news release 82/2011, June 2011.
9. China is not a liberalized economy by capital or current account transactions, but is liberalized enough to give access to FDI companies to its market on several conditions.
10. China faces the problem of a rapidly aging population and rising dependency ratios that will have an important influence on consumption as well as production in the future. It is estimated that the Chinese population at working age will reach a maximum in 2015 (European Commission, 2004, p. 236).
11. Despite China's impressive industrialization, its urbanization process is far from complete, due most of all to domestic migration control by the government, the 'hukou' system. As a result of such control, more than 50 per cent of the total population resides in rural areas.

12. This is the state-designed guide for the foreign direct investors, which identifies the preferred projects and industries in line with Chinese authorities' economic and social development goals. The current catalogue is distributed by China's National Development and Reform Commission (NDRC) and Ministry of Commerce (MOFCOM). It was amended on 24 December 2011 and approved by the State Council. It came into effect on 30 January 2012.
13. See Economist Intelligence Unit (2011) report for a detailed analysis of current and future Chinese exports, the future in the composition of the trade flows with China and how this will affect European markets.
14. Judging by the share of people depending on incomes from agriculture, Ghosh et al. (2009, p. 51) evaluate that 'the factory of the world' is still an agricultural country. Moreover, the Chinese economy is fragmented by considerable regional disparities. According to Ghosh et al. (2009, p. 50), 'the top ten coastal provinces including Beijing hosted about 40% of China's population, but produced more than 60% of its GDP, accounted for more than 90% of China's foreign trade and attracted about 80% of foreign direct investment'.
15. Author's estimation based on FDI statistics as reported by national central banks.
16. All this is explained by Rodrik (2011), Spence (2011), Sachs (2011) and Samuelson (1948, 2004).
17. See Anastasakis and Watson (2011) and Bastian (2011) for a discussion of foreign anchors in the SEE region.
18. The Heritage Foundation's 'China Global Investment Tracker' provides estimated figures for China's non-bond foreign investments, reported by countries and industries.

REFERENCES

Anastasakis, O. and M. Watson (2011), 'Reform challenges and growth prospects in South East Europe', in O. Anastasakis, M. Watson and J. Bastian (eds), *From Crisis to Recovery: Sustainable Growth in South East Europe*, Oxford: ESC, St Antony's College, pp. 1–12.
Arora, V. and A. Vamvakidis (2010), 'China's economic growth: international spillovers', IMF Working Paper, WP/10/165.
Autor, David H., David Dorn and Gordon H. Hanson (2011), 'The China syndrome: local labour market effects of import competition in the United States', MIT Working Paper, August.
Bastian, J. (2011), 'Assisting South East Europe through external anchors', in O. Anastasakis, M. Watson and J. Bastian (eds), *From Crisis to Recovery: Sustainable Growth in South East Europe*, Oxford: ESC, St Antony's College, pp. 73–94.
Economist Intelligence Unit (2011), 'Heavy duty: China's next wave of exports', available at https://www.eiu.com/public/topical_report.aspx?campaignid=hea vyduty_Aug11.
European Commission (2004), 'The challenge to the EU of a rising Chinese economy', European Competitiveness Report, Commission staff working document SEC (2004) 1397, Enterprise and Industry publications, Ch. 5, pp. 235–77.
European Commission (2009), 'The Western Balkans in transition', *European Economy, Occasional Papers*, **46**, European Commission Directorate-General for Economic and Financial Affairs, May.
Fidrmuc, J. and R. Martin (2011), 'FDI trade and growth in CESEE countries',

Focus on European Economic Integration Q1/11, Oesterreichische Nationalbank, pp. 70–82.

Fullani, Ardian (2012), 'Southeast European cooperation: a window of opportunity for sustainable economic prosperity', forthcoming in South East European Studies at Oxford.

Ghosh, J., P. Havlik, M.P. Ribeiro and W. Urban (2009), 'Models of BRICs' economic development and challenges for EU competitiveness', Research Reports 359, wiiw, December.

IMF (2011), 'Navigating stormy waters', *Regional Economic Outlook: Europe*, World Economic and Financial Surveys, October.

Kaoudis, G., V. Metaxas, N. Stavrianou, D. Tsoudis and A.T. Vouldis (2011), 'Financial market aspects of the crisis in South East Europe', in O. Anastasakis, M. Watson and J. Bastian (eds), *From Crisis to Recovery: Sustainable Growth in South East Europe*, Oxford: ESC, St Antony's College, pp. 53–72.

Kinoshita, Yuko (2011), 'Sectoral composition of the FDI and external vulnerability in Eastern Europe', IMF WP/11/123, May.

Landesmann, M.A. (2010), 'Which growth model for Central and Eastern Europe after the crisis?', FIW, Research Centre for International Economics, Policy Brief No. 4, May.

Li, L., M. Dunford and G. Yeung (2012), 'International trade and industrial dynamics: geographical and structural dimensions of Chinese and Sino-EU merchandise trade', *Applied Geography*, **32**, 130–42.

Minchev, O., O. Stojkovski, S. Ralchev and M. Lessenski (2010), 'Western Balkans: between the economic crisis and the European perspective', Institute for Regional and International Studies, http://www.iris-bg.org/files/TheWesternBalkans.pdf, September.

Pllaha, A. (2011), 'Free trade agreements and trade integration among South Eastern European countries: gravity model estimations', forthcoming Bank of Albania Working Paper series.

Poulain, L. (2011), 'China's new Balkan strategy', *Central Europe Watch*, **1** (2), August.

Rodrik, D. (2011), 'The manufacturing imperative', www.project-syndicate.org/commentary/rodrik60/English, 10 August.

Sachs, J.D. (2011), 'Globalization's government', www.project-syndicate.org/commentary/sachs182/English, 30 September.

Samuelson, P. (1948), 'The international trade and the equalization of factor prices', *The Economic Journal*, **58**(230), 163–84.

Samuelson, P. (2004), 'Where Ricardo and Mill rebut and confirm arguments of mainstream economists supporting globalization', *The Journal of Economic Perspectives*, **18**(3), 135–46.

Schadler, S. (2011), 'Rethinking the South East European convergence model', in O. Anastasakis, M. Watson and J. Bastian (eds), *From Crisis to Recovery: Sustainable Growth in South East Europe*, Oxford: ESC, St Antony's College, pp. 37–52.

Spence, M. (2011), 'The global jobs challenge', http://www.project-syndicate.org/commentary/spence28/English, 17 October.

Winkler, A. (2009), 'Southeastern Europe: financial deepening, foreign banks and sudden stops in capital flows', *Focus on European Economic Integration*, Q1/09, Oesterreichische Nationalbank, pp. 84–9.

16. The sustainability of the catching-up process – a multidimensional take

Frank Moss[1]

This contribution is intended to complement the views provided by four other authors.[2] Its main purpose is to emphasize certain issues addressed in each of the four contributions, rather than providing an additional view on the sustainability of the catching-up process of Central, Eastern and South-Eastern European (CESEE) countries.

The chapter focuses on four issues: first, credit growth and boom–bust cycles, which in the case of a number of CESEE countries are linked to a special additional challenge, namely the provision of credit in foreign currency; second, the concept of internal devaluation as a means to boost competitiveness in countries with fixed exchange rates, which is a feature of a number of CESEE countries; third, the concept of sustainable convergence, which – as with the previous concept – is not only of relevance for many CESEE countries, but also for EU and even euro area countries; and fourth, some key policy lessons for CESEE countries.

Before addressing these four points, let me first of all put the economic outlook of the region in perspective, complementing Schneider's contribution (Chapter 14). For small open economies such as the CESEE countries, situated in the close neighbourhood of the euro area, not only is the global economic picture of relevance, but more specifically also that of the euro area. As regards the macroeconomic picture, the ECB staff projections on the global outlook are by and large the same as those of the OECD.[3] Advanced economies, coming out of a severe, though fairly short-lived downturn in the wake of the financial crisis, will be facing for some time to come the headwinds of balance sheet repair. This implies that emerging economies have become the primary driving force for global growth. The need for balance sheet repair is also clearly visible in the euro area, particularly for the public and the financial sector. The ongoing tensions in euro area financial markets, moreover, are having unfavourable effects on financing conditions and confidence, and are therefore likely to dampen the pace of economic growth in the euro area going forward. At the time of writing the ECB is expecting a significant downward revision to the projections for euro area real GDP growth in 2012, with something of a halt in growth in the period around the turn of the year. Pending the release in December 2011 of the latest staff projections, the autumn 2011 forecast of the European Commission provided confirmation that the upturn after end-2011 will probably be weak in the euro area and the EU.[4] Moreover, uncertainty is extremely high and a number of downside risks can be identified, which might make a very moderate growth upturn in 2012 seem a likely outcome.

In this unappealing external environment, CESEE countries cannot expect to reap much of an external demand dividend. Unsurprisingly, therefore, emerging Europe is being accredited by the IMF, among other forecasters, as the region with the slowest rate of growth in 2012 of all emerging and developing-country regions.[5] Still, such an outcome cannot be ascribed to external factors alone. As the crisis and post-crisis diagnostics of individual CESEE countries demonstrate, different countries have been affected by, and have coped with, the crisis in different ways. Some could indeed be seen as innocent bystanders whereas for others the crisis in advanced economies acted as a trigger in exposing their own underlying imbalances. Hence country situations and economic structures, but also economic policies do matter in determining growth outcomes and hence influencing the convergence path, as Tanku's contribution (Chapter 15) illustrates.

CREDIT GROWTH AND BOOM–BUST CYCLES

One structural break arising from the crisis is what Schneider refers to as the 'new normal', involving a repricing of risk and a higher cost of capital than was considered the normal situation before 2008. A higher cost of capital, in turn, may dampen future credit growth and therefore lower the potential for 'boom–bust cycles' to emerge again. Recent research, including work by BIS and ECB researchers, has confirmed that credit growth is among the most robust leading indicators for banking crises (Borio and Drehmann, 2009) and costly asset price boom–bust cycles (Alessi and Detken, 2009). Similar studies have also been performed using long historical data sets (Schularick and Taylor, 2012), underpinning the thesis that excessive credit growth and too much leverage in the financial sector were indeed at the root of most past financial crises. For the 2009 contraction, past credit growth also explains relatively well the dispersion of recessions across European countries (see Figure 16.1), which is, as argued above, also the result of additional factors such as policy responses to the

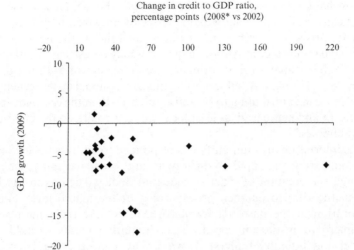

Change in credit to GDP ratio,
percentage points (2008* vs 2002)

Notes: *Figures for 2006 in the case of credit/GDP used in case of Iceland.
Countries shown in this figure include Albania, Bosnia–Herzegovina, Croatia, FYR
Macedonia, Serbia, Turkey, Ukraine, Bulgaria, Czech Republic, Estonia, Hungary, Latvia,
Lithuania, Poland, Romania, Iceland, Russia, Ireland, Spain, Greece, Portugal, Italy,
Slovenia, Slovakia.

Sources: IMF and ECB calculations.

Figure 16.1 Credit booms (2002–08) versus GDP contractions in 2009

crisis. It is hard to dispute, however, that even when excluding an obvious
outlier such as Iceland, a figure of 40 percentage points or more change
in credit to GDP ratio over a period of several years (2002–08 in Figure
16.1) can be deemed excessive when the modal figure, and hence a reasonable yardstick, appears to be more in the range of 28 percentage points
(which corresponds to the mean in Figure 16.1) even when accounting for
catching-up in terms of financial development.

Similarly, in the case of China, the IMF recently warned about emerging risks in the financial sector (IMF, 2011b). The risks pointed out by
the IMF include – in addition to risks stemming from China's persistent
imbalanced growth model – (i) the impact of the recent sharp credit expansion on banks' asset quality; (ii) the rise of off-balance-sheet exposures and
of lending outside the formal banking sector; and (iii) the relatively high
level of real-estate prices. All these risks sound from a European perspective very familiar and should not be underestimated. A peculiar aspect in
the case of China is perhaps the two components of the non-formal or

shadow banking sector, as Taube has highlighted (Chapter 17): one is the statistically registered shadow banking sector, in which non-bank financial enterprises provide banking services; the other is the non-registered informal banking sector. Although the latter may be less significant overall than Taube estimates (most estimates are in a range of 5–10 per cent of GDP), and is certainly subject to significant regional heterogeneity, its importance in contributing to overall credit growth in the economy can be significant and hence lead, at least locally or regionally, to the build-up of credit bubbles.

The international community has responded to address the challenges stemming from too rapid credit growth and over-leveraging, *inter alia* through the creation of macro-prudential bodies (such as in the USA and in the EU) to dampen procyclicality at the macro level, and the elaboration of the Basel III framework, to achieve the same result at the micro or institution-specific level (requiring banks to hold more capital and liquidity buffers). However, at a more general level, the problem may be more fundamental since we do not exactly know what is the optimal size of the financial sector in the economy. Therefore macro-prudential supervisors can so far not rely on quantitative and transparent targets for, for example, the optimal level of credit in an economy. Still, it will be important for CESEE countries to heed the lessons drawn at the global level and to start implementing the newly agreed standards at the level of the G20, which also includes China and Russia.

FOREIGN EXCHANGE LENDING AND THE EUROPEAN SYSTEMIC RISK BOARD (ESRB)

One specific financial stability risk for the CESEE countries consists of foreign currency lending to unhedged borrowers. Such lending entails several micro-prudential risks for borrowers and lenders (ECB, 2010). First, it exposes unhedged borrowers to exchange rate risk. Financial institutions granting such loans are exposed to 'indirect exchange rate risk', which can materialize as credit risk in a situation when unhedged borrowers are not able to fully repay their foreign currency loans as any depreciation of the local currency inflates the value of debt repayments in that currency. In such circumstances, credit quality typically also deteriorates owing to a worsening of the macroeconomic environment (in particular because of a rise in unemployment) so that foreign currency loans expose financial institutions to correlated market and credit risk. In addition, financial institutions granting foreign currency loans may be exposed to funding risk if they rely heavily on wholesale and parent bank financing rather than on local deposits.

Lending in foreign currency can also increase macro-prudential risks since it tends to foster excessive credit growth as lower foreign interest rates lead to additional demand for loans. For example, there seems to be a strong link between rapid credit growth and borrowing in foreign currencies in non-euro area EU countries in Central and Eastern Europe (ECB, 2010). Countries that had experienced particularly strong credit growth before the global financial crisis also tended to have a higher share of foreign currency loans. In turn, excessive credit growth can lead to the build-up of asset price bubbles, in particular in the case of house prices, when lending is concentrated in the real-estate sector. To the extent that foreign currency lending is financed by capital inflows, for example via parent banks to local subsidiaries, it can also foster unsustainable external imbalances (see also IMF, 2010).

Finally, lending in foreign currencies also has macroeconomic costs since it can impair the interest rate channel of monetary policy. A restrictive monetary policy leads to a decrease in domestic currency lending but can simultaneously accelerate the growth of foreign-currency-denominated loans (Brzoza-Brzezina et al., 2010). In addition, the benefit of currency depreciation via an increase in competitiveness can, to some extent, be offset by negative balance sheet effects. In extreme cases, depreciations can be contractionary owing to a high level of foreign currency lending (Galindo et al., 2003). Therefore many authorities in countries with a high level of foreign currency debt pursue contractionary policies to stabilize the exchange rate during a crisis in order to avoid negative financial stability implications via balance sheet effects. In the academic literature this response to depreciation pressures is often referred to as 'fear of floating' (see Hausmann et al., 2001; Towbin and Weber, 2011). It should be noted that such policies may even be optimal *ex post*, since the loss in output owing to the monetary tightening can be more than offset by the benefits of avoiding the fallout from negative balance sheet effects. *Ex ante*, however, the build-up of currency mismatches is fostered if economic agents anticipate this type of policy response (Caballero and Krishnamurthy, 2005).

While most observers have recently focused on developments with respect to lending denominated in Swiss francs, it should be stressed that unhedged lending in all foreign currencies is risky, irrespective of the exchange rate regime in place. Indeed, exchange rate crises cannot be ruled out and past readings of exchange rate volatility are not always a reliable measure of risks building up. This view is shared by the European Systemic Risk Board (ESRB), which issued recommendations on foreign exchange lending on 21 September 2011. These recommendations, which have also been conveyed to EU candidate countries for their information, are expected to mitigate the 'flow problem' of foreign exchange loans, because their implementation will make new foreign exchange lending more expensive. Addressing the 'stock problem' of foreign exchange loans is even more challenging. It should be noted, however, that the ESRB recommendation that supervisors require institutions to 'hold adequate capital to cover risks associated with loans denominated in a foreign currency' is not restricted to new loans in foreign currency, but applies to the whole stock.

INTERNAL DEVALUATIONS

Moving to the notion of 'internal devaluation' which is extensively presented in Åslund's contribution (Chapter 13) for the case of Latvia, it should be acknowledged that this is an instrument that can help countries with a fixed exchange rate regime to regain competitiveness. As such, this adjustment method is also of relevance for euro area countries in need of correcting past losses in competitiveness. However, a few words of caution are warranted, given that the effectiveness of the instrument is highly dependent on the degree of downward wage and price flexibility. Recent evidence in the euro area seems to show that in particular wage moderation is playing a more limited role in the adjustment of countries under EU/IMF programmes than in other countries such as the Baltics, mainly on account of less flexible labour markets (which is also influenced by cross-border labour migration). In addition, it has to be borne in mind that adjustments in unit labour costs at the level of the overall economy can be influenced by changes in the composition of output so that unit labour cost adjustments on the surface may not necessarily imply a genuine gain in competitiveness (IMF, 2011c). Moreover, statistical improvements in competitiveness may also materialize through recessionary channels rather than productivity improvements. In essence, therefore, gains in competitiveness can only be achieved in a sustainable manner if wage and cost moderation is accompanied by structural reforms that will generate new sources of employment and growth.

It should also be kept in mind that in countries with high debt levels, 'internal devaluations' ultimately bear the risk of a debt–deflation spiral:[6] if wages and prices are falling and debt remains unchanged in nominal terms, the real value of previously accumulated financial imbalances will increase. During an external adjustment process, the necessary measures to restrain domestic demand and import growth such as fiscal consolidation should thus be commensurate with a policy objective of maintaining price stability (i.e. also avoiding deflations). Once again, the macroeconomic adjustment efforts will need to be complemented with structural measures to increase the flexibility of the economy, which will not only remove existing rigidities but also enhance the long-term growth potential of the economy and make it more resilient in the face of future shocks.

SUSTAINABLE CONVERGENCE

Shocks can throw countries off their convergence path. In this context, the appropriate measure is that of real convergence, not of nominal convergence as is applied in the context of the EU Treaty to measure a country's degree of readiness to join the euro area (in addition to the sustainability of the levels of nominal convergence reached). Schneider and Tanku in their contributions (Chapters 14 and 15) spoke of 'good' and 'bad' convergence as real convergence in the direction of the higher or the lower performer, respectively. I would prefer to refer to 'good' and 'bad' convergence as real convergence that is on a sustainable or a non-sustainable path. When applying such a concept of 'sustainable convergence' it should first be acknowledged – after a great deal of optimism about catching up during the 2000s – that convergence takes time. In fact, in GDP per capita terms, emerging Europe (including also South-East Europe) still stands at only around 45 per cent of the euro area after almost 20 years of convergence. Second, the quality of convergence is essential, and this is where sustainability becomes key. In most CESEE countries, growth was driven primarily by domestic demand and the non-tradable sector, in particular construction. As a result, large external (current account deficits) and internal imbalances (excessive credit growth) emerged before the bust of the credit cycle. Russia and China are special cases in this context: in Russia, the growth base is too narrowly based in the natural resource sector; and non-oil deficits are widening (this applies to both the fiscal and external balance). In China financial market and capital restrictions have artificially boosted the contribution of investment-led and export-led growth (but with the side effects of a declining incremental capital–output ratio and an exorbitantly large stock of official reserve holdings).

'Sustainable convergence' requires that external deficits and increases in domestic demand be intertemporally matched by improvements on the supply side. This necessitates structural reforms and good institutions to boost the tradable sector, improve price and non-price competitiveness and raise total factor productivity to allow for real per capita incomes to grow. Schneider's contribution shows that, in terms of labour supply, there is little left to catch up for CESEE countries. In terms of capital stock building, it seems difficult for countries to persistently outperform others (unless one is a giant such as China that is able to skew incentives to that effect). Of course, foreign direct investment can make a difference, as Tanku has demonstrated, but for such a situation to persist, structural reforms and good institutions are necessary, that is, the same policy set that will attract FDI will also help to raise the productivity of domestic factors of production (see IMF, 2011a). Hence increases in total factor productivity are the key to 'sustainable convergence'.

CONCLUSION

I conclude with five key lessons that I draw from the contributions mentioned earlier. Lesson one: excessive credit growth was at the root of many financial crises, this time around more in advanced than in emerging countries. Still, some of the CESEE countries have their own tale to tell. Lesson two: real convergence takes time and policy makers need to consistently undertake efforts, not only in terms of preserving macroeconomic stability and pursuing structural reforms, but also in terms of institution building as they climb up the technology ladder. Only under those conditions will they be in a position to put and keep their country on a sustainable real convergence path. Lesson three: maintaining competitiveness is a crucial ingredient of sustainable convergence. Correcting for losses in competitiveness can benefit from internal or external devaluation/depreciation, depending on the exchange rate regime in place, but ultimate success will hinge on the right mixture of accompanying policies and conditions in place. Lesson four: deeper economic integration with neighbours pays off in that it allows for comparative advantages to be better exploited: either neighbours are relatively poorer, in which case parts of the production chain can be shifted; or they are relatively wealthier, in which case parts of the production chain can be exported and technological advances imported. Lesson five: a rapid entry into the euro area cannot provide a short cut to sustainable real convergence, just as asset and liability euroization cannot provide a short cut to sustainable nominal convergence. If there is one silver lining to the financial crisis of recent years, it is that these lessons have become much better understood by policy makers in CESEE countries as well as elsewhere.

NOTES

1. The views expressed in this contribution do not necessarily reflect those of the European Central Bank. The author would like to thank Roland Beck for his research assistance.
2. See Chapters 13–15 and 17.
3. See for instance ECB (2011).
4. See European Commission (2011).
5. See IMF (2011a).
6. See Fischer (1933).

REFERENCES

Alessi, L. and C. Detken (2009), 'Real time early warning indicators for costly asset price boom/bust cycles: a role for global liquidity', ECB Working Paper 1039, March. 2009; reprinted as'Quasi real time early warning indicators for costly asset price boom/bust cycles: a role for global liquidity', *European Journal of Political Economy*, **27**(3) (2011), 520–33.
Borio, C. and M. Drehmann (2009), 'Assessing the risk of banking crises – revisited', *BIS Quarterly Review*, March, 29–46.
Brzoza-Brzezina, M., T. Chmielewski and J. Niedźwiedzińska (2010), 'Substitution between domestic and foreign currency loans in Central Europe. Do central banks matter?', Working Paper Series, No 1187, ECB, Frankfurt am Main, May.
Caballero, R. and A. Krishnamurthy (2005), 'Inflation targeting and sudden stops', in B. Bernanke and M. Woodford (eds), *The Inflation-Targeting Debate*, Chicago, IL: National Bureau of Economic Research, pp. 423–46.
ECB (2010), *Financial Stability Review*, special feature on 'Addressing risks associated with foreign currency lending in EU Member States', Frankfurt am Main, June.
ECB (2011), *Monthly Bulletin*, November.
European Commission (2011), 'European economic forecast – autumn 2011', DG ECFIN, *European Economy*, No. 6/2011.
European Systemic Risk Board (2011), 'Recommendation of the European Systemic Risk Board of 21 September 2011 on lending in foreign currencies' (ESRB/2011/1).
Fischer, I. (1933), 'The debt–deflation theory of great depressions', *Econometrica*, **1**(4), 337–57.
Galindo, A., U. Panizza and F. Schiantarelli (2003), 'Debt composition and balance sheet effects of currency depreciation: a summary of the micro evidence', *Emerging Markets Review*, **4**(4), 330–39.
Hausmann, R., U. Panizza and E. Stein (2001), 'Why do countries float the way they float?', *Journal of Development Economics*, **66**(2), 387–414.
IMF (2010), *Regional Economic Outlook for Europe*, October.
IMF (2011a), *Regional Economic Outlook for Europe*, October.
IMF (2011b), *People's Republic of China: Financial System Stability Assessment*, November.
IMF (2011c), *Ireland: First and Second Reviews Under the Extended Arrangement and Request for Rephasing of the Arrangement*, May.

Schularick, M. and A. Taylor (2012), 'Credit booms gone bust: monetary policy, leverage cycles, and financial crises, 1870–2008', *American Economic Review*, **102**(2).
Towbin, P. and S. Weber (2011), 'Limits of floating exchange rates: the role of foreign currency debt and import structure', IMF Working Papers 11/42.

PART V

Banking and financial stability

17. China's shadow banking sector – pillar or threat to the system?

Markus Taube

It is not long ago that the Western world was watching developments in China with a mixture of patrimonial pride – because its rapid development and growth seemed to be based on classical Western recipes of marketization and internationalization – and a peculiar fascination with calamity – because the Chinese 'economic miracle' seemed to be destined for ruin as its banking sector was burdened with dramatic levels of non-performing loans (NPL) (e.g. Chang, 2001). Today the situation has changed. While the triad economies are trying to stay afloat in a series of system-shattering crises, the Chinese economy is still on its trajectory of high-speed growth and development, with its banking sector having reduced its NPL ratio to a minuscule 1.1 per cent (CBRC, 2011; Bloomberg, 2011) and IMF-accredited crisis resilience (IMF, 2011). Today anxious eyes are fixed on China, seen as the final anchor of stability and the potential saviour of a faltering Western system poisoned by complex financial products; it seems to have lost the capacity to control excessive sovereign debt.

But is China's economy really as stable and strong as these hopes express? Probably not. A whole range of problems has evolved in the shadow of the country's rapid economic rise, ready to become nuclei of serious crises once the dynamics of China's catching-up growth break down. One of these potentially destabilizing parameters rests in China's informal banking sector, which, unnoticed by most observers, has not only grown to very significant size, but is also standing completely beyond the reach of China's regulators. This chapter will try to shed some light on a few aspects of this phenomenon, trying to determine the role of China's informal financial sector for the Chinese economic system as well as its potential to destabilize the Chinese economy. In order to do so, Section 1 will first of all identify the two major spheres of shadow banking in the Chinese economy, before Section 2 focuses on the working mechanisms and specific manifestations of China's informal shadow banking sector. Section 3 concludes with a discussion of the positive as well as negative impacts of informal shadow banking on the Chinese economy.

1. MANIFESTATIONS OF SHADOW BANKING IN CHINA

Shadow banking is anything but a new phenomenon in China and has been a permanent companion of China's formal banking sector since the market-oriented reform movement re-monetized the Chinese economy (Peebles, 1991; World Bank, 1990) and established a commercial banking sector from the 1980s onwards. However, it is necessary to differentiate between two different types of shadow banking that have evolved in different economic spheres, address different types of clients and have a different impact on the overall economic system and its macroeconomic stability.

The first type of shadow banking activities is deeply rooted in and actually originating from the formal financial sector. Its evolution is motivated by entrepreneurs inside the formal sector, who try to circumnavigate regulatory obstacles and restrictions that prevent them from expanding their operations and balance sheets. This 'formal' sector shadow banking includes activities and organizations such as off-balance-sheet lending, offshore borrowing, special purpose vehicle lending, direct company-to-company lending, trust companies and wealth management organizations, leasing companies, regulated pawnshops, loan guarantee companies, small loan companies and microfinance organizations and so on. Shadow banking activities of this type can be observed in more or less all economies. Wherever there are restrictions to potentially profitable finance transactions, entrepreneurial ingenuity is challenged to circumvent these restrictions – inside the latitude existing in the legal system, or even outside. China's 'formal sector shadow banking' addressed here should be understood to exist predominantly inside the boundaries of the Chinese legal system. Statistical data covering some of its business models indicate that these transactions had a volume equal to not less than 25 per cent of formal RMB lending activities in recent years (World Bank, 2011).

The second type of 'informal' institutional solution to financial intermediation is different in so far as it evolved spontaneously as a substitute and complement to the formal financial sector. This evolution has for many years been driven by the incompleteness of China's institutional reforms in the formal financial sector and its discrimination against the (semi-) private enterprise sector as well as its disregard of the demand for loans by households. In this environment entrepreneurial actors have been motivated to establish a parallel world of financial intermediation that caters to the needs of all those who cannot gain access to the formal banking sector. Manifestations of this type of 'informal' financial intermediation include private peer-to-peer lending activities, rotating savings and credit associations (ROSCA), 'Associations for Mutual

Assistance' unregulated pawnshops as well as private money houses and underground banks. No reliable information is available on the size of this type of informal financial intermediation. What is known, however, is that these mechanisms are employed all over the country, although in greatly varying intensities. They are most widespread in areas with a long tradition (post-Mao) and a high density of private entrepreneurship like Wenzhou (Zhejiang), the Pearl River Delta (Guangdong) and so on, as well as under-regulated peripheral areas such as Ordos in Inner Mongolia. Estimates of the transaction volumes reach up to more than 50 per cent of the formal sector lending activities in certain localities.

The following analysis will focus on this latter segment of China's shadow banking sector.

2. WORKING MECHANISMS OF CHINA'S 'INFORMAL SHADOW BANKING'

The crucial role that China's 'informal shadow banking' sector has been playing in the country's economic rise becomes particularly obvious when China's rapid economic development is analysed from the perspective of the 'law, finance and growth' literature. Taking this school's assertion that the capacity for growth and development of an economy hinges on the quality of its financial system and the legal protection of creditor rights (Levine, 1997, 1999) as a benchmark and comparing this with the reality of China's formal financial sector and the formal legal protection available for creditors during the first two to three decades of economic reforms, one wonders how China has been able to grow at all (Yao and Yueh, 2009).

One answer to this riddle lies in the observation that the formal financial sector has been focusing on the financial needs of the state-owned enterprise sector and operated in a hybrid institutional framework between plan and market. The 'law, finance and growth' literature, with its analytical foundation in the institutional framework of private markets, is not defined for these environments. Even more important, however, is the observation that the financial requirements of the most dynamic sector of the Chinese economy have not been coordinated in the realm of the formal financial sector (Huang, 2003, 2008). China's booming (semi-) private enterprises have rather been forced to look for alternative solutions to their financing needs.

Starting in the late 1970s, China's gradual reform and liberalization process has unleashed a large demand for finance and start-up capital by China's new entrepreneurial class. Rejected by the formal financial system, which continued to concentrate its activities on the state-owned enterprise sector, these new entrepreneurs had to look for alternative institutional solutions for financial interaction and often found them in the context of either traditional social networks (clans, village communities etc.) or those that they had been forced to join in the framework of the New China's quest for a socialist economic and social system (e.g. in the countryside the People's Communes respectively their brigades; in urban areas enterprise *danweis*, neighbourhoods, affiliations to party and military organizations etc.) (Taube, 2009).

2.1 A Taxonomy of Informal Financial Intermediation in China

The financial arrangements that developed in China's informal financial sector can be described in the framework of an extended 'financing technologies' matrix as introduced by Berger and Udell (2006) and Udell (2008). Berger and Udell differentiate between transaction-based activities relying on hard information and relationship-based activities relying on soft information. Transaction-based activities are to be understood as financial transactions based on a set of formal institutional arrangements. Due to their foundation in standardized legal requirements, each transaction request can be evaluated and implemented independently from other activities conducted by the (potential) contractors. 'History', in the sense of the 'reputation' of the transaction partners, does not – at least in principle – play a role in the evaluation and implementation of a (potential) transaction. This type of transaction includes a broad range of operations such as financial statement lending, asset-based lending, factoring, leasing, small business credit scoring, equipment lending, real-estate-based lending and so on. All of them require a specific mix of legal infrastructure elements such as commercial laws on collateral, bankruptcy, licensing, credit scoring, information publicity and so on (Udell, 2008). Relationship-based activities are, in comparison, based on the accumulation of soft information about a potential borrower made available by a high frequency (in dense networks usually complemented by multiplexity[1]) of interaction between the latter and individuals in a position to determine capital allocation decisions. 'History' and reputation effects play a crucial role in this type of transaction.

While providing a powerful means for a structured taxonomy of financial transactions and their institutional foundations, this classification appears to be insufficient if applied outside the context of highly developed industrialized economies. The concept was developed by Berger and Udell with reference to the US financial system only. In this institutional environment, transaction-based as well as relationship-based financial transactions rely on a universalistic, highly formalized legal system for the delineation and enforcement of the property rights arrangements underlying a specific financial transaction. In order to capture the realities of less developed economies and those less based on universalistic legal systems of order such as China, it becomes necessary to split up the property rights regime and differentiate between two modes of governance: third-party and second-party enforcement. Third-party enforcement relates to the 'standard' environment envisaged by Berger and Udell, where universalistic legal systems and state agencies like courts or (supranational) arbitration courts provide the necessary property rights protection. Second-party enforcement regimes, in contrast, function on the basis of particularistic ordering systems based on 'dense networks' and the disciplining power of closed, exclusive socioeconomic communities.

Combining these dimensions, we can construct a matrix of four types of potential financing technologies featuring various information-gathering and enforcement regimes (Table 17.1).

In the framework of this taxonomy, the financing arrangements that have evolved in China's informal financial sector fall in the category 'second-party enforcement/soft information'. For China's new private entrepreneurs, the social networks and 'clubs', which had become a central element of Chinese society, now became the basis for their entrepreneurial activities, financing needs and protection of property rights. Given a high frequency as well as a considerable degree of multiplexity in the interaction among network members, they were able to convey sufficient credible information on their integrity as well as entrepreneurial capability in order to solve the cooperation dilemma underlying intertemporal financial transactions. As Bradsher (2004, p. 68) observes:

Borrowers default on nearly half the loans issued by the state-owned banks, but seldom do so here on money that is usually borrowed from relatives, neighbors or people in the same industry. Residents insist that the risk of ostracism for failing to repay a loan is penalty enough to ensure repayment of most loans. Although judges have ruled that handwritten i.o.u.'s are legally binding, creditors seldom go to court to collect. 'If it is a really good friend, I would lose face if I sued them in court,' said Tu Shangyun, the owner of a local copper smelter and part-time 'silver bearer' – a broker who puts lenders and borrowers in touch with each other, 'and if it weren't a good friend, I wouldn't lend the money in the first place.' Violence is extremely rare, but the threat of it does exist as the ultimate guarantor that people make every effort to repay debts. 'Someone can hire a killer who will chase you down, beat you up and maybe even kill you,' said Ma Jinlong, who oversaw market-driven financial changes in the 1990's in Wenzhou as director of the municipal economic reform committee and is now an economics professor at Wenzhou University.[2]

Table 17.1   Financing technologies

	Hard information	Soft information
Third-party enforcement	Standard object of analysis in the law, finance and growth literature. Standardized information regime combined with highly formalized universalistic legal system	'Relationship lending' of the law, finance and growth literature. The evaluation of potential financial transactions is primarily based on information gathered by informal institutional arrangements. Ensuing financial transactions are embedded in formal justiciable contractual relations
Second-party enforcement	Requires close relationship between transaction partners in order to facilitate property rights enforcement inside a social network and without recourse to an external 'umpire'. Given this close relationship, hard information can be expected to be systemically less important than soft information for most financial transactions. Hostage-based transactions may constitute one of the few possible transactions classifying for this category	Obstacles to cooperation like adverse selection and *ex post* opportunism, i.e. property rights enforcement, are solved by informal mechanisms, first of all social networks based on particularistic ordering regimes. Information required to make financing decisions is gathered in non-standardized form in the context of the underlying social network by means of frequent and multiplex interaction

Source: Taube and Conlé (2011).

2.2   Informal Financial Arrangements – Some Examples

In the following we shall take a closer look at the working mechanisms of some specific lending technologies that may serve as examples for the operation of this kind of financial arrangement.

2.2.1   '*Guanxi* lending' (*minjian jiedai*)
Lending activities among family members, friends and close acquaintances integrated in close social networks (*guanxi*) traditionally play an

important role in financing the needs of Chinese households, especially in the countryside. Mostly the funds taken up are employed in consumptive purposes, the organization of wedding ceremonies, funerals, to pay for medical treatment and so on. Usually taking place in the context of dense social networks providing a high degree of bondage as well as massive threats of social ostracism in case of failure to fulfil implicit lending contracts (Ben-Porath, 1980), such transactions are overwhelmingly conducted without a written receipt or lending contract. However, debt obligations are understood not to expire with the death of the debtor, but to be inherited in his family over the generations (Feng, 2006).

Most private *guanxi* lending activities involve only comparatively small amounts of money and are provided interest-free. If larger amounts of money are required, which may not be mobilized inside the confines of a given dense network (family/clan, friends, neighbourhood, military 'buddies' or alumni network etc.), intermediaries (*dangshou*) can be employed in order to make the necessary contacts to other networks and individuals.[3] These intermediaries may be understood to rent out their reputation to the debtor and thereby provide the necessary signalling to the lender that the transaction is 'safe'.[4] For such financial transactions interest is usually charged in a range of 1–2 per cent per month, and simple written receipts are more common than in unmediated transactions.

With the rise of (semi-) private enterprises, the form of *guanxi* lending has also been employed in order to mobilize working capital and bridge liquidity shortages in the context of specific business activities (Hu, 1998). While in principle relying on the same networks and social relationships, such transactions usually involve larger amounts of money and interest payments and are usually documented by simple IOUs. Mostly lender and borrower are both (private) entrepreneurs and are in a position to evaluate the soundness of the debtor's enterprise and the underlying business model.

2.2.2 Rotating savings and credit associations (*hehui, lunhui, biaohui, paihui*)

Rotating savings and credit associations have been developed individually all over the world and are known to have been employed in China for many centuries (Geertz, 1962). ROSCAs come in all kinds of variations, but the underlying concept is invariably that of a fixed number of people committing themselves to putting a fixed amount of money in a 'pot' for a fixed number of rounds (usually equivalent to the number of participants). In each period this pot is made available for one of the participants in order to finance consumptive or business-related expenses. Those who have been provided with the pot will in all following periods pay an interest rate on the money received, which is determined either as a fixed rate, derived in a bidding process, or other form. The later a participant receives the pot during the life cycle of a ROSCA, the more he uses this arrangement as a savings instrument collecting net-interest proceeds; the earlier a participant receives the pot, the greater the lending character of his participation and the greater the net-interest payments he has to make (Besley et al., 1993).

Being extremely flexible vehicles, ROSCAs may evolve spontaneously wherever net savers and entrepreneurs with investment and business ideas convene in a social group. ROSCAs hinge on the prime reputation of its 'master' and the soft information this 'master' possesses about (potential) participants, their trustworthiness and entrepreneurial capabilities. As such, the reach of a ROSCA is usually limited to a specific social network and cannot be approached from the outside. This exclusive element allows ROSCAs to dispense with any monitoring of participants who have been awarded the pot. The screening implicit in becoming a member of the network (and upholding this membership status) from which the ROSCA participants are recruited is understood to make this unnecessary.

The life cycle of a specific ROSCA is short and usually spans no more than a couple of months. Once settled and dissolved, no infrastructure or other sunk investments remain of a specific ROSCA but the reputation earned by its master and members in honouring or breaking their obligations in the transaction.[5]

In principle, a ROSCA can be established irrespective of the external environment (business cycle, economic or political crises etc.). From this perspective, ROSCAs may be understood as institutional arrangements for the facilitation of financial interaction that are highly crisis-resilient. ROSCAs may even rise in importance as savers and investors retreat from the formal financial sector due to unattractive interest rate levels, a 'liquidity crunch' or increased administrative requirements and 'red tape'.

2.2.3   Credit broker (*yinbei*) and (illegal) money houses (*qianzhuang*)

Although some ROSCAs – especially those established among private entrepreneurs – are known to be able to mobilize substantial amounts of money, other institutional arrangements seem to feature comparative advantages when larger amounts of money are involved in financial transactions. In this context highly specialized financial intermediaries acting in a more professional manner and mobilizing larger amounts of money than the *dangshou* intermediaries discussed above are of particular importance.

Following the notion that informational frictions, that is, asymmetric (and proprietary) information, provide the most fundamental explanation for the existence of (financial) intermediaries (Bhattacharya and Thakor, 1993; Boot, 2000), the Chinese financial intermediaries discussed here may be understood as entrepreneurs who enlarge the scope of reputation-based economic interaction between otherwise unconnected players and earn a rent from opening a transaction channel formerly blocked by prohibitive transaction costs. The (potential) lender does not have to investigate and evaluate the reputation and entrepreneurial capabilities of a prospective borrower, but bases his decision solely on his evaluation of the intermediary. The intermediary, on the other hand, has a strong incentive to mediate financial flows only to borrowers whom he is certain possess the will and capability to repay the loan. His 'reputation capital' among creditors is based on the implicit guarantee to establish transaction bridges to trustworthy and capable borrowers only. As such, intermediaries will uphold a high frequency of contact with their potential (borrower) customer basis in order to monitor their behaviour and collect sufficient soft information.

Bringing this business to scale, some intermediaries have started to create specific tools and consultancy services that tend to crowd out individual intermediaries and lead to the establishment of (illegal) money houses, that is, second economy proto banks (Feng, 2006). These illegal proto banks feature a couple of characteristics that turn them into powerful competitors for the formal banking sector (Bradsher, 2004). First of all they are not subjected to the central bank's interest rate regulation and are therefore free to construct their specific interest rate structure. Second, they have evolved in a bottom-up fashion and therefore feature a strong embeddedness in local society, endowing them with substantial start-up 'trust capital'. The case of Hebei Dawu Agriculture and Animal Husbandry Group Ltd constitutes a particularly well-documented case where a company more or less spontaneously turned into a proto bank as its peculiar grain futures business became increasingly attractive to local society.[6] Other examples of 'underground banks' have been documented especially for the Wenzhou area but also other regions in China, where 'old men's societies' and specific 'mutual assistance societies' (*huzhu hui*) have been collecting millions of yuan RMB which they lend out to local SMEs (Tsai, 2002; Feng, 2006).

3. PILLAR OR THREAT? THE IMPACT OF 'INFORMAL SHADOW BANKING' ON THE CHINESE ECONOMY

Seen in perspective, the 'informal shadow banking' sector may be understood to have been of paramount importance in the realization of China's economic 'miracle' since the beginning of the reform movement in the late 1970s. It has been this sector that has been providing the (semi-) private sector with the necessary financial means to evolve and establish a strong SME sector in Chinese industry. And the 'informal shadow banking' sector has not only been able to fulfil this role because of the failure of the formal sector to service (semi-) private entrepreneurs. It has also been better equipped to do so. In contrast to the transaction-based formal sector, which relies on standardized (hard) information packages, the informal sector has been able to access more comprehensive, although non-standardized, packages of (hard and soft) information, available to actors conducting intra-network transactions only. This understanding is based on the observation that reputation effects generated in social networks carry information not only on the integrity of a specific actor but also on his capabilities (Nooteboom, 2007). In this understanding, entrepreneurial savvy is much easier to determine inside a social group than from the outside, where information on the (entrepreneurial) capabilities of a specific actor is mostly not verifiable.

Given the advantage of soft information/second-party-enforcement-based financing technologies in ascertaining the integrity as well as entrepreneurial savvy and capability of start-up entrepreneurs, the Chinese 'informal shadow banking' sector's financing technologies may have provided just the necessary institutional arrangements for a 'market' dominated by venture capital and start-up financing activities. A lack of these financial technologies and stronger reliance on the formal banking sector (third-party enforcement) may not have resulted in a better fulfilment of the requirements of China's upcoming entrepreneurs during the 1980s and 1990s, but rather stymied the entrepreneurial activity driving China's bottom-up industry and service sector revolution (Lin and Sun, 2005).

This 'pillar function' of China's shadow banking, which has been providing important services for the creation of a second – non-state enterprise – sector in the context of a hybrid transition economy located somewhere between state planning and market competition, must today be qualified as the Chinese economic system has advanced a long way on the road to a fully functioning market economy. In this new environment the formerly beneficial shadow banking activities may now become increasingly harmful for the economy's overall development.

China's 'informal shadow banking' sector has always stood outside the country's legal system. For many years it has been tolerated as it has been able to improve overall economic efficiency by facilitating the circumvention or substitution of deficient institutional arrangements.

As such, shadow banking activities have created positive externalities according to which the personal gains of the parties to a transaction were complemented by social welfare improvements (respectively: economic growth) that would not have been realized otherwise, or only later. This 'functionality', however, has been eroding substantially in recent years. With the formal institutional framework crossing a threshold line of market coordination capacity, the potential of shadow banking to bridge institutional deficiencies in the formal system and provide for financial coordination in 'forgotten' sectors of the economy has been significantly reduced. Instead the negative aspects of China's shadow banking sector have become more pronounced. As the sector stands completely outside the realm of the country's (macroeconomic) regulators, it is increasingly turning into a threat to the government's endeavours to rein in lending activities and control the speculative inflow of money to the bubbling stock markets and especially the real-estate sector.

The latter aspect harbours an additional danger. With substantial amounts of speculative money flowing into China's asset bubbles financed via the 'informal shadow banking sector', an implosion of the real-estate bubble may bring dozens and hundreds of local ROSCAs and proto banks to the verge of collapse. Accounts in the Chinese media of whole villages having been thrown into poverty because of disintegrating shadow banking schemes already indicate the dangers to social stability in the country if a collapse of shadow banking activities should hit larger regions.

The problem is to a certain extent self-inflicted: with deposit rates in the formal banking sector administratively kept at below inflation rate levels, private households have been incentivized to bring their money to the informal shadow banking sector. Here they can expect decent interest rate income, be it with ROSCA arrangements or proto banks, which over the years have been paying a decent 15 per cent on deposits.

The difficult task Chinese regulators face today is therefore to integrate the various formal and informal spheres of China's financial system into one 'greater financial system' that allows for better control and macroeconomic direction. This implies the need to broaden the business scope of formal sector actors and to legalize certain activities that right now exist 'in the wild'. If they are brought into the formal sector, they will become subject to better control and central regulation. Other activities, which may prove themselves to be non-internalizable, must be contained – without stifling the potentially superior capabilities of soft information/second-party enforcement-based financing technologies in the identification of entrepreneurial talent.

NOTES

1. 'Multiplexity' relates to the co-occurrence of distinct social roles in a dyadic relationship (e.g. father/son + employer/employee + neighbour/neighbour) and/or the overlap of different exchanges or activities in a specific social relationship (i.e. the relationship has more than one focus of interaction) and/or the common membership in more than one organization, peer group, kindred group, neighbourhood etc.
2. The breakdown of a ROSCA in Leqing County, Wenzhou, in 1986 resulted in the death of three people and the kidnapping of another 53 people held responsible for the breakdown. The collapse of two ROSCAs in Pingyang County, Wenzhou, in 1988 and 1989 led to the 'abnormal death of several dozens of members' (Feng, 2006, p. 54).
3. In the framework of network analysis these intermediaries may be understood to constitute bridges across 'structural holes' (Burt, 1992). By establishing contact points between otherwise independent and isolated networks, these intermediaries profit from the rents created.
4. In this context, see also the discussion on credit broker (*yinbei*) and (illegal) money houses (*qianzhuang*) below.
5. For a detailed description and analysis of various manifestations of ROSCAs in contemporary China, see Feng (2004, 2006) and Hu (2005).
6. In this way, increasingly crowding out the formal banking sector, however, proved to be one success too much for the company. Its owner/entrepreneur Sun Dawu as well as the company as a juridical entity were prosecuted and convicted for illegally taking deposits from the public. The Dawu case constitutes a further idiosyncrasy in so far as the money collected from the local population was mostly not lent out to other borrowers, but rather used for the company's own expansion and investment needs. For a detailed account see Feng (2006).

REFERENCES

Ben-Porath, Y. (1980), 'The F-connection: families, friends, and firms and the organization of exchange', *Population and Development Review*, **6**, 1–30.

Berger, Allen N. and Gregory F. Udell (2006), 'A more complete conceptual framework for SME finance', *Journal of Banking and Finance*, **30**(11), 2945–66.

Besley, Timothy, Stephen Coate and Glen Loury (1993), 'The economics of rotating savings and credit associations', *The American Economic Review*, **83**(4), 792–810.

Bhattacharya, Sudipto and Anjan V. Thakor (1993), 'Contemporary banking theory', *Journal of Financial Intermediation*, **3**(1), 2–50.

Boot, Arnoud W.A. (2000), 'Relationship banking: what do we know?', *Journal of Financial Intermediation*, **9**, 7–25.

Bradsher, Keith (2004), 'China's informal lenders pose risks to its banks', *The New York Times*, 9 November.

Burt, Ronald S. (1992), *Structural Holes. The Social Structure of Competition*, Boston, MA: Harvard University Press.

Chang, Gordon (2001), *The Coming Collapse of China*, New York: Random House.

Feng, Xingyuan (2004), 'Toushi Zhedong hehui xianxiang' [Analysis of the ROSCA phenomenon in East-Zhejiang], mimeo.

Feng, Xingyuan (2006), *Case Studies on Informal Finance in Rural China*, Beijing: World Bank Consultancy Report.

Geertz, Clifford (1962), 'The rotating credit association. A "middle rung" in development', *Economic Development and Cultural Change*, **10** (April), 241–63.
Hu, Biliang (1998), *Fazhan lilun yu Zhongguo* [Development Theory and China], Beijing.
Hu, Biliang (2005), 'Laizi yige Zhongguo cunzhuang de biaohui baogao' [Report on a ROSCA in a Chinese village], mimeo.
Huang, Yasheng (2003), *Selling China: Foreign Direct Investment During the Reform Era*, New York: Cambridge University Press.
Huang, Yasheng (2008), *Capitalism with Chinese Characteristics: Entrepreneurship and the State*, Cambridge: Cambridge University Press.
IMF (2011), *People's Republic of China: Financial System Stability Assessment*, IMF Country Report No. 11/321, Washington, DC: IMF.
Levine, Ross (1997), 'Financial development and economic growth: views and agenda', *Journal of Economic Literature*, **35**(2), 688–726.
Levine, Ross (1999), 'Law, finance, and economic growth', *Journal of Financial Intermediation*, **8**, 8–35.
Lin, Yifu and Sun Xifang (2005), 'Xinxi, feizhenggui jinrong yu zhingxiao qiye rongzi' [Information, Informal Finance and SME Financing], in *Jingji Yanjiu*, July, 35–44.
Nooteboom, Bart (2007), 'Social capital, institutions and trust', *Review of Social Economy*, **65**(1), 29–53.
Peebles, Gavin (1991), *Money in the People's Republic of China. A Comparative Perspective*, Sydney, London and Boston, MA: Allen and Unwin.
Taube, Markus (2009), 'Principles of property rights evolution in China's rural industry', in Thomas Heberer and Gunter Schubert (eds), *Regime Legitimacy in Contemporary China. Institutional Change and Stability*, London and New York: Routledge, pp. 108–28.
Taube, Markus and Marcus Conlé (2011), 'The Chinese law, finance & growth paradox – lending channels in the Chinese formal and informal financial sectors', in Ma Ying, Markus Taube and Dieter Cassel (eds), *Economic Growth in China and Europe: Development in the Financial Sector and the Labor Market*, Economic Studies on Asia Series, **10**, Marburg: Metropolis-Verlag, pp. 63–82.
Tsai, Kelly S. (2002), *Back-Alley Banking. Private Entrepreneurs in China*, Ithaca, NY: Cornell University Press.
Udell, Gregory F. (2008), 'What's in a relationship? The case of commercial lending', *Business Horizons*, **51**, 93–103.
World Bank (1990), *China: Financial Sector Policies and Institutional Development*, Washington, DC: World Bank.
World Bank (2011), *China Quarterly Update*, Washington, DC and Beijing: World Bank.
Yao, Yang and Linda Yueh (2009), 'Law, finance, and economic growth in China: an introduction', *World Development*, **37**(4), 753–62.

Interactive Databases:

Bloomberg, www.bloomberg.com.
CBRC, www.cbrc.gov.cn.21.

18. Banking and financial stability in the light of the crisis from the perspective of UniCredit

Gianni Franco Papa

Question: In terms of instruments aimed at maintaining banking and financial stability in the light of the crisis, which instruments have been most effective in maintaining stability in Central and Eastern Europe and for the countries UniCredit is represented in? What additional instruments might be needed?

Papa: I'm trying to give a commercial spin to that question. We have seen a number of policy actions taking place in 2011 in light of the current phase of uncertainty that is also touching the CEE region. Some of these actions stem from the crisis in 2008 and were aimed at containing the spillover effect the crisis might have also on the CEE region. First, the presence of the IMF was very important as the IMF adopted a more flexible approach and reacted in strong coordination with the EU. It is present through stand-by programmes or flexible credit lines and continues to support a balance-of-payment adjustment or readjustment of countries. Second, we had and have the action of central banks that are responding in accordance with the local specificities. On the one hand, we have central banks providing liquidity to the interbank market (for instance the Central Bank of Russia); then we have some central banks tightening reserve requirements in order to cool down lending growth or in order to decrease liquidity and contain speculation on the local currency. In some countries where the FX weakness does not pose a risk to financial stability, central banks have allowed devaluation of the local currency in order to boost exports and support growth. On the other hand, some central banks in the region did exactly the opposite by tightening liquidity whenever it became excessive, also through outright effects of market intervention. Last but not least, the 'Vienna Initiative' is definitely one of the most important initiatives that have helped CEE. As part of the 'Vienna Initiative', we committed to keeping capital and funding to the subsidiaries constant throughout the crisis. This has unquestionably been a success story and played a crucial role in avoiding a full-fledged crisis in CEE. I do believe that – in light of the economic context in which we are working at the time of writing – it is going to be essential to have a direct dialogue with international financial institutions and with home and host regulators in order to avoid a new debt crisis.

Question: What do you think are the implications of the new ESRB recommendations (see Chapter 16)? Is now the right time to rethink this product? What is a reasonable strategy for that?

Papa: Clearly, solvency problems related to the existing stock of FX lending remain an issue. All banks need to monitor constantly, especially in those countries where we have a higher exposure. Throughout the crisis, banks have been very carefully monitoring the implications of devaluation pressures on CEE currencies for customers' solvency; and as a matter of fact, banks have taken a number of proactive actions to ease their problems.

In most cases they have already discontinued the riskiest form of foreign currency lending. The new ESRB recommendations are clearly addressing the problem. I am convinced that the regulators should make full use of the tools available within the pillar 2 framework of the existing Basel Accord to deal with the concentration risk associated with foreign currency lending in observation of the specific characteristics of the bank and its credit portfolio. An appropriate solution to the risk embedded in lending should always be taken into consideration. Then we have to look where we have a structural shortness of local currencies. This situation brings a constraint to lending in local currencies in many countries.

However, it is of the utmost importance that an optimal exit strategy always involves a coordinated approach among all relevant stakeholders in order to avoid inflicting large losses on banks with repercussions on financial stability, as happened for instance in Hungary, where most of the burden is put on banks.

Question: Why have banks and maybe also authorities such a short memory and why do we seem to fall into the same traps again and again?

Papa: Well, let's put it in a politically correct way: financial innovation is faster than the ability of regulators to catch up with it. It is probably a reality that anytime you try to regulate something you will have a whiz kid coming up with something new. And then you have to catch up again to cover it. In addition, there is also an emotional component: people constantly think that next time it is going to be different – what happened in the previous crisis is not going to repeat itself. This means, we always try to find an excuse for ourselves. This applies to everybody – financial institutions, probably regulators, politicians, all stakeholders. We saw an increase in local regulations in 2010 and 2011 and we are sure that this will change things in the future. But in an increasingly interdependent world, close cooperation and coordination is needed. I don't have any other answer to that.

Question: As the head of UniCredit's CEE Division, how do you see business in the region and the future of UniCredit in the region?

Papa: We are living in a new normal – we are not going to see double-digit growth in CEE as we did before the crisis in 2007; this is impossible to have. Therefore diversification will become more and more important and more relevant. As far as UniCredit is concerned, being a commercial banking group with the leading position in CEE countries, we will continue to support and remain interested in the growth and prosperity of the region, although under different approaches from before.

19. Banking and financial stability in the light of the crisis

Dejan Šoškić

Question: It's always very interesting to hear what banks want to get, but what is the official side willing to give?

Šoškić: Let me respond to this question with reference to the crisis in 2007 and 2008. On an international level, the policy response consisted essentially of the provision of supporting instruments by the IMF and of the Vienna Initiative, which has basically substantially decreased the funding risk for many of the subsidiaries and branch offices of Western banks in Central, Eastern and South-Eastern Europe. Those were the two very important instruments on the international side, which have, I would say, induced and stabilized the financial situation in Central, Eastern and South-Eastern Europe. What is also important is the recapitalization of financial institutions that has occurred through various channels through international financial institutions. That has provided additional long-term financing for some of the banks and therefore stabilized their financial position. But from the point of view of Serbia I would like to add something that was, let's say, a more country-specific side of circumstances and measures that have helped.

First of all, for instance, Serbia had subsidiaries rather than branch offices of Western banks. That has, in our view, proven to be a very important difference concerning the potential spillover effects and in terms of preserving the overall financial stability of our financial system. Second, we had a relatively conservative banking portfolio structure. We have not been, as many other banks unfortunately have, exposed to the complex financial instruments, mortgage-backed securities, collateralized debt obligations, and also we have not had so many instruments that would induce leverage within the banks, meaning mainly derivative instruments. So, this, let's say conservative, structure of banks' balance sheets has proven to have been very useful. Furthermore, we had an immediate response from the government of the Republic of Serbia in the sense that there was a substantial increase in deposit insurance, up to €50000 per deposit holder, which prevented any excessive banking panic. We also introduced the waiver of taxes on bank deposits and that has also helped. Still, in the first wave of the crisis at the end of 2008, we experienced what you might call a real-life stress test because on some not so favourable news in the media, deposit holders tried to withdraw their deposits and all their deposits were honoured in a timely manner. That was a stress test which, I believe, has also been useful in order to overcome the potential lack of confidence in the following years. And I'm glad to say that until now, the overall confidence of deposit holders in the banks in my country has been preserved. Throughout the period from the beginning of 2009 we have had a gradual increase in deposits and at the time this book goes to press deposits have rebounded to well above pre-crisis levels. All in all, there has been a mixture of internationally induced measures and country-specific policies, which have helped to preserve financial stability, especially in the case of Serbia.

Question: The foreign currency lending issue (FX risk) is something the Serbian central bank has been very vocal about. The question always is: why were these products necessary in the first instance? Plus: you have introduced a number of measures to reduce this. What is your experience and what is your way forward?

Šoškić: It is a fact that, prior to the introduction of foreign banks and FX lending, there was a lack of long-term financial instruments in the market place in many of the CESEE countries. I do recognize that, in the early stages, FX lending was a way to increase the maturity of financial products offered in the marketplace. In this respect, FX lending was successful. At the same time, and on a more fundamental note, FX risk in lending is not just an issue of an individual bank's solvency. Hence we should not monitor FX lending from the perspective of a single bank. Obviously, this is a much larger problem, especially if it is a persistent one and dominant in the financial system of a country. It is something that, obviously, can very much influence overall systemic risk in the country. We are not dealing here with something that can influence just the quality of the balance sheet of a single bank. Much rather, FX lending basically creates a potential of contagion throughout the system. In addition, there is a very high degree of correlation between exchange rate movements and developments in non-performing loans. Beside the increase in non-performing loans, in some countries banks' capital base is denominated in the local currency – so you can have a deterioration in capital adequacy as well, and then you basically have a serious system-wide systemic risk on your hands. And this is something that really needs to be dealt with.

Our belief is that it takes market-based fine-tuning measures rather than administrative measures to tackle this problem, because the market-based measures are going to gradually align the interests of individual banks and their parent banks with the interest of long-term stability and quality of the local financial system. The high level of FX-denominated instruments in the system is something that goes even beyond the implications sketched so far. High FX levels can very much influence and potentially hamper the effectiveness of the monetary policy tools used by central banks, and it is also something that can substantially affect the degree of potential flexibility economies have got concerning the movement of the FX rate. If some of the countries have flexible exchange rates and if they cannot use that potential advantage because a depreciation can suddenly increase the overall level of non-performing loans in the system and decrease capital adequacy – that is, threaten the solvency of not just individual banks but the solvency of the banking system as a whole – then you basically have a situation which is tying down and reducing many potential advantages of certain policy measures and regimes. Serbia has approached this issue. We have taken, I would say, positive steps in the right direction for quite some time now. Let me mention below some of the measures that we have introduced.

First of all, banks need to meet reserve requirements, which are differentiated between the local currency and FX sources of funding. If banks rely on FX sources of funding, our idea and understanding of the situation was that we should, basically, discourage the creation of FX-denominated liabilities in order to discourage the shift of the underlying FX risks towards unhedged borrowers, both households and corporates. So, the reserve requirements are higher for FX-denominated sources of funding, namely 30 per cent for shorter maturities, and 25 per cent for longer maturities (above two years). Not so for the local currency-denominated sources of funding where we do not impose any reserve requirements if the maturity is above two years; and if it is below two years, there is a 5 per cent reserve requirement. Furthermore, we also introduced a differentiation concerning the loan-to-value ratio (LTV). So, if a mortgage is FX-denominated it should not go beyond a loan-to-value of 80 per cent. Also, we have administratively banned other types of indexation like indexation to Swiss francs, Japanese yen, US dollars and other currencies, which do not have relatively low volatility of FX rate against the value of the local currency. Therefore, the only possibility regarding the FX indexation in our system now is to have euro loans and euro-indexed loans.

We have also enhanced consumer protection. First of all, we require banks to provide full information on what the real and effective interest rate is that the customer is going to be paying but also what the currency risk is if the borrower is unhedged. Also, banks are now obliged to offer first a local-currency-denominated financial instrument, and then, on customer request, the FX-denominated financial instrument – if the customer wishes to engage in such a financial product.

Concerning the implementation of Basel II, we also oblige banks to monitor the interconnectedness between the market (FX) and credit risk, which is very important for most of the unhedged borrowers. You can obviously have exceptions to these rules, if households have FX-denominated income or if corporates are exporting, especially on a long-term basis, since such customers are naturally hedged. In these cases the approach can be slightly different. The FX risk in the system is also something that needs to be addressed by fiscal policy as well. In line with this, we have only one fiscal policy measure at the time this book goes to press which enables the local-currency-denominated deposits in the banks to be free of income tax. Deposits which are FX-denominated are not exempted from tax and there is a 10 per cent tax on their interest income. I believe all of these measures are something we need to be persistent with and that we need to be dedicated to this goal jointly with the financial institutions and the government. By providing long-term financial stability, the financial system as a whole can develop in a much more sustainable manner.

Question: Providing long-term financial stability is, of course, one of the key goals of central banks. What about the importance of providing long-term local currency financing?

Šoškić: Long-term local currency financing certainly plays a key role in ensuring long-term financial stability. First of all, as I have already mentioned, our reserve requirements framework is based on a staggered system, so we really promote the creation of longer-term local currency sources of funding. Then, we must not forget that deposits are not the only source of funding. Banks are fully free to issue local currency-denominated financial instruments, like bonds, and offer them to domestic investors, or potentially to non-residents and, therefore, to create the needed structure of liabilities, in order to promote the longer-term local currency financing within the system. This process can be substantially facilitated by international financial institutions with their guarantees, or stand-alone local-currency-denominated long-term bond issues. So, I believe that there is a range of possibilities and that there are different ways to increase the local currency portion of the liabilities of the financial system. Having recognized the importance of this concept, some international financial institutions are already offering support in the creation of local-currency-denominated bond markets as well as guarantees for local-currency-denominated instruments issued on the local markets. These are all interesting elements that combined can create a different environment with much more incentives to promote the use of the local currency, both in liabilities and assets within the banking system of the countries, which otherwise can be quite vulnerable.

Question: Why do banks and maybe also authorities have such a short memory – why do we seem to fall into the same traps again and again? Governor Šoškić, what is your opinion on this? Of course, everybody thinks that this time it's different but isn't there a certain danger that we will get into the opposite oversteering and try to regulate in such a way that this will harm a reasonably sustainable growth?

Šoškić: We should obviously always take into account and try to understand fully the types of risks within the financial system. As the late Hyman Minsky used to say, concerning his depiction of what creates a financial boom and an eventual crisis, the increase in the number of highly leveraged agents acting on the verge of being a Ponzi scheme is something that inevitably leads to financial instability. Now, there is a perception, among all of us as human beings, to think of present circumstances as if they are there to stay for a long time. And then we sometimes do make decisions, long-term decisions, which are made on presumptions that are based on very short experiences that we had in previous periods of time. There is this something that led also Alan Greenspan to talk about irrational exuberance. These behaviours lead to the creation of the bubbles. But I would say that, from the institutional point of view, we have made a step forward. Stress tests should be the way to cool heads, to see how we are going to fare out if things turn sour. Are we capable of creating scenarios which are realistic enough – that is a different question. But I would say that we have made a step in a good direction, introducing some of the measures of new regulatory requirements which are internationally accepted. But there are still lots of things that need to be done, especially in terms of curbing the potential leverages in the system. If we allow derivative instruments to be issued without a specific and complete analysis of the volumes and the exposures toward specific financial institutions, and towards the system as a whole, we are bound to get into trouble sooner or later.

So, I would say that the international initiatives aimed at ensuring that derivative instruments are conducted under the standardized contracts and centrally cleared are steps in a good direction. Everything which can trigger off-balance-sheet obligations on the side of the financial institution is potentially dangerous. On the side of the households, I would say that we need to go back to the old and well-known mechanisms and instruments such as loan-to-value (LTV) and debt-payment-to-income (DTI) because these instruments can help us to control the overall risk of leverage. But, frankly speaking, if we look also at the tax system and at international accounting standards, we find that leverage is being promoted. If you take on debt, it is treated more favourably in tax terms than if you take equity as a source of financing. And that is also something that, I would say, deserves a cautious look through a magnifying glass to see whether we possibly have a system which is basically promoting leverage.

On a final note, let me say that markets are, as a rule, always ahead of regulators. That is, I would say, more or less a fact. The other fact is that markets are globalized and that regulation and supervision is not. So, my message would be: as regulators, we need to make every effort to understand the markets and risks, and cooperate as much as possible.

Index

advanced economies 9, 10, 15, 16, 25, 148, 150–56
agricultural prices 106, 149
agricultural products 99, 106, 149
Albania 159, 160, 161, 169
apparel and textiles sectors 111, 112, 115, 116
ASEAN 83, 84, 85–8
Asia 46, 47, 108, 109, 110, 111
asset price boom-bust cycles 63, 64, 178–80, 181, 183, 199, 209
Austria 11, 12, 40, 57, 58, 64, 152, 161

balance of payments, Russia 123–5
banking regulation 131, 170–71, 180, 198, 199, 202–3, 205, 207–8, 209, 210
banking regulation deficits 149, 189, 190, 191, 198–9
banking sector 8, 127–8, 130, 149, 163, 171–2, 190, 191–2, 194, 198, 199, 202–10
see also banking regulation; banking regulation deficits; shadow banking in China
bilateral trade agreements 74, 76, 80
bonds 15–16, 27, 39, 40, 61, 130, 147, 208–9
Bosnia-Herzegovina 160, 161, 162, 168
Bradsher, Keith 193, 197
budget deficits 125–6, 131, 134, 135, 136, 142
Bulgaria 40–41, 130, 131, 132, 133–4, 135, 136, 137–40, 141, 142, 143, 144, 145, 161
business environment 132, 137–8, 139

capital accumulation 19, 151–2, 153
capital adequacy 18, 28, 172, 182, 202–3, 205, 206–7

capital cost increases 151–2, 178
capital flows 37, 39, 40, 55–6, 62, 63–4
capital inflows 5, 17, 39, 159
capital outflows 125, 131, 149–50, 163
capital products 38, 82, 94, 95, 96, 97, 106, 184
CEE (Central and Eastern Europe) 9, 12, 61, 98–9, 100, 103, 108–9, 110, 111, 150, 151, 152, 157, 159–61, 164, 172, 202–4
see also CESEE (Central, Eastern and South-Eastern Europe)
central banks 56, 66, 125, 197, 202, 206, 207
see also European Central Bank (ECB); National Bank of Serbia
CESEE (Central, Eastern and South-Eastern Europe)
business environment 132, 137–8, 139
capital flows 5, 131, 159
chemical and manufacturing sectors 159
competition 88, 89, 91, 94, 95, 96, 97, 101–4
country size 3, 4, 142
credit growth 178–9, 180–81, 183
current account 131, 133, 178, 183
domestic market demand 183
economic decline 130
economic growth 5, 87, 88, 89, 130, 133, 134, 135, 137, 140, 141–3, 145–6, 157, 158–62, 177
economic growth strategies 5, 7, 130
economic outcomes versus PIGS (Portugal, Italy, Greece and Spain) 133–43
European convergence 145–6, 157, 158–60